"... wise, rich, witty and indispe——
—JOHN LEONARD, *The New York Times*

"Dr. May offers an intensity and an intelligence that might make a difference in all our lives. LOVE AND WILL is a book to study and cherish, for those daring enough to study and cherish our human heritage and potential ... a book that might save us!"
—*San Francisco Examiner*

"... a closely reasoned and eloquent work [that seeks] the restoration of man's wholeness and confidence."
—*Los Angeles Times*

"... a rich and useful book, one that deserves a thoughtful audience." —*Saturday Review*

"An analysis of modern love and life ... brilliant, impeccable, full of encouraging insight."
—*Chicago Sun-Times*

"... an excellent book; it can serve as a mirror that reflects insight and understanding to a troubled world ... the type of book that could go far in establishing a common ground for today's much discussed 'generation gap.'" —*Cincinnati Enquirer*

ROLLO MAY is a practicing psychoanalyst who is internationally known not only for his scholarly and pioneering contributions in his writing but as an eminently successful practitioner. He began his studies in Vienna and completed his doctorate in psychology and his psychoanalytic training in New York City. In addition to his clinical practice, he has been affiliated with the William Alanson White Institute of Psychiatry, Psychoanalysis and Psychology, and has taught at Harvard and Princeton. He is the author of *The Meaning of Anxiety, Man's Search for Himself* (Delta Books), and *Power and Innocence*.

By the same author

MAN'S SEARCH FOR HIMSELF
  (*available in a Delta edition*)

THE MEANING OF ANXIETY

THE ART OF COUNSELING

PSYCHOLOGY AND THE HUMAN DILEMMA

SPRINGS OF CREATIVE LIVING

DREAMS AND SYMBOLS (*with Leopold Caligor*)

EXISTENCE: A NEW DIMENSION IN
  PSYCHIATRY AND PSYCHOLOGY
  (*with Angel and Ellenberger*)

EXISTENTIAL PSYCHOLOGY (*Ed.*)

SYMBOLISM IN RELIGION AND
  LITERATURE (*Ed.*)

ROLLO MAY

Love
and
Will

A LAUREL EDITION

Published by
DELL PUBLISHING CO., INC.
1 Dag Hammarskjold Plaza,
New York, New York 10017

Published by arrangement with
W. W. Norton & Company, Inc.
For information contact
W. W. Norton & Company, Inc.
55 Fifth Avenue
New York, New York 10003
Printed in the United States of America
First Laurel Printing—March 1974

CONTENTS

Part II: WILL

Part III: LOVE AND WILL

FOREWORD

Some readers will wonder at the juxtaposition of love and will in the title of this book. I have long believed that love and will are interdependent and belong together. Both are conjunctive processes of being—a reaching out to influence others, molding, forming, creating the consciousness of the other. But this is only possible, in an inner sense, if one opens oneself at the same time to the influence of the other. And will without love becomes manipulation—of which the age just preceding the First World War is replete with examples. Love without will in our own day becomes sentimental and experimental.

I take the author's usual pride, as well as responsibility, for the ideas in this book. But in the eight years it was in process of being written a number of friends read and discussed chapters with me. I want to thank them: Jerome Bruner, Doris Cole, Robert Lifton, Gardner Murphy, Elinor Roberts, Ernest Schachtel, and the late Paul Tillich. Jessica Ryan has given the intuitive understanding, combined with practical suggestions, that an author always feels deserve more than gratitude.

During the long summers in New Hampshire when this book was being written I would often get up early in the morning and go out on my patio where the valley, stretching off to the mountain ranges in the north and east, was silver with predawn mist. The birds, eloquent voices in an otherwise silent world, had already begun their hallelujah chorus to welcome in the new day. The song sparrow sings with an enthusiasm which rocks him almost off his perch atop the apple tree, and the goldfinch chimes in with his obligato. The thrush in the woods is so full of song he can't contain himself. The woodpecker beats on the hollow beech tree. The loons over on the lake erupt with their plaintive and tormented daemonic, to save the whole thing from being too sweet. Then the sun comes up over the mountain range revealing an incredibly green New Hampshire overflowing through the whole long valley with a richness that is almost too abundant. The trees seem to have grown several inches overnight, and the meadow is bursting with a million brown-eyed Susans.

I feel again the everlasting going and coming, the eternal return, the growing and mating and dying and growing again. And I know that human beings are part of this eternal going and returning, part of its sadness as well as its song. But man, the seeker, is called by his consciousness to transcend the eternal return. I am no different from anyone else—except in the choice of areas for the quest. My own conviction has always been to seek the inner reality, with the belief that the fruits of future values will be able to grow only after they are sown by the values of our history. In this transitional twentieth century, when the full results of our bankruptcy of inner values is brought home to us, I believe it is especially important that we seek the source of love and will.

ROLLO MAY

Holderness,
New Hampshire, 1969

Love
and
Will

ONE

INTRODUCTION: OUR SCHIZOID WORLD

Cassandra: Apollo was the seer who set me this
work. . . .
Chorus: Were you already ecstatic in the skills of
God?
Cassandra: Yes; even then I read my city's destinies.
—FROM *Agamemnon,* BY AESCHYLUS

The striking thing about love and will in our day is that,
whereas in the past they were always held up to us as the
answer to life's predicaments, they have now themselves
become the *problem.* It is always true that love and will
become more difficult in a transitional age; and ours is an
era of radical transition. The old myths and symbols by
which we oriented ourselves are gone, anxiety is rampant;
we cling to each other and try to persuade ourselves that
what we feel is love; we do not will because we are
afraid that if we choose one thing or one person we'll lose
the other, and we are too insecure to take that chance.
The bottom then drops out of the conjunctive emotions
and processes—of which love and will are the two fore-
most examples. The individual is forced to turn inward;
he becomes obsessed with the new form of the problem
of identity, namely, Even-if-I-know-who-I-am, I-have-no-
significance. I am unable to influence others. The next
step is apathy. And the step following that is violence.
For no human being can stand the perpetually numbing
experience of his own powerlessness.

So great was the emphasis on love as the resolution to
life's predicament that people's self-esteem ascended or
fell depending on whether or not they had achieved it.
Those who believed they had found it indulged in self-
righteousness, confident in their visible proof of salvation
as the Calvinist's wealth used to be tangible evidence of

his being numbered among the elect. Those who failed to find it felt not simply bereft to a greater or lesser extent, but, on a deeper and more damaging inner level, their self-esteem was undermined. They felt marked as a new species of pariah, and would confess in psychotherapy that they awoke in the small hours of the morning not necessarily especially lonely or unhappy but plagued with the gnawing conviction that they had somehow missed the great secret of life. And all the while, with rising divorce rates, the increasing banalization of love in literature and art, and the fact that sex for many people has become more meaningless as it is more available, this "love" has seemed tremendously elusive if not an outright illusion. Some members of the new political left came to the conclusion that love is destroyed by the very nature of our bourgeois society, and the reforms they proposed had the specific purpose of making "a world in which love is more possible."[1]

In such a contradictory situation, the sexual form of love—lowest common denominator on the ladder of salvation—understandably became our preoccupation; for sex, as rooted in man's inescapable biology, seems always dependable to give at least a facsimile of love. But sex, too, has become Western man's test and burden more than his salvation. The books which roll off the presses on technique in love and sex, while still best-sellers for a few weeks, have a hollow ring: for most people seem to be aware on some scarcely articulated level that the frantic quality with which we pursue technique as our way to salvation is in direct proportion to the degree to which we have lost sight of the salvation we are seeking. It is an old and ironic habit of human beings to run faster when we have lost our way; and we grasp more fiercely at research, statistics, and technical aids in sex when we have lost the values and meaning of love. Whatever merits or failings the Kinsey studies and the Masters-Johnson research have in their own right, they are symptomatic of a culture in which the personal meaning of love has been progressively lost. Love had been assumed to be a motivating force, a power which could be relied upon to push us onward in life. But the great shift in our day indicates that the motivating force itself is now called into question. Love has become a problem to itself.

So self-contradictory, indeed, has love become that some of those studying family life have concluded that "love" is simply the name for the way more powerful members of the family control other members. Love, Ronald Laing maintains, is a cover for violence.

The same can be said about will. We inherited from our Victorian forefathers the belief that the only real problem in life was to decide rationally *what* to do—and then *will* would stand ready as the "faculty" for making us do it. Now it is no longer a matter of deciding what to do, but of *deciding how to decide. The very basis of will itself is thrown into question.*

Is will an illusion? Many psychologists and psychotherapists, from Freud down, have argued that it is. The terms "will power" and "free will," so necessary in the vocabulary of our fathers, have all but dropped completely out of any contemporary, sophisticated discussion; or the words are used in derision. People go to therapists to find substitutes for their lost will: to learn how to get the "unconscious" to direct their lives, or to learn the latest conditioning technique to enable them to behave, or to use new drugs to release some motive for living. Or to learn the latest method of "releasing affect," unaware that affect is not something you strive for in itself but a by-product of the way you give yourself to a life situation. And the question is, What are they going to use the stiuation *for?* In his study of will, Leslie Farber asserts that in this failure of will lies the central pathology of our day, and that our time should be called the "age of the disordered will."[2]

In such an age of radical transition, the individual is driven back into his own consciousness. When the foundations of love and will have been shaken and all but destroyed, we cannot escape the necessity of pushing below the surface and searching within our own consciousness and within the "collective unarticulated consciousness" of our society for the sources of love and will. I use the term "source" as the French speak of the "source" of a river—the springs from which the water originally comes. If we can find the sources from which love and will spring, we may be able to discover the new forms which these essential experiences need in order to become viable in the new age into which we are moving. In this sense, our quest, like every such exploration, is a moral quest, for we are seeking the bases on which a morality for a new age can be founded. Every sensitive person finds himself in Stephen Dedalus' position: "I go forth . . . to forge in the smithy of my soul the uncreated conscience of my race."

My term "schizoid," in the title of this chapter, means *out of touch; avoiding close relationships; the inability to feel.* I do not use the term as a reference to psychopathology, but rather as a general condition of our culture and the tendencies of people which make it up. Anthony Storr, describing it more from the point of view of individual psychopathology, holds that the schizoid person is cold, aloof, superior, detached. This may erupt in violent aggression. All of which, says Storr, is a complex mask for a repressed longing for love. The detachment of the schizoid is a defense against hostility and has its source in a distortion of love and trust in infancy which renders him forever fearing actual love "because it threatens his very existence."[3]

I agree with Storr as far as he goes, but I am contending that the schizoid condition is a general tendency in our transitional age, and that the "helplessness and disregard" in infancy to which Storr refers comes not just from parents but from almost every aspect of our culture. The parents are themselves helpless and unwitting expressions of their culture. The schizoid man is the natural product of the technological man. It is one way to live and is increasingly utilized—and it may explode into violence. In its "normal" sense, the schizoid does not require repression. Whether the schizoid character state later breaks down into a schizophrenic-like state in any given case, only the future can decide. But this is much less apt to happen, as in the case with many patients, if the individual can frankly admit and confront the schizoid characteristic of his present state. Anthony Storr goes on to indicate that the schizoid character has a "conviction of being unlovable, and a feeling of being attacked and humiliated by criticism."[4]

While I value Storr's description, there is one point

where it breaks down. This is in his citing Freud, Descartes, Schopenhauer, and Beethoven as examples of the schizoid. "In the case of Descartes and Schopenhauer, it is their very alienation from love which has given birth to their philosophies." And with Beethoven,

> In compensation for his disappointment with, and resentment of, actual human beings, Beethoven imagined an ideal world of love and friendship. . . . His music, perhaps more obviously than that of any other composer, displays considerable aggression in the sense of power, forcefulness and strength. It is easy to imagine that, had he not been able to sublimate his hostility in his music, he might well have succumbed to a paranoid psychosis.[5]

Storr's dilemma is that if these men are seen as psychopathological and then had assumedly been "cured," we would not have had their creations. Thus, I believe it must be admitted that the schizoid state can be a constructive way of dealing with profoundly difficult situations. Whereas other cultures pushed schizoid persons toward being creative, our culture pushed people toward becoming more detached and mechanical.

In centering upon the problems of love and will, I do not forget the positive characteristics of our time and the potentialities for individual fulfillment. It is an obvious fact that when an age is torn loose from its moorings and everyone is to some degree thrown on his own, more people can take steps to find and realize themselves. It is also true that we hear most hue and cry about the power of the individual when the individual has least. But I write about the problems; they are what clamor for our attention.

The problems have a curious characteristic not yet adequately appreciated: *they predict the future*. The problems of a period are the existential crises of what can be, but hasn't yet been, resolved; and regardless of how seriously we take that word "resolved," if there were not some new possibility, there would be no crisis—there would be only despair. Our psychological enigmas express our unconscious desires. Problems arise where we meet

our world and find it inadequate to ourselves or ourselves
inadequate to it; something hurts, clashes, and, as Yeats
puts it,

> We . . . feel
> The pain of wounds,
> The labour of the spear. . . .

PROBLEMS AS PROPHETIC

I write this book on the basis of my experience of twen-
ty-five years of working intensively as a psychoanalytic
therapist with persons trying to meet and work through
their conflicts. Particularly in the last decade or so, these
conflicts have generally been based upon some aspect of
love or will gone wrong. In one sense, every therapist is,
or ought to be, engaged in *research* all the time—research,
as the word itself states, as a "search" for the sources.

At this point, I hear my experimental-psychologist colleagues challenging me with the argument that the data we
get in therapy are impossible to formulate mathematical-
ly and that they come from persons who represent the
psychological "misfits" of the culture. At the same time,
I hear philosopher friends insisting to me that no model
of man can be based centrally on data from neuroses or
character disorders. With both of these cautions I agree.

But neither these psychologists in their laboratories nor
those philosophers in their studies can ignore the fact
that we do get tremendously significant and often unique
data from persons in therapy—data which are revealed
only when the human being can break down the customary pretenses, hypocrisies, and defenses behind which we
all hide in "normal" social discourse. It is only in the
critical situation of emotional and spiritual suffering—
which is the situation that leads them to seek therapeutic
help—that people will endure the pain and anxiety of un-
covering the profound roots of their problems. There is
also the curious situation that unless we are oriented toward *helping* the person, he won't, indeed in some ways
cannot, reveal the significant data. Harry Stack Sullivan's
remark on research in therapy is still as cogent as
when he first made it: "Unless the interviews are de-

signed to help the person, you'll get artifacts, not real data."[6]

True, the information we get from our patients may be hard or even impossible to codify more than superficially. But this information speaks so directly out of the human being's immediate conflicts and his living experience that its richness of meaning more than makes up for its difficulty in interpretation. It is one thing to discuss the hypothesis of aggression as resulting from frustration, but quite another to see the tenseness of a patient, his eyes flashing in anger or hatred, his posture clenched into paralysis, and to hear his half-stifled gasps of pain from reliving the time a score of years ago when his father whipped him because, through no fault of his own, his bicycle was stolen—an event giving rise to a hatred which for that moment encompasses every parental figure in his whole world, including me in the room with him. Such data are empirical in the deepest meaning of the term.

With respect to the question of basing a theory of man on data from "misfits" I would, in turn, challenge my colleagues: *Does not every human conflict reveal universal characteristics of man as well as the idiosyncratic problems of the individual?* Sophocles was not writing merely about one individual's pathology when he showed us, step by step, through the drama of King Oedipus, the agonizing struggle of a man to find out "who I am and where I came from." Psychotherapy seeks the most specific characteristics and events of the given individual's life—and any therapy will become weakened in vapid, unexistential, cloudy generalities which forgets this. But psychotherapy also seeks the elements of the human conflict of this individual which are basic to the perdurable, persistent qualities of every man's experience as man— and any therapy will tend to shrink the patient's consciousness and make life more banal for him if it forgets that.

Psychotherapy reveals *both* the immediate situation of the individual's "sickness" *and* the archetypal qualities and characteristics which constitute the human being as human. It is the latter characteristics which have gone awry in specific ways in a given patient and have resulted in the former, his psychological problems. The interpretation of a patient's problems in psychotherapy is also a partial revelation of man's self-interpretation of himself through history in the archetypal forms in literature. Aeschylus' *Orestes* and Goethe's *Faust,* to take two diverse examples, are not simply portrayals of two given characters, one back in Greece in the fifth century B.C. and the other in eighteenth-century Germany, but presentations of the struggles we all, of whatever century or race, go through in growing up, trying to find identity as individual beings, striving to affirm our being with whatever power we have, trying to love and create, and doing our best to meet all the other events of life up to and including our own death. One of the values of living in a transitional age—an "age of therapy"—is that it forces upon us this opportunity, even as we try to resolve our individual problems, to uncover new meaning in perennial man and to see more deeply into those qualities which constitute the human being as human.

Our patients are the ones who express and live out the subconscious and unconscious tendencies in the culture. The neurotic, or person suffering from what we now call character disorder, is characterized by the fact that the usual defenses of the culture do not work for him—a generally painful situation of which he is more or less aware.[7] The "neurotic" or the person "suffering from character disorders" is one whose problems are so severe that he cannot solve them by living them out in the normal agencies of the culture, such as work, education, and religion. Our patient cannot or will not adjust to the society. This, in turn, may be due to one or both of the two following interrelated elements. First, certain traumatic or unfortunate experiences have occurred in his life which make him more sensitive than the average person and less able to live with and manage his anxiety. Second, he may possess a greater than ordinary amount of originality and potential which push for expression and, when blocked off, make him ill.

THE ARTIST AND THE NEUROTIC

The relation between the artist and the neurotic, often considered mysterious, is entirely understandable from the

viewpoint presented here. Both artist and neurotic speak
and live from the subconscious and unconscious depths of
their society. The artist does this positively, communicating what he experiences to his fellow men. The neurotic
does this negatively. Experiencing the same underlying
meanings and contradictions of his culture, he is unable
to form his experiences into communicable meaning for
himself and his fellows.

Art and neurosis both have a *predictive* function. Since
art is communication springing from unconscious levels, it
presents to us an image of man which is as yet present
only in those members of the society who, by virtue of
their own sensitized consciousness, live on the frontier of
their society—live, as it were, with one foot in the future.
Sir Herbert Read has made the case that the artist antici-
pates the later scientific and intellectual experience of the
race.[8] The water reeds and ibis legs painted in triangular
designs on neolithic vases in ancient Egypt were the
prediction of the later development of geometry and
mathematics by which the Egyptian read the stars and
measured the Nile. In the magnificent Greek sense of
proportion of the Parthenon, in the powerful dome of
Roman architecture, and in the medieval cathedral, Read
traces how, in a given period of history, art expresses the
meanings and trends which are as yet unconscious, but
which will later be formulated by the philosophers, religious leaders, and scientists of the society. The arts anticipate the future social and technological development by
a generation when the change is more superficial, or by
centuries when the change, as the discovery of mathematics, is profound.

By the same token, we find the artists expressing the
conflicts in the society before these conflicts emerge consciously in the society as a whole. The artist—who is the
"antennae of the race," to use Ezra Pound's phrase—is
living out, in forms that only he can create, the depths of
consciousness which he experiences in his own being as
he struggles with and molds his world.

Here we are plunged immediately into the center of
the issues raised in this book. For the world presented by
our contemporary painters and dramatists and other artists is a *schizoid world*. They present the condition of our

world which makes the tasks of loving and willing peculiarly difficult. It is a world in which, amid all the vastly developed means of communication that bombard us on all sides, actual personal communication is exceedingly difficult and rare. The most significant dramatists of our time, as Richard Gilman reminds us, are those who take as their subject matter precisely this loss of communication—who show, as do Ionesco and Genet and Beckett and Pinter, that our present fate as man is to exist in a world where communication between persons is all but destroyed. We live out our lives talking to a tape recorder, as in Beckett's *Krapp's Last Tape;* our existence becomes more lonely as the radios and TVs and telephone extensions in our houses become more numerous. Ionesco has a scene in his play, *The Bald Soprano,* in which a man and woman happen to meet and engage in polite, if mannered, conversation. As they talk they discover that they both came down to New York on the ten o'clock train that morning from New Haven, and, surprisingly, the address of both is the same building on Fifth Avenue. Lo and behold, they also both live in the same apartment and both have a daughter seven years old. They finally discover to their astonishment that they are man and wife.

We find the same situation among the painters. Cézanne, the acknowledged father of the modern art movement, a man who in his own life was as undramatic and bourgeois as only a middle-class Frenchman can be, paints this schizoid world of spaces and stones and trees and faces. He speaks to us out of the old world of mechanics but forces us to live in the new world of free-floating spaces. "Here we are beyond causes and effects," writes Merleau-Ponty of Cézanne; "both come together in the simultaneity of an eternal Cézanne who is at the same time the formula of what he wanted to be and what he wanted to do. There is a rapport between Cézanne's schizoid temperament and his work because the work reveals a metaphysical sense of the disease. . . . In this sense to be schizoid and to be Cézanne come to the same thing."[9] Only a schizoid man could paint a schizoid world; which is to say, only a man sensitive enough to penetrate to the underlying psychic conflicts could present our world as it is in its deeper forms.

But in the very grasping of our world by art there is also *our protection from* the dehumanizing effects of technology. The schizoid character lies in both the confronting of the depersonalizing world and the refusing to be depersonalized by it. For the artist finds deeper planes of consciousness where we can participate in human experience and nature below superficial appearances. The case may be clearer in Van Gogh, whose psychosis was not unconnected with his volcanic struggle to paint what he perceived. Or in Picasso, flamboyant as he may seem to be, whose insight into the schizoid character of our modern world is seen in the fragmented bulls and torn villagers in *Guernica*, or in the distorted portraits with mislocated eyes and ears—paintings not named but numbered. It is no wonder that Robert Motherwell remarks that this is the first age in which the artist does not have a community; he must now, like all of us, make his own.

The artist presents the broken image of man but transcends it in the very act of transmuting it into art. It is his creative act which gives meaning to the nihilism, alienation, and other elements of modern man's condition. To quote Merleau-Ponty again when he writes of Cézanne's schizoid temperament, "Thus the illness ceases to be an absurd fact and a fate, and becomes a general possibility of human existence."[10]

The neurotic and the artist—since both live out the unconscious of the race—reveal to us what is going to emerge endemically in the society later on. The neurotic feels the same conflicts arising from his experience of nihilism, alienation, and so on, but he is unable to give them meaningful form; he is caught between his incapacity to mold these conflicts into creative works on one hand and his inability to deny them on the other. As Otto Rank remarked, the neurotic is the "artiste manqué," the artist who cannot transmute his conflicts into art.

To admit this as a reality not only gives us our liberty as creative persons but also the basis of our freedom as human beings. By the same token, confronting at the outset the fact of the schizoid state of our world may give us a basis for discovering love and will for our own age.

THE NEUROTIC AS PREDICTIVE

Our patients predict the culture by living out *consciously* what the masses of people are able to keep *unconscious* for the time being. The neurotic is cast by destiny into a Cassandra role. In vain does Cassandra, sitting on the steps of the palace at Mycenae when Agamemnon brings her back from Troy, cry, "Oh for the nightengale's pure song and a fate like hers!"[11] She knows, in her ill-starred life, that "the pain flooding the song of sorrow is [hers] alone,"[12] and that she must predict the doom she sees will occur there. The Mycenaeans speak of her as mad, but they also believe she does speak the truth, and that she has a special power to anticipate events. Today, the person with psychological problems bears the burdens of the conflicts of the times in his blood, and is fated to predict in his actions and struggles the issues which will later erupt on all sides in the society.

The first and clearest demonstration of this thesis is seen in the sexual problems which Freud found in his Victorian patients in the two decades before World War I. These sexual topics—even down to the words—were entirely denied and repressed by the accepted society at the time.[13] But the problems burst violently forth into endemic form two decades later after World War II. In the 1920's, everybody was preoccupied with sex and its functions. Not by the furthest stretch of the imagination can anyone argue that Freud "caused" this emergence. He rather reflected and interpreted, through the data revealed by his patients, the underlying conflicts of the society, which the "normal" members could and did succeed in repressing for the time being. Neurotic problems are the language of the unconscious emerging into social awareness.

A second, more minor example is seen in the great amount of hostility which was found in patients in the 1930's. This was written about by Horney, among others, and it emerged more broadly and openly as a conscious phenomenon in our society a decade later.

A third major example may be seen in the problem of anxiety. In the late 1930's and early 1940's, some therapists, including myself, were impressed by the fact that in many of our patients anxiety was appearing *not merely as a symptom of repression or pathology, but as a generalized character state.* My research on anxiety,[14] and that of Hobart Mowrer and others, began in the early 1940's. In those days very little concern had been shown in this country for anxiety other than as a symptom of pathology. I recall arguing in the late 1940's, in my doctoral orals, for the concept of normal anxiety, and my professors heard me with respectful silence but with considerable frowning.

Predictive as the artists are, the poet W. H. Auden published his *Age of Anxiety* in 1947, and just after that Bernstein wrote his symphony on that theme. Camus was then writing (1947) about this "century of fear," and Kafka already had created powerful vignettes of the coming age of anxiety in his novels, most of them as yet untranslated.[15] The formulations of the scientific establishment, as is normal, lagged behind what our patients were trying to tell us. Thus, at the annual convention of the American Psychopathological Association in 1949 on the theme "Anxiety," the concept of normal anxiety, presented in a paper by me, was still denied by most of the psychiatrists and psychologists present.

But in the 1950's a radical change became evident; everyone was talking about anxiety and there were conferences on the problem on every hand. Now the concept of "normal" anxiety gradually became accepted in the psychiatric literature. Everybody, normal as well as neurotic, seemed aware that he was living in the "age of anxiety." What had been presented by the artists and had appeared in our patients in the late 30's and 40's was now endemic in the land.

Our fourth point brings us to contemporary issues—the problem of identity. This was first a concern of therapists with their patients in the late 40's and early 50's. It was described on the basis of data from psychological studies by Erikson in *Childhood and Society* in 1950, by myself in *Man's Search for Himself* in 1953, by Allen Wheelis in *The Quest for Identity* in 1958, and by other interpreters in psychotherapy and psychoanalysis. We find the problem of identity becoming a concern on every sophisticated person's lips in the last of that decade and the early 60's; it has taken its place as a "steady" in *New*

Yorker cartoons, and the spate of books dealing with it became best-sellers in their fields. The cultural values by which people had gotten their sense of identity had been wiped away.[16] Our patients were aware of this *before* society at large was, and they did not have the defenses to protect themselves from its disturbing and traumatic consequences.

All of these problems, to be sure, carry a certain momentum related to the ups and downs of fashion. But it would fail entirely to do justice to the dynamic historical emergence of psychological problems and of social change to dismiss them as *mere* fashions. Indeed, van den Berg, in a stimulating and provocative book, argues that *all* psychological problems are a product of the sociohistorical changes in culture. He believes that there is no "human nature" but only a changing nature of man depending on the changes in the society, and that we should call the conflicts of our patients not "neurosis" but "sociosis."[17] We need not go all the way with van den Berg: I, for one, believe psychological problems are produced by a three-cornered dialectical interplay of biological *and* individual *and* historical-social factors. Nevertheless, he makes clear what a gross and destructive oversimplification it is to assume that psychological problems emerge "out of the blue" or simply because society is now aware of the problem, or to assume that the problems exist merely because we have found new words to diagnose them. We *find* new words because something of importance is happening on unconscious, unarticulated levels and is pushing for expression; and our task is to do our best to understand and express these emergent developments.

Freud's patients were mostly hysterics who, by definition, carried repressed energy which could be released by the therapist's naming of the unconscious. Today, however, when practically all our patients are compulsive-obsessional neurotics (or character problems, which is a more general and less intense form of the same thing), we find that the chief block to therapy is the incapacity of the patient to feel. These patients are persons who can talk from now till doomsday about their problems, and are generally well-practiced intellectuals; but they cannot experience genuine feelings. Wilhelm Reich described compulsive characters as "living machines," and in his book, David Shapiro refers to this as well as to the "restraint and evenness in living and thinking" of these compulsive-obsessives. Reich, here, was ahead of his time in insight into the problems of twentieth-century patients.[18]

THE EMERGENCE OF APATHY

Earlier, I quoted Leslie Farber's assertion that our period should be called the "age of disordered will." But what underlies this disordered will?

I shall take my own leap in proposing an answer. I believe it is a state of feelinglessness, the despairing possibility that nothing matters, a condition very close to apathy. Pamela H. Johnson, after reporting the murders on the moors of England, found herself unable to shake loose her conviction that "We may be approaching the state which the psychologists call affectlessness."[19] If apathy or affectlessness is a dominant mood emerging in our day, we can understand on a deeper level why love and will have become so difficult.

What some of us were nonplussed to find in our patients in the 1950's has, in its predictive fashion, during the last few years, emerged as an overt issue gravely troubling our whole society. I wish to quote from my book, *Man's Search for Himself,* written in 1952 and published the following year:

It may sound surprising when I say, on the basis of my own clinical practice as well as that of my psychological and psychiatric colleagues, that the chief problem of people in the middle decade of the twentieth century is *emptiness*.[20]

While one might laugh at the meaningless boredom of people a decade or two ago, the emptiness has for many now moved from the state of boredom to a state of futility and despair which holds promise of dangers.[21]

. . . The human being cannot live in a condition of emptiness for very long: if he is not growing *toward* something, he does not merely stagnate; the pent-up potentialities turn into morbidity and despair, and eventually into destructive activities.[22]

The *feeling* of emptiness or vacuity . . . generally comes from people's feeling that they are *powerless* to do anything effective about their lives or the world they live in. Inner vacuousness is the long-term, accumulated result of a person's particular conviction about himself, namely his conviction that he cannot act as an entity in directing his own life, or change other people's attitudes toward him, or effectually influence the world around him. Thus he gets the deep sensé of despair and futility which so many people in our day have. And soon, since what he wants and what he feels can make no real difference, he gives up wanting and feeling.[23]

. . . Apathy and lack of feeling are also defenses against anxiety. When a person continually faces danger he is powerless to overcome, his final line of defense is at last to avoid even feeling the dangers.[24]

It was not until the mid-60's that this problem erupted in the form of several incidents that shook us to the very foundations. Our "emptiness" had been turning into despair and destructiveness, violence and assassination; it is now undeniable that these go hand in hand with apathy. "For more than half an hour, 38 respectable, law-abiding citizens in Queens," reported *The New York Times* in March, 1964, "watched a killer stalk and stab a woman in three separate attacks in Kew Gardens."[25] In April of the same year, the *Times* said, in an impassioned editorial about another event in which a crowd urged a deranged youth who was clinging to a hotel ledge to jump, calling him "chicken" and "yellow": "Are they any different from the wild-eyed Romans watching and cheering as men and beasts tore each other apart in the Colosseum? . . . Does the attitude of that Albany mob bespeak a way of life for many Americans? . . . If so, the bell tolls for all of us."[26] In May of that year, a *Times* article was headed "Rape Victim's Screams Draw 40 But No One Acts."[27] A number of similar events occurred during the next months which awakened us from our apathy long enough to realize how apathetic we had become, and how much modern city existence had developed in us the habit of uninvolvement and unfeeling detachment.

I am aware how easy it is to exaggerate specific events, and I have no wish to overstate my case. Nevertheless, I do believe that there is in our society a definite trend toward a state of affectlessness as an attitude toward life, a character state. The anomie about which intellectuals had speculated earlier seemed now to emerge with a hideous reality on our very streets and in our very subways.

What shall we call this state reported by so many of our contemporaries—estrangement, playing it cool, alienation, withdrawal of feeling, indifference, anomie, depersonalization? Each one of these terms expresses a part of the condition to which I refer—a condition in which men and women find themselves experiencing a distance between themselves and the objects which used to excite their affection and their will.[28] I wish to leave open for the moment what the sources of this are. When I use the term "apathy," despite its limiting connotations, it is because its literal meaning is the closest to what I am describing: "want of feeling; lack of passion, emotion or excitement, indifference." Apathy and the schizoid world go hand in hand as cause and effect of each other.

Apathy is particularly important because of its close relation to love and will. Hate is not the opposite of love, apathy is. The opposite of will is not indecision—which actually may represent the struggle of the *effort* to decide, as in William James—but being uninvolved, detached, unrelated to the significant events. Then the issue of will never can arise. The interrelation of love and will inheres in the fact that both terms describe a person in the process of reaching out, moving toward the world, seeking to affect others or the inanimate world, and opening himself to be affected; molding, forming, relating to the world or requiring that it relate to him. This is why love and will are so difficult in an age of transition, when all the familiar mooring places are gone. The blocking of the ways in which we affect others and are affected by them is the essential disorder of both love and will. Apathy, or a-pathos, is a withdrawal of feeling; it may begin as playing it cool, a studied practice of being unconcerned and unaffected. "I did not want to get involved," was the consistent response of the thirty-eight ciizens of Kew Gardens when they were questioned as to why they had not acted. Apathy, operating like Freud's "death instinct," is a gradual letting go of involvement until one finds that life itself has gone by.

Viewing the society freshly, students often have a clearer insight into this than older adults—though they tend, in oversimplified fashion, to blame it on the institutions. "We have just not been given any passionate sense of the excitement of intellectual life around here," said the editor of the Columbia *Spectator*.[29] A student columnist in *The Michigan Daily* wrote, "This institution has dismally failed to inculcate, in most of its undergraduates at least, anything approaching an intellectual appetite." He spoke of the drift "towards something worse than mediocrity—and that is absolute indifference. An indifference towards perhaps even life itself."[30] "We were all divided up into punches on an IBM card," a Berkeley student remarked. "We decided to punch back in the riots of 1964, but the *real* revolution around here will come when we decide to burn computer cards as well as draft cards."[31]

There is a dialectical relationship between apathy and violence. To live in apathy provokes violence; and, in incidents like those cited above, violence promotes apathy. Violence is the ultimate destructive substitute which surges in to fill the vacuum where there is no relatedness.[32] There are degrees of violence, from the relatively normal shock effect of many forms of modern art, through pornography and obscenity—which achieve their desired reaction through violence to our forms of life—to the extreme pathology of assassinations and the murders of the moors. When inward life dries up, when feeling decreases and apathy increases, when one cannot affect or even genuinely *touch* another person, violence flares up as a daimonic necessity for contact, a mad drive forcing touch in the most direct way possible.[33] This is one aspect of the well-known relationship between sexual feelings and crimes of violence. To inflict pain and torture at least proves that one can affect somebody. In the alienated state of mass communication, the average citizen knows dozens of TV personalities who come smiling into his living room of an evening—but he *himself is never known*. In this state of alienation and anonymity, painful for anyone to bear, the average person may well have fantasies which hover on the edge of real pathology. The mood of the anonymous person is, If I cannot affect or touch anybody, I can at least shock you into some feeling, force you into some passion through wounds and pain; I shall at least make sure we both feel something, and I shall force you to see me and know that I also am here! Many a child or adolescent has forced the group to take cognizance of him by destructive behavior; and though he is condemned, at least the community notices him. To be actively hated is almost as good as to be actively liked; it breaks down the utterly unbearable situation of anonymity and aloneness.

But having seen the serious affects of apathy, we need now to turn to the fact of its necessity; and, in its "normal schizoid" form, how it can be turned into a constructive function. Our tragic paradox is that in contemporary history, we *have* to protect ourselves by some kind of apathy. "Apathy is a curious state," remarks Harry Stack Sullivan; "It is a way used to survive defeat without material damage, although if it endures too long one is damaged by the passage of time. Apathy seems to me to be a miracle of protection by which a personality in utter fiasco rests until it can do something else."[34] The longer the situation goes unmet, the more apathy is prolonged; and it sooner or later becomes a character state. This affectlessness is a shrinking up in the winds of continuous demands, a freezing in the face of hyperstimuli, letting the current go by since one fears he would be overwhelmed if he responded to it. No one who has ever ridden the subway at rush hour, with its cacophonous din and hordes of anonymous humanity, will be surprised at this.

It is not difficult to appreciate how people living in a schizoid age have to protect themselves from tremendous overstimulation—protect themselves from the barrage of words and noise over radio and TV, protect themselves from the assembly line demands of collectivized industry and gigantic factory-modeled multiversities. In a world where numbers inexorably take over as our means of identification, like flowing lava threatening to suffocate and fossilize all breathing life in its path; in a world where "normality" is defined as keeping your cool; where sex is so available that the only way to preserve any inner center is to learn to have intercourse without committing yourself—in such a schizoid world, which young people experience more directly since they have not had time to build up the defenses which dull the senses of their elders, it is not surprising that will and love have become increasingly problematic and even, as some people believe, impossible of achievement.

But what of the constructive use of this schizoid situation? We have seen how Cézanne could turn his schizoid personality into a way of expressing the most significant forms of modern life, and could stand against the debilitating tendencies in our society by means of his art. We have seen that the schizoid stand is necessary; now we shall inquire how, in its healthy dimensions, it can also be turned to good. The constructive schizoid person stands against the spiritual emptiness of encroaching technology and does not let himself be emptied by it. He lives and works with the machine without becoming a machine. He finds it necessary to remain detached enough to get meaning from the experience, but in doing so to protect his own inner life from impoverishment.

Dr. Bruno Bettelheim finds the same supremacy of the aloof person—whom I would call schizoid—in his experiences in the concentration camps during World War II.

> According to psychoanalytic convictions then current . . . aloofness from other persons and emotional distance from the world were viewed as weakness of character. My comments . . . on the admirable way in which a group of what I call "annointed persons" behaved in the concentration camps suggest how struck I was with these very aloof persons. They were very much out of contact with their unconscious but nevertheless retained their old personality structure, stuck to their values in the face of extreme hardships, and as persons were hardly touched by the camp experience. . . . These very persons who, according to existing psychoanalytic theory, should have had weak personalities apt to readily disintegrate, turned out to be heroic leaders, mainly because of the strength of their character.[35]

Indeed, studies have shown that the persons who survive most effectively in space ships, and who can adjust to the sensory deprivation necessary for such a life—our comrades of the twenty-first century—are those who can detach and withdraw into themselves. "There are reasons to believe," writes Arthur J. Brodbeck after summarizing the evidence, "that it may well be the schizoid personality that will be best able to endure the requirements of extended space travel."[36] They preserve the inner world which the very hyperstimuli of our age would take away. These introverts can continue to exist despite the overpowering stimuli or lack of it, for they have learned to develop a "constructive" schizoid attitude toward life. Since we must live in the world as we find it, this distinguishing of the constructively schizoid attitude is an important part of our problem.

Apathy is the withdrawal of will and love, a statement that they "don't matter," a suspension of commitment. It is necessary in times of stress and turmoil; and the present great quantity of stimuli is a form of stress. But apathy, now in contrast to the "normal" schizoid attitude, leads to emptiness and makes one less able to defend oneself, less able to survive. However understandable the state we are describing by the term apathy is, it is also essential that we seek to find a new basis for the love and will which have been its chief casualties.

PART I

Love

TWO

PARADOXES OF
SEX AND LOVE

Sexual intercourse is the human counterpart of the
cosmic process.   —PROVERB OF ANCIENT CHINA

A patient brought in the following dream: "I am in
bed with my wife, and between us is my accountant.
He is going to have intercourse with her. My feeling
about this is odd—only that somehow it seemed
appropriate."   —REPORTED BY DR. JOHN SCHIMEL

There are four kinds of love in Western tradition. One
is *sex*, or what we call lust, libido. The second is *eros*,
the drive of love to procreate or create—the urge, as the
Greeks put it, toward higher forms of being and relationship. A third is *philia*, or friendship, brotherly love. The
fourth is *agape* or *caritas* as the Latins called it, the love
which is devoted to the welfare of the other, the prototype of which is the love of God for man. Every human
experience of authentic love is a blending, in varying
proportions, of these four.

We begin with sex not only because that is where our
society begins but also because that is where every man's
biological existence begins as well. Each of us owes his
being to the fact that at some moment in history a man
and a woman leapt the gap, in T. S. Eliot's words, "between the desire and the spasm." Regardless of how much
sex may be banalized in our society, it still remains the
power of procreation, the drive which perpetuates the
race, the source at once of the human being's most intense pleasure and his most pervasive anxiety. It can, in
its daimonic form, hurl the individual into sloughs of
despond, and, when allied with eros, it can lift him out
of his despondency into orbits of ecstasy.

The ancients took sex, or lust, for granted just as they

took death for granted. It is only in the contemporary age that we have succeeded, on a fairly broad scale, in singling out sex for our chief concern and have required it to carry the weight of all four forms of love. Regardless of Freud's overextension of sexual phenomena as such—in which he is but the voice of the struggle of thesis and antithesis of modern history—it remains true that sexuality is basic to the ongoing power of the race and surely has the *importance* Freud gave it, if not the *extension*. Trivialize sex in our novels and dramas as we will, or defend ourselves from its power by cynicism and playing it cool as we wish, sexual passion remains ready at any moment to catch us off guard and prove that it is still the *mysterium tremendum*.

But as soon as we look at the relation of sex and love in our time, we find ourselves immediately caught up in a whirlpool of contradictions. Let us, therefore, get our bearings by beginning with a brief phenomenological sketch of the strange paradoxes which surround sex in our society.

SEXUAL WILDERNESS

In Victorian times, when the denial of sexual impulses, feelings, and drives was the mode and one would not talk about sex in polite company, an aura of sanctifying repulsiveness surrounded the whole topic. Males and females dealt with each other as though neither possessed sexual organs. William James, that redoubtable crusader who was far ahead of his time on every other topic, treated sex with the polite aversion characteristic of the turn of the century. In the whole two volumes of his epoch-making *Principles of Psychology*, only one page is devoted to sex, at the end of which he adds, "These details are a little unpleasant to discuss. . . ."[1] But William Blake's warning a century before Victorianism, that "He who desires but acts not, breeds pestilence," was amply demonstrated by the later psychotherapists. Freud, a Victorian who did look at sex, was right in his description of the morass of neurotic symptoms which resulted from cutting off so vital a part of the human body and the self.

Then, in the 1920's, a radical change occurred almost

overnight. The belief became a militant dogma in liberal circles that the opposite of repression—namely, sex education, freedom of talking, feeling, and expression—would have healthy effects, and obviously constituted the only stand for the enlightened person. In an amazingly short period following World War I, we shifted from acting as though sex did not exist at all to being obsessed with it. We now placed more emphasis on sex than any society since that of ancient Rome, and some scholars believe we are more preoccupied with sex than any other people in all of history. Today, far from not talking about sex, we might well seem, to a visitor from Mars dropping into Times Square, to have no other topic of communication.

And this is not solely an American obsession. Across the ocean in England, for example, "from bishops to biologists, everyone is in on the act." A perceptive front-page article in *The Times Literary Supplement,* London, goes on to point to the "whole turgid flood of post-Kinsey utilitarianism and post-Chatterley moral uplift. Open any newspaper, any day (Sunday in particular), and the odds are you will find some pundit treating the public to his views on contraception, abortion, adultery, obscene publications, homosexuality between consenting adults or (if all else fails) contemporary moral patterns among our adolescents."[2]

Partly as a result of this radical shift, many therapists today rarely see patients who exhibit repression of sex in the manner of Freud's pre-World War I hysterical patients. In fact, we find in the people who come for help just the opposite: a great deal of talk about sex, a great deal of sexual activity, practically no one complaining of cultural prohibitions over going to bed as often or with as many partners as one wishes. But what our patients do complain of is lack of feeling and passion. "The curious thing about this ferment of discussion is how little anyone seems to be *enjoying* emancipation."[3] So much sex and so little meaning or even fun in it!

Where the Victorian didn't want anyone to know that he or she had sexual feelings, we are ashamed if we do not. Before 1910, if you called a lady "sexy" she would be insulted; nowadays, she prizes the compliment and rewards you by turning her charms in your direction. Our patients often have the problems of frigidity and impotence, but the strange and poignant thing we observe is how desperately they struggle not to let anyone find out they don't feel sexually. The Victorian nice man or woman was guilty if he or she did experience sex; now we are guilty if we *don't*.

One paradox, therefore, is that enlightenment has not solved the sexual problems in our culture. To be sure, there are important positive results of the new enlightenment, chiefly in increased freedom for the individual. Most external problems are eased: sexual knowledge can be bought in any bookstore, contraception is available everywhere except in Boston where it is still believed, as the English countess averred on her wedding night, that sex is "too good for the common people." Couples can, without guilt and generally without squeamishness, discuss their sexual relationship and undertake to make it more mutually gratifying and meaningful. Let these gains not be underestimated. External social anxiety and guilt have lessened; dull would be the man who did not rejoice in this.

But *internal* anxiety and guilt have increased. And in some ways these are more morbid, harder to handle, and impose a heavier burden upon the individual than external anxiety and guilt.

The challenge a woman used to face from men was simple and direct—would she or would she not go to bed?—a direct issue of how she stood vis-à-vis cultural mores. But the question men ask now is no longer, "Will she or won't she?" but "Can she or can't she?" The challenge is shifted to the woman's personal adequacy, namely, her own capacity to have the vaunted orgasm—which should resemble a *grand mal* seizure. Though we might agree that the second question places the problem of sexual decision more where it should be, we cannot overlook the fact that the first question is much easier for the person to handle. In my practice, one woman was afraid to go to bed for fear that the man "won't find me very good at making love." Another was afraid because "I don't even know how to do it," assuming that her lover would hold this against her. Another was scared to death of the second marriage for fear that she wouldn't be able to have the orgasm as she had not in her first. Often the woman's hesitation is formulated as, "He won't like me well enough to come back again."

In past decades you could blame society's strict mores and preserve your own self-esteem by telling yourself what you did or didn't do was society's fault and not yours. And this would give you some time in which to decide what you do want to do, or to let yourself grow into a decision. But when the question is simply how you can perform, your own sense of adequacy and self-esteem is called immediately into question, and the whole weight of the encounter is shifted inward to how you can meet the test.

College students, in their fights with college authorities about hours girls are to be permitted in the men's rooms, are curiously blind to the fact that rules are often a boon. Rules give the student time to find himself. He has the leeway to consider a way of behaving without being committed before he is ready, to try on for size, to venture into relationships tentatively—which is part of any growing up. Better to have the lack of commitment direct and open rather than to go into sexual relations under pressure—doing violence to his feelings by having physical commitment without psychological. He may flout the rules; but at least they give some structure to be flouted. My point is true whether he obeys the rule or not. Many contemporary students, understandably anxious because of their new sexual freedom, repress this anxiety ("one should *like* freedom") and then compensate for the additional anxiety the repression gives them by attacking the parietal authorities for not giving them more freedom!

What we did not see in our short-sighted liberalism in sex was that throwing the individual into an unbounded and empty sea of free choice does not in itself give freedom, but is more apt to increase inner conflict. The sexual freedom to which we were devoted fell short of being fully human.

In the arts, we have also been discovering what an illusion it was to believe that mere freedom would solve our problem. Consider, for example, the drama. In an article entitled "Is Sex Kaput?," Howard Taubman, former drama critic of *The New York Times*, summarized what we have all observed in drama after drama: "Engaging in sex was like setting out to shop on a dull afternoon; desire had nothing to do with it and even curiosity was faint."[4] Consider also the novel. In the "revolt against the Victorians," writes Leon Edel, "the extremists have had their day. Thus far they have impoverished the novel rather than enriched it."[5] Edel perceptively brings out the crucial point that in sheer realistic "enlightenment" there has occurred a *dehumanization* of sex in fiction. There are "sexual encounters in Zola," he insists, "which have more truth in them than any D. H. Lawrence described—and also more humanity."[6]

The battle against censorship and for freedom of expression surely was a great battle to win, but has it not become a new strait jacket? The writers, both novelists and dramatists, "would rather hock their typewriters than turn in a manuscript without the obligatory scenes of unsparing anatomical documentation of their characters' sexual behavior. . . ."[7] Our "dogmatic enlightenment" is self-defeating: it ends up destroying the very sexual passion it set out to protect. In the great tide of realistic chronicling, we forgot, on the stage and in the novel and even in psychotherapy, that imagination is the life-blood of eros, and that realism is neither sexual nor erotic. Indeed, there is nothing *less* sexy than sheer nakedness, as a random hour at any nudist camp will prove. It requires the infusion of the imagination (which I shall later call intentionality) to transmute physiology and anatomy into *interpersonal* experience—into art, into passion, into eros in a million forms which has the power to shake or charm us.

Could it not be that an "enlightenment" which reduces itself to sheer realistic detail is itself an escape from the anxiety involved in the relation of human imagination to erotic passion?

SALVATION THROUGH TECHNIQUE

A second paradox is that *the new emphasis on technique in sex and love-making backfires.* It often occurs to me that there is an inverse relationship between the number of how-to-do-it books perused by a person or rolling off the presses in a society and the amount of sexual passion or even pleasure experienced by the persons involved.

Certainly nothing is wrong with technique as such, in playing golf or acting or making love. But the emphasis beyond a certain point on technique in sex makes for a mechanistic attitude toward love-making, and goes along with alienation, feelings of loneliness, and depersonalization.

One aspect of the alienation is that the lover, with his age-old art, tends to be superseded by the computer operator with his modern efficiency. Couples place great emphasis on bookkeeping and timetables in their love-making—a practice confirmed and standardized by Kinsey. If they fall behind schedule they become anxious and feel impelled to go to bed whether they want to or not. My colleague, Dr. John Schimel, observes, "My patients have endured stoically, or without noticing, remarkably destructive treatment at the hands of their spouses, but they have experienced falling behind in the sexual time-table as a loss of love."[8] The man feels he is somehow losing his masculine status if he does not perform up to schedule, and the woman that she has lost her feminine attractiveness if too long a period goes by without the man at least making a pass at her. The phrase "between men," which women use about their affairs, similarly suggests a gap in time like the *entr'acte*. Elaborate accounting- and ledger-book lists—how often this week have we made love? did he (or she) pay the right amount of attention to me during the evening? was the foreplay long enough?—make one wonder how the spontaneity of this most spontaneous act can possibly survive. The computer hovers in the stage wings of the drama of love-making the way Freud said one's parents used to.

It is not surprising then, in this preoccupation with techniques, that the questions typically asked about an act of love-making are not, Was there passion or meaning or pleasure in the act? but, How well did I perform?[9] Take, for example, what Cyril Connolly calls "the tyranny of the orgasm," and the preoccupation with achieving a simultaneous orgasm, which is another aspect of the alienation. I confess that when people talk about the "apocalyptic orgasm," I find myself wondering, Why do they have to try so hard? What abyss of self-doubt, what inner void of loneliness, are they trying to cover up by this great concern with grandiose effects?

Even the sexologists, whose attitude is generally the more sex the merrier, are raising their eyebrows these days about the anxious overemphasis on achieving the orgasm and the great importance attached to "satisfying" the partner. A man makes a point of asking the woman if she "made it," or if she is "all right," or uses some other euphemism for an experience for which obviously no euphemism is possible. We men are reminded by Simone de Beauvoir and other women who try to interpret the love act that this is the last thing in the world a woman wants to be asked at that moment. Furthermore, the technical preoccupation robs the woman of exactly what she wants most of all, physically and emotionally, namely the man's spontaneous abandon at the moment of climax. This abandon gives her whatever thrill or ecstasy she and the experience are capable of. When we cut through all the rigmarole about roles and performance, what still remains is how amazingly important the sheer fact of intimacy of relationship is—the meeting, the growing closeness with the excitement of not knowing where it will lead, the assertion of the self, and the giving of the self—in making a sexual encounter memorable. Is it not this intimacy that makes us return to the event in memory again and again when we need to be warmed by whatever hearths life makes available?

It is a strange thing in our society that what goes into building a relationship—the sharing of tastes, fantasies, dreams, hopes for the future, and fears from the past— seems to make people more shy and vulnerable than going to bed with each other. They are more wary of the tenderness that goes with psychological and spiritual nakedness than they are of the physical nakedness in sexual intimacy.

THE NEW PURITANISM

The third paradox is that our highly-vaunted sexual freedom has turned out to be a new form of puritanism. I spell it with a small "p" because I do not wish to confuse this with the original Puritanism. That, as in the passion of Hester and Dimmesdale in Hawthorne's *The Scarlet Letter,* was a very different thing.[10] I refer to puritanism as it came down via our Victorian grandparents and became allied with industrialism and emotional and moral compartmentalization.

I define this puritanism as consisting of three elements. First, *a state of alienation from the body.* Second, *the separation of emotion from reason.* And third, *the use of the body as a machine.*

In our new puritanism, bad health is equated with sin.[11] Sin used to mean giving in to one's sexual desires; it now means not having full sexual expression. Our contemporary puritan holds that it is immoral *not* to express your libido. Apparently this is true on both sides of the ocean: "There are few more depressing sights," the London *Times Literary Supplement* writes, "than a progressive intellectual determined to end up in bed with someone from a sense of moral duty. . . . There is no more high-minded puritan in the world than your modern advocate of salvation through properly directed passion. . . ."[12] A woman used to be guilty if she went to bed with a man; now she feels vaguely guilty if after a certain number of dates she still refrains; her sin is "morbid repression," refusing to "give." And the partner, who is always completely enlightened (or at least pretends to be) refuses to allay her guilt by getting overtly angry at her (if she could fight him on the issue, the conflict would be a lot easier for her). But he stands broadmindedly by, ready at the end of every date to undertake a crusade to assist her out of her fallen state. And this, of course, makes her "no" all the more guilt-producing for her.

This all means, of course, that people not only have to learn to perform sexually but have to make sure, at the same time, that they can do so without letting themselves go in passion or unseemly commitment—the latter of which may be interpreted as exerting an unhealthy demand upon the partner. *The Victorian person sought to have love without falling into sex; the modern person seeks to have sex without falling into love.*

I once diverted myself by drawing an impressionistic sketch of the attitude of the contemporary enlightened person toward sex and love. I would like to share this picture of what I call the new sophisticate:

The new sophisticate is not castrated by society,

but like Origen is self-castrated. Sex and the body are for him not something to be and live out, but tools to be cultivated like a T.V. announcer's voice. The new sophisticate expresses his passion by devoting himself passionately to the moral principle of dispersing all passion, loving everybody until love has no power left to scare anyone. He is deathly afraid of his passions unless they are kept under leash, and the theory of total expression is precisely his leash. His dogma of liberty is his repression; and his principle of full libidinal health, full sexual satisfaction, is his denial of eros. The old Puritans repressed sex and were passionate; our new puritan represses passion and is sexual. His purpose is to hold back the body, to try to make nature a slave. The new sophisticate's rigid principle of full freedom is not freedom but a new straitjacket. He does all this because he is afraid of his body and his compassionate roots in nature, afraid of the soil and his procreative power. He is our latter-day Baconian devoted to gaining power *over* nature, gaining knowledge in order to get more power. And you gain power over sexuality (like working the slave until all zest for revolt is squeezed out of him) precisely by the role of full expression. Sex becomes our tool like the caveman's bow and arrows, crowbar, or adz. Sex, the new machine, the *Machina Ultima*.

This new puritanism has crept into contemporary psychiatry and psychology. It is argued in some books on the counseling of married couples that the therapist ought to use only the term "fuck" when discussing sexual intercourse, and to insist the patients use it; for any other word plays into the patients' dissimulation. What is significant here is not the use of the term itself: surely the sheer lust, animal but self-conscious, and bodily abandon which is rightly called fucking is not to be left out of the spectrum of human experience. But the interesting thing is that the use of the once-forbidden word is now made into an *ought*—a duty for the moral reason of honesty. To be sure, it *is* dissimulation to use the term fuck for the sexual experience when what we seek is a relationship of personal intimacy which is more than a release of sexual tension, a personal intimacy which will be remembered tomorrow and many weeks after tomorrow. The former is dissimulation in the service of inhibition; the latter is dissimulation in the service of alienation of the self, a defense of the self against the anxiety of intimate relationship. As the former was the particular problem of Freud's day, the latter is the particular problem of ours.

The new puritanism brings with it a depersonalization of our whole language. Instead of making love, we "have sex"; in contrast to intercourse, we "screw"; instead of going to bed, we "lay" someone or (heaven help the English language as well as ourselves!) we "are laid." This alienation has become so much the order of the day that in some psychotherapeutic training schools, young psychiatrists are taught that it is "therapeutic" to use solely the four-letter words in sessions; the patient is probably masking some repression if he talks about making love; so it becomes our righteous duty—the new puritanism incarnate!—to let him know he only fucks. Everyone seems so intent on sweeping away the last vestiges of Victorian prudishness that we entirely forget that these different words refer to different kinds of human experience. Probably most people have experienced the different forms of sexual relationship described by the different terms and don't have much difficulty distinguishing among them. I am not making a value judgment among these different experiences; they are all appropriate to their own kinds of relationship. Every woman wants at some time to be "laid"—transported, carried away, "made" to have passion when at first she has none, as in the famous scene between Rhett Butler and Scarlett O'Hara in *Gone with the Wind*. But if being "laid" is all that ever happens in her sexual life, then her experience of personal alienation and rejection of sex are just around the corner. If the therapist does not appreciate these diverse kinds of experience, he will be presiding at the shrinking and truncating of the patient's consciousness, and will be confirming the narrowing of the patient's bodily awareness as well as his or her capacity for relationship. This is the chief criticism of the new puritanism: it grossly limits feelings, it blocks the infinite variety and richness of the act, and it makes for emotional impoverishment.

It is not surprising that the new puritanism develops smoldering hostility among the members of our society. And that hostility, in turn, comes out frequently in references to the sexual act itself. We say "go fuck yourself" or "fuck you" as a term of contempt to show that the other is of no value whatever beyond being used and tossed aside. The biological lust is here in its *reductio ad absurdum*. Indeed, the word fuck is the most common expletive in our contemporary language to express violent hostility. I do not think this is by accident.

FREUD AND PURITANISM

How Freudian psychoanalysis was intertwined with both the new sexual libertarianism and puritanism is a fascinating story. Social critics at cocktail parties tend to credit Freud with being the prime mover of, or at least the prime spokesman for, the new sexual freedom. But what they do not see is that Freud and psychoanalysis reflected and expressed the new puritanism in both its positive and negative forms.

The psychoanalytic puritanism is positive in its emphasis on rigorous honesty and cerebral recitude, as exemplified in Freud himself. It is negative in its providing a new system by which the body and self can be viewed, rightly or wrongly, as a mechanism for gratification by way of "sexual objects." The tendency in psychoanalysis to speak of sex as a "need" in the sense of a tension to be reduced plays into this puritanism.

We thus have to explore this problem to see how the new sexual values in our society were given a curious twist as they were rationalized psychoanalytically. "Psychoanalysis is Calvinism in Bermuda shorts," pungently stated Dr. C. Macfie Campbell, president of the American Psychiatric Association in 1936-37, discussing the philosophical aspects of psychoanalysis. The aphorism is only half true, but that half is significant. Freud himself was an excellent example of a puritan in the positive sense in his strength of character, control of his passions, and compulsive work. Freud greatly admired Oliver Cromwell, the Puritan commander, and named a son after him. Philip Rieff, in his study *Freud: The Mind of the Mor-*

alist, points out that this "affinity for militant puritanism was not uncommon among secular Jewish intellectuals, and indicates a certain preferred character type, starched with independence and cerebral rectitude rather than a particular belief or doctrine."[13] In his ascetic work habits, Freud shows one of the most significant aspects of puritanism, namely the use of *science as a monastery.* His compulsive industry was rigorously devoted to achieving his scientific goals, which transcended everything else in life (and, one might add, life itself) and for which he sublimated his passion in a quite real rather than figurative sense.

Freud himself had a very limited sexual life. His own sexual expression began late, around thirty, and subsided early, around forty, so his biographer Ernest Jones tells us. At forty-one, Freud wrote to his friend Wilhelm Fliess complaining of his depressed moods, and added, "Also sexual excitation is of no more use to a person like me." Another incident points to the fact that around this age his sexual life had more or less ended. Freud reports in *The Interpretation of Dreams* that at one time, in his forties, he felt physically attracted to a young woman and reached out half-voluntarily and touched her. He comments on how surprised he was that he was "still" able to find the possibility for such attraction in him.[14]

Freud believed in the control and channeling of sexuality, and was convinced that this had specific value both for cultural development and for one's own character. In 1883, during his prolonged engagement to Martha Bernays, the young Freud wrote to his future wife:

> . . . it is neither pleasant nor edifying to watch the masses amusing themselves; we at least don't have much taste for it. . . . I remember something that occurred to me while watching a performance of *Carmen:* the mob gives vent to its appetites, and we deprive ourselves. We deprive ourselves in order to maintain our integrity, we economize in our health, our capacity for enjoyment, our emotions; we save ourselves for something, not knowing for what. And this constant suppression of natural instincts gives us the quality of refinement. . . . And the extreme case of people like ourselves who chain themselves to-

gether for life and death, who deprive themselves and pine for years so as to remain faithful, who probably wouldn't survive a catastrophe that robbed them of their beloved. . . ."[15]

The basis of Freud's doctrine of sublimation lies in this belief that libido exists in a certain quantity in the individual, that you can deprive yourself, "economize" emotionally in one way to increase your enjoyment in another, and that if you spend your libido in direct sexuality you will not have it for utilization, for example, in artistic creation. In a positive statement of appreciation of Freud's work, Paul Tillich nevertheless remarks that the "concept of sublimation is Freud's most puritanical belief."[16]

I am not making a simple derogatory value judgment about psychoanalysis when I point out the association between it and puritanism. The *original* Puritan movement, in its best representatives and before its general deterioration into the moralistic compartments of Victorianism at the end of the nineteenth century, was characterized by admirable qualities of dedication to integrity and truth. The progress of modern science owes a great deal to it and, indeed, would probably not have been possible without these virtues of the secular monks in their scientific laboratories. Furthermore, a cultural development like psychoanalysis is always effect as well as cause: it *reflects* and *expresses* the emerging trends in the culture, as well as molds and influences these trends. If we are conscious of what is going on, we can, in however slight a way, influence the direction of the trends. We can then hopefully develop new values which will be relevant to our new cultural predicament.

But if we try to take the content of our values from psychoanalysis, we are thrown into a confusing contradiction not only of the values themselves but of our own self-image. It is an error to expect psychoanalysis to carry the burden of providing our values. Psychoanalysis can, by its unfolding and revealing of previously denied motives and desires and by enlarging consciousness, prepare the way for the patient's working out values by means of which he can change. But it can never, in itself, carry the burden for the value decisions which do change a person's life. The great contribution of Freud was his carrying of the Socratic injunction "Know thyself" into new depths that comprise, in effect, a new continent, the continent of repressed, unconscious motives. He also developed techniques in the personal relationships in therapy, based on the concepts of transference and resistance, for bringing these levels into conscious awareness. Whatever the ebb and flow of the popularity of psychoanalysis, it will remain true that Freud's discoveries and those of the others in this field are an invaluable contribution not only to the area of psychological healing but also to morality in clearing away hypocritical debris and self-deceit.

What I wish to make clear is that many people in our society, yearning for the nirvana of automatic change in their characters and relief from responsibility that comes from handing over one's psyche to a technical process, have actually in their values of "free expression" and hedonism simply *bootlegged in from psychoanalysis new contents to their old puritanism*. The fact that the change in sexual attitudes and mores occurred so quickly—virtually in the one decade of the 1920's—also argues for the assumption that we changed our clothes and our roles more than our characters. What was omitted was the opening of our senses and imaginations to the enrichment of pleasure and passion and the meaning of love; we relegated these to technical processes. In this kind of "free" love, one does not learn to love; and freedom becomes not a liberation but a new straitjacket. The upshot was that our sexual values were thrown into confusion and contradiction, and sexual love presented the almost insoluble paradoxes we are now observing.

I do not wish to overstate the case, nor to lose sight at any point of the positive benefits of the modern fluidity in sexual mores. The confusions we are describing go hand in hand with the real possibilities of freedom for the individual. Couples are able to affirm sex as a source of pleasure and delight; no longer hounded by the misconception that sex as a natural act is evil, they can become more sensitive to the actual evils in their relationships such as manipulation of each other. Free to a degree Victorians never were, they can explore ways of making their relationship more enriching. Even the growing frequency of divorce, no matter how sobering the problems it raises, has the positive psychological effect of mak-

ing it harder for couples to rationalize a bad marriage by
the dogma that they are "stuck" with each other. The
possibility of finding a new lover makes it more necessary
for us to accept the responsibility of choosing the one we
do have if we stay with him or her. There is the possibility of developing a courage that is midway between—
and includes both—biological lust on one hand and on
the other the desire for meaningful relationship, a deepening awareness of each other, and the other aspects of
what we call human understanding. Courage can be
shifted from simply fighting society's mores to the inward
capacity to commit one's self to another human being.

But these positive benefits, it is now abundantly clear,
do not occur automatically. They become possible only as
the contradictions which we have been describing are understood and worked through.

MOTIVES OF THE PROBLEM

In my function as a supervisory analyst at two analytic
institutes, I supervise one case of each of six psychiatrists
or psychologists who are in training to become analysts. I
cite the six patients of these young analysts both because
I know a good deal about them by now and also because,
since they are not my patients, I can see them with a more
objective perspective. Each one of these patients goes to
bed without ostensible shame or guilt—and generally with
different partners. The women—four of the six patients
—all state that they don't feel much in the sex act. The
motives of two of the women for going to bed seem to
be to hang on to the man and to live up to the standard that sexual intercourse is "what you do" at a certain stage. The third woman has the particular motive of
generosity: she sees going to bed as something nice you
give a man—and she makes tremendous demands upon
him to take care of her in return. The fourth woman
seems the only one who does experience some real sexual
lust, beyond which her motives are a combination of generosity to and anger at the man ("I'll *force* him to give
me pleasure!"). The two male patients were originally impotent, and now, though able to have intercourse, have
intermittent trouble with potency. But the outstanding

fact is they never report getting much of a "bang" out of their sexual intercourse. Their chief motive for engaging in sex seems to be to demonstrate their masculinity. The specific purpose of one of the men, indeed, seems more to tell his analyst about his previous night's adventure, fair or poor as it may have been, in a kind of backstage interchange of confidence between men, than to enjoy the love-making itself.

Let us now pursue our inquiry on a deeper level by asking, What are the underlying motives in these patterns? What drives people toward the contemporary compulsive preoccupation with sex in place of their previous compulsive denial of it?

The struggle to prove one's identity is obviously a central motive—an aim present in women as well as men, as Betty Friedan in *The Feminine Mystique* made clear. This has helped spawn the idea of *egalitarianism* of the sexes and the *interchangeability* of the sexual roles. Egalitarianism is clung to at the price of denying not only biological differences—which are basic, to say the least—between men and woman, but emotional differences from which come much of the delight of the sexual act. The self-contradiction here is that the compulsive need to prove you are identical with your partner means that you repress your own unique sensibilities—and this is exactly what undermines your own sense of identity. This contradiction contributes to the tendency in our society for us to become machines even in bed.

Another motive is the individual's hope to overcome his own solitariness. Allied with this is the desperate endeavor to escape feelings of emptiness and the threat of apathy: partners pant and quiver hoping to find an answering quiver in someone else's body just to prove that their own is not dead; they seek a responding, a longing in the other to prove their own feelings are alive. Out of an ancient conceit, this is called love.

One often gets the impression, amid the male's flexing of sexual prowess, that men are in training to become sexual athletes. But what is the great prize of the game? Not only men, but women struggle to prove their sexual power—they too must keep up to the timetable, must show passion, and have the vaunted orgasm. Now it is well accepted in psychotherapeutic circles that, dynamically, the overconcern with potency is generally a compensation for feelings of impotence.

The use of sex to prove potency in all these different realms has led to the increasing emphasis on technical performance. And here we observe another curiously self-defeating pattern. It is that the excessive concern with technical performance in sex is actually correlated with the reduction of sexual feeling. The techniques of achieving this approach the ludicrous: one is that an anesthetic ointment is applied to the penis before intercourse. Thus feeling less, the man is able to postpone his orgasm longer. I have learned from colleagues that the prescribing of this anesthetic "remedy" for premature ejaculation is not unusual. "One male patient," records Dr. Schimel, "was desperate about his 'premature ejaculations,' even though these ejaculations took place after periods of penetration of ten minutes or more. A neighbor who was a urologist recommended an anesthetic ointment to be used prior to intercourse. This patient expressed complete satisfaction with the solution and was very grateful to the urologist."[17] Entirely willing to give up any pleasure of his own, he sought only to prove himself a competent male.

A patient of mine reported that he had gone to a physician with the problem of premature ejaculation, and that such an anesthetic ointment has been prescribed. My surprise, like Dr. Schimel's, was particularly over the fact that the patient had accepted this solution with no questions and no conflicts. Didn't the remedy fit the necessary bill, didn't it help him turn in a better performance? But by the time that young man got to me, he was impotent in every way imaginable, even to the point of being unable to handle such scarcely ladylike behavior on the part of his wife as her taking off her shoe while they were driving and beating him over the head with it. By all means the man was impotent in this hideous caricature of a marriage. And his penis, before it was drugged senseless, seemed to be the only character with enough "sense" to have the appropriate intention, namely to get out as quickly as possible.

Making one's self *feel less* in order to *perform better!* This is a symbol, as macabre as it is vivid, of the vicious circle in which so much of our culture is caught. The more one must demonstrate his potency, the more he treats sexual intercourse—this most intimate and personal of all acts—as a performance to be judged by exterior requirements, the more he then views himself as a machine to be turned on, adjusted, and steered, and the less feeling he has for either himself or his partner; and the less feeling, the more he loses genuine sexual appetite and ability. The upshot of this self-defeating pattern is that, in the long run, *the lover who is most efficient will also be the one who is impotent.*

A poignant note comes into our discussion when we remind ourselves that this excessive concern for "satisfying" the partner is an expression, however perverted, of a sound and basic element in the sexual act: the pleasure and experience of self-affirmation in being able to *give* to the partner. The man is often deeply grateful toward the woman who lets herself be gratified by him —lets him give her an orgasm, to use the phrase that is often the symbol for this experience. This is a point midway between lust and tenderness, between sex and agapé —and it partakes of both. Many a male cannot feel his own identity either as a man or a person in our culture until he is able to gratify a woman. The very structure of human interpersonal relations is such that the sexual act does not achieve its full pleasure or meaning if the man and woman cannot feel they are able to gratify the other. And it is the inability to experience this pleasure at the gratification of the other which often underlies the exploitative sexuality of the rare type and the compulsive sexuality of the Don Juan seduction type. Don Juan has to perform the act over and over again because he remains forever unsatisfied, quite despite the fact that he is entirely potent and has a technically good orgasm.

Now the problem is not the desire and need to satisfy the partner as such, but the fact that this need is interpreted by the persons in the sexual act in only a technical sense—giving physical sensation. What is omitted even from our very vocabulary (and thus the words may sound "square" as I say them here) is the experience of giving feelings, sharing fantasies, offering the inner psychic richness that normally takes a little time and enables sensation to transcend itself in emotion and emotion to transcend itself in tenderness and sometimes love.

It is not surprising that contemporary trends toward

the mechanization of sex have much to do with the problem of impotence. The distinguishing characteristic of the machine is that it can go through all the *motions* but it never *feels*. A knowledgeable medical student, one of whose reasons for coming into anaylsis was his sexual impotence, had a revealing dream. He was asking me in the dream to put a pipe in his head that would go down through his body and come out at the other end as his penis. He was confident in the dream that the pipe would constitute an admirably strong erection. What was entirely missing in this intelligent scion of our sophisticated times was an understanding at all that *what he conceived of as his solution was exactly the cause of his problem*, namely the image of himself as a "screwing machine." His symbol is remarkably graphic: the brain, the intellect, is included, but true symbol of our alienated age, his shrewd system bypasses entirely the seats of emotions, the thalamus, the heart and lungs, even the stomach. Direct route from head to penis—but what is lost is the heart![18]

I do not have statistics on hand concerning the present incidence of impotence in comparison with past periods, nor does anyone else so far as I have been able to discover. But my impression is that impotence is increasing these days despite (or is it because of) the unrestrained freedom on all sides. All therapists seem to agree that more men are coming to them with that problem—though whether this represents a real increase in the prevalence of sexual impotence or merely a greater awareness and ability to talk about it cannot be definitely answered. Obviously, it is one of those topics on which meaningful statistics are almost impossible to get. The fact that the book dealing with impotence and frigidity, *Human Sexual Response*, clung near the top of the best-seller lists for so many months, expensive and turgidly-written as it was, would seem to be plenty of evidence of the urge of men to get help on impotence. Whatever the reason, it is becoming harder for the young man as well as the old to take "yes" for an answer.

To see the curious ways the new puritanism shows itself, you have only to open an issue of *Playboy*, that redoubtable journal reputedly sold mainly to college students and clergymen. You discover the naked girls with silicated breasts side by side with the articles by reputable authors, and you conclude on first blush that the magazine is certainly on the side of the new enlightenment. But as you look more closely you see a strange expression in these photographed girls: detached, mechanical, uninviting, vacuous—the typical schizoid personality in the negative sense of that term. You discover that they are not "sexy" at all but that *Playboy* has only shifted the fig leaf from the genitals to the face. You read the letters to the editor and find the first, entitled "Playboy Priest," telling of a priest who "lectures on Hefner's philosophy to audiences of young people and numerous members of the clergy," that "true Christian ethics and morality are not incompatible with Hefner's philosophy," and—written with enthusiastic approbation—that "most clergymen in their fashionable parsonages live more like playboys than ascetics."[19] You find another letter entitled "Jesus was a playboy," since he loved Mary Magdalene, good food, and good grooming, and castigated the Pharisees. And you wonder why all this religious justification and why people, if they are going to be "liberated," can't just enjoy their liberation?

Whether one takes the cynical view that letters to the editor are "planted," or the more generous one that these examples are selected from hundreds of letters, it amounts to the same thing. An image of a type of American male is being presented—a suave, detached, self-assured bachelor, who regards the girl as a "Playboy accessory" like items in his fashionable dress. You note also that *Playboy* carries no advertising for trusses, bald heads, or anything that would detract from this image. You discover that the good articles (which, frankly, can be bought by an editor who wants to hire an assistant with taste and pay the requisite amount of money) give authority to this male image.[20] Harvey Cox concludes that *Playboy* is basically antisexual, and that it is the "latest and slickest episode in man's continuing refusal to be human." He believes "the whole phenomenon of which *Playboy* is only a part vividly illustrates the awful fact of the new kind of tyranny."[21] The poet-sociologist Calvin Herton, discussing *Playboy* in connection with the fashion and entertainment world, calls it the new sexual fascism.[22]

Playboy has indeed caught on to something significant

in American society: Cox believes it to be "the repressed fear of involvement with women."[23] I go farther and hold that it, as an example of the new puritanism, gets its dynamic from a repressed anxiety in American men that underlies even the fear of involvement. This is the repressed anxiety about impotence. Everything in the magazine is beautifully concocted to bolster the *illusion of potency* without ever putting it to the test or challenge at all. Noninvolvement (like playing it cool) is elevated into the ideal model for the Playboy. This is possible because the illusion is air-tight, ministering as it does to men fearful for their potency, and capitalizing on this anxiety. The character of the illusion is shown further in the fact that the readership of *Playboy* drops off significantly after the age of thirty, when men cannot escape dealing with real women. This illusion is illustrated by the fact that Hefner himself, a former Sunday-school teacher and son of devout Methodists, practically never goes outside his large establishment in North Chicago. Ensconced there, he carries on his work surrounded by his bunnies and amidst his nonalcoholic bacchanals on Pepsi-Cola.

THE REVOLT AGAINST SEX

With the confusion of motives in sex that we have noted above—almost every motive being present in the act except the desire to make love—it is no wonder that there is a diminution of feeling and that passion has lessened almost to the vanishing point. This diminution of feeling often takes the form of a kind of anesthesia (now with no need of ointment) in people who can perform the mechanical aspects of the sexual act very well. We are becoming used to the plaint from the couch or patient's chair that "We made love, but I didn't feel anything." Again, the poets tell us the same things as our patients. T. S. Eliot writes in *The Waste Land* that after "lovely woman stoops to folly," and the carbuncular clerk who seduced her at tea leaves,

> She turns and looks a moment in the glass,
> Hardly aware of her departed lover;
> Her brain allows one half-formed thought to pass;

"Well now that's done: and I'm glad it's over."
When lovely woman stoops to folly and
Paces about her room again, alone,
She smoothes her hair with automatic hand,
And puts a record on the gramophone.

(III:249—256)

Sex is the "last frontier," David Riesman meaningfully phrases it in *The Lonely Crowd*. Gerald Sykes, in the same vein, remarks, "In a world gone grey with market reports, time studies, tax regulations and path lab analyses, the rebel finds sex to be the one green thing."[24] It is surely true that the zest, adventure, and trying out of one's strength, the discovering of vast and exciting new areas of feeling and experience in one's self and in one's relations to others, and the validation of the self that goes with these are indeed "frontier experiences." They are rightly and normally present in sexuality as part of the psychosocial development of every person. Sex in our society did, in fact, have this power for several decades after the 1920's, when almost every other activity was becoming "other-directed," jaded, emptied of zest and adventure. But for various reasons—one of them being that sex by itself had to carry the weight for the validation of the personality in practically all other realms as well —the frontier freshness, newness, and challenge become more and more lost.

For we are now living in the post-Riesman age, and are experiencing the long-run implications of Riesman's "other-directed" behavior, the radar-reflected way of life. The last frontier has become a teeming Las Vegas and no frontier at all. Young people can no longer get a bootlegged feeling of personal identity out of revolting in sexuality since there is nothing there to revolt against. Studies of drug addiction among young people report them as saying that the revolt against parents, the social "kick of feeling their own oats" which they used to get from sex, they now have to get from drugs. One such study indicates that students express a "certain boredom with sex, while drugs are synonymous with excitement, curiosity, forbidden adventure, and society's abounding permissiveness."[25]

It no longer sounds new when we discover that for

many young people what used to be called love-making is now experienced as a futile "panting palm to palm," in Aldous Huxley's predictive phrase; that they tell us that it is hard for them to understand what the poets were talking about, and that we should so often hear the disappointed refrain, "We went to bed but it wasn't any good."

Nothing to revolt against, did I say? Well, there is obviously one thing left to revolt against, and that is sex itself. The frontier, the establishing of identity, the validation of the self can be, and not infrequently does become for some people, a revolt against sexuality entirely. I am certainly not advocating this. What I wish to indicate is that the very revolt against sex—this modern Lysistrata in robot's dress—is rumbling at the gates of our cities or, if not rumbling, at least hovering. The sexual revolution comes finally back on itself not with a bang but a whimper.

Thus it is not surprising that, as sex becomes more machinelike, with passion irrelevant and then even pleasure diminishing, the problem has come full circle. And we find, *mirabile dictu,* a progression from an *anesthetic* attitude to an *antiseptic* one. Sexual contact itself then tends to get put on the shelf and to be avoided. This is another and surely least constructive aspect of the new puritanism: it returns, finally, to a new asceticism. This is said graphically in a charming limerick that seems to have sprung up on some sophisticated campus:

> The word has come down from the Dean
> That with the aid of the teaching machine,
>   King Oedipus Rex
>   Could have learned about sex
> Without ever touching the Queen.

Marshall McLuhan, among others, welcomes this revolt against sex. "Sex as we now think of it may soon be dead," write McLuhan and Leonard. "Sexual concepts, ideals and practices already are being altered almost beyond recognition. . . . The foldout playmate in *Playboy* magazine—she of outsize breast and buttocks, pictured in sharp detail—signals the death throes of a departing age."[26] McLuhan and Leonard then go on to predict that eros will not be lost in the new sexless age but diffused, and that all life will be more erotic than now seems possible.

This last reassurance would be comforting indeed to believe. But as usual, McLuhan's penetrating insights into *present* phenomena are unfortunately placed in a framework of history—"pretribalism" with its so-called lessened distinction between male and female—which has no factual basis at all.[27] And he gives us no evidence whatever for his optimistic prediction that new eros, rather than apathy, will succeed the demise of *vive la difference*. Indeed, there are amazing confusions in this article arising from McLuhan's and Leonard's worship of the new electric age. In likening Twiggy to an X-ray as Sophia Loren to a Rubens, they ask, "And what does an X-ray of a woman reveal? Not a realistic picture, but a deep, involving image. Not a specialized female, but a *human being*."[28] Well! An X-ray actually reveals not a human being at all but a depersonalized, fragmentized segment of bone or tissue which can be read only by a highly specialized technician and from which we could never in a thousand years recognize a human being or any man or woman we know, let alone one we love. Such a "reassuring" view of the future is frightening and depressing in the extreme.

And may I not be permitted to prefer Sophia Loren over Twiggy for an idle erotic daydream without being read out of the New Society?

Our future is taken more seriously by the participants in the discussion on this topic at the Center for the Study of Democratic Institutions at Santa Barbara. Their report, called "The A-Sexual Society," frankly faces the fact that "we are hurtling into, not a bisexual or a multisexual, but an a-sexual society: the boys grow long hair and the girls wear pants. . . . Romance will disappear; in fact, it has almost disappeared now. . . . Given the Guaranteed Annual Income and The Pill, will women choose to marry? Why should they?"[29] Mrs. Eleanor Garth, a participant in the discussion and writer of the report, goes on to point out the radical change that may well occur in having and rearing children. "What of the time when the fertilized ovum can be implanted in the womb of a mercenary, and one's progeny selected from a sperm-bank? Will the lady choose to reproduce her husband, if there still are such things? . . . No problems, no jealousy, no love-transference. . . . And what of the children, incubated under glass? . . . Will communal love develop the human qualities that we assume emerge from the present rearing of children? Will women under these conditions lose the survival drive and become as death-oriented as the present generation of American men? . . . I don't raise the question in advocacy," she adds, "I consider some of the possibilities horrifying."[30]

Mrs. Garth and her colleagues at the Center recognize that the real issue underlying this revolution is not what one does with sexual organs and sexual functions per se, but what happens to man's humanity. "What disturbs me is the real possibility of the disappearance of our humane, life-giving qualities with the speed of developments in the life sciences, and the fact that no one seems to be discussing the alternative possibilities for good and evil in these developments."[31]

The purpose of our discussion in this book is precisely to raise the questions of the alternative possibilities for good and evil—that is, the destruction or the enhancement of the qualities which constitute man's "humane, life-giving qualities."

THREE
EROS IN CONFLICT
WITH SEX

Eros, the god of love, emerged to create the earth.
Before, all was silent, bare, and motionless. Now all
was life, joy, and motion. —EARLY GREEK MYTH

Several beautiful children were born to Aphrodite
and Ares. . . . Eros, their little son, was appointed
god of love. Although nursed with tender solicitude,
this second-born child did not grow as other children
do, but remained a small, rosy, chubby child, with
gauzy wings and roguish, dimpled face. Alarmed for
his health, Aphrodite consulted Themis, who oracu-
larly replied, "Love cannot grow without Passion."
—LATER GREEK MYTH

In the last chapter, we observed that the contemporary
paradoxes in sex and love have one thing in common,
namely *the banalization of sex and love.* By anesthetizing
feeling in order to perform better, by employing sex as a
tool to prove prowess and identity, by using sensuality to
hide sensitivity, we have emasculated sex and left it vapid
and empty. The banalization of sex is well-aided and
-abetted by our mass communication. For the plethora of
books on sex and love which flood the market have one
thing in common—they oversimplify love and sex, treating the topic like a combination of learning to play tennis
and buying life insurance. In this process, we have robbed
sex of its power by sidestepping eros; and we have ended
by dehumanizing both.

My thesis in this chapter is that what underlies our
emasculation of sex is the *separation of sex from eros.*
Indeed, we have set sex over *against* eros, used sex precisely to avoid the anxiety-creating involvements of eros.
In ostensibly enlightened discussions of sex, particularly

those about freedom from censorship, it is often argued that all our society needs is full freedom for the expression of eros. But what is revealed beneath the surface in our society, as shown not only in patients in therapy but in our literature and drama and even in the nature of our scientific research, is just the opposite. We are in a flight from eros—and we use sex as the vehicle for the flight.

Sex is the handiest drug to blot out our awareness of the anxiety-creating aspects of eros. To accomplish this, we have had to define sex ever more narrowly: the more we became preoccupied with sex, the more truncated and shrunken became the human experience to which it referred. We fly to *the sensation of sex in order to avoid the passion of eros.*

THE RETURN OF REPRESSED EROS

My thesis was formulated out of several strange phenomena I observed in my patients as well as in our society— psychic eruptions which have a curiously explosive quality. These phenomena occurred in areas in which, from any common-sense point of view, they would be least expected in our day. Most people live in the confidence that our technological developments have largely freed us from the risks of unchosen pregnancy and venereal disease and, therefore, *ipso facto,* the anxiety people used to feel about sex and love is now banished forever to the museum. The vicissitudes about which the novelists of previous centuries wrote—when a woman gave herself to a man, it meant illegitimate pregnancy and social ostracism, as in *The Scarlet Letter;* or the tragic break-up of the family structure and suicide, as in *Anna Karenina;* or venereal disease, as in the market place of social reality—have been outgrown. Now, thank God and science, we tell ourselves, we are rid of all that! The implication is that sex is free and that love is easy and comes in readily procurable packages like what the students call "instant Zen." And any talk of the deeper conflicts which used to be associated with the tragic and daimonic elements is anachronistic and absurd.

But I shall be impolite enough to ask, May there not

be a gigantic and extensive repression underlying all this? A repression not of sex, but of something underlying body chemistry, some psychic needs more vital, deeper, and more comprehensive than sex. A repression that is socially sanctioned, to be sure—but just for that reason harder to discern and more effective in its results. I am obviously not questioning contemporary medical and psychological advances as such: no one in his right mind would fail to be grateful for the development of contraceptives, estrogen, and cures for venereal disease. And I count it good fortune indeed to be born into this age with its freedom of possibilities rather than in the Victorian period with its rigid mores. But that issue is fallacious and a red herring. Our problem is more profound and starkly real.

We pick up the morning paper and read that there are a million illegal abortions in enlightened America each year; that premarital pregnancies are increasing on all sides. One girl out of six who is now thirteen will, according to present statistics, become illegitimately pregnant before she is twenty—two and a half times the incidence of ten years ago.[1] The increase is mainly among girls of the proletarian classes, but there is enough increase among girls of middle and upper classes to prove that this is not a problem solely of disadvantaged groups. Indeed, the radical increase is not among Puerto Rican or Negro girls but among *white* girls—the jump of percentage of illegitimate births to all live births being from 1.7 ten years ago to 5.3 last year. We are confronted by the curious situation of *the more birth control, the more illegitimate pregnancies*. As the reader hastens to cry that what is necessary is to change barbaric abortion laws and give more sex education, I would not disagree; but I could, and should, raise a caveat. The blanket advising of more sex education can act as a reassurance by means of which we escape having to ask ourselves the more frightening questions. May not the real issue be not on the level of conscious, rational intentions at all? May it not be in a deeper realm of what I shall later call intentionality?

Kenneth Clark points out, for example, with respect to the lower-class Negro girl, "The marginal Negro female uses her sex to gain personal affirmation. She is desired, and that is almost enough . . . a child is a symbol that she is a woman, and she may gain from having something on her own."[2] This struggle to prove one's identity and personal worth may be more outspoken with lower-class girls, but it is just as present in middle-class girls who can cover it up better by socially skillful behavior.

Let us take as an example a female patient from an upper middle-class background with whom I worked. Her father had been a banker in a small city, and her mother a proper lady who had always assumed a "Christian" attitude toward everyone but who seemed, from the data which came up in the therapy, to be unusually rigid and had actually resented having this girl when she was born. My patient was well educated, already in her early thirties a successful editor in a large publishing house, and obviously was not the slightest deficient in knowledge of sex or contraception. Yet she had had two illegitimate pregnancies in her mid-twenties several years before she began treatment with me. Both of these pregnancies gave her painful feelings of guilt and conflict, yet she went from one directly into the other. She had been married for two years in her early twenties to a man who, an intellectual like herself, was emotionally detached, and each had tried by various kinds of aggressive-dependency nagging to get the other to infuse some meaning and vitality into an empty marriage. After her divorce, while she lived alone, she volunteered to do some evening reading to the blind. She became pregnant by the young blind man to whom she read. Though this, and its subsequent abortion, upset her greatly, she became pregnant again shortly after her first abortion.

Now it is absurd to think we can understand this behavior on the basis of "sexual needs." Indeed, the fact that she did *not feel* sexual desire was actually more influential in leading her into the sexual relations which caused the pregnancies. We must look to her image of herself and her ways of trying to find a meaningful place for herself in her world if we are to have any hope of discovering the dynamics of the pregnancies.

She was, diagnostically speaking, what is called a typically contemporary schizoid personality: intelligent, articulate, efficient, successful in work, but detached in personal intercourse and afraid of intimate relationships. She had always thought of herself as an empty person who never could feel much on her own or experience anything lastingly even when she took LSD—the kind of person who cries out to the world to give her some passion, some vitality. Attractive, she had a number of men friends but the relationships with them also had a "dried up" quality and lacked the zest for which she fervently longed. She described sleeping with the one with which she was most intimate at the time as if they were two animals clinging together for warmth, her feeling being a generalized despair. She had a dream early in the therapy which recurred in varying form, of herself in one room and her parents in the next room separated by a wall which went not quite up to the ceiling; and no matter how hard she knocked on the wall or cried out to them in the dream, she could not get them to hear her.

She arrived for her therapy hour one day having just come from an art exhibit, to tell me she had discovered the symbol most accurately describing her feelings about herself: the lonely figures of Edward Hopper, in his paintings in which there is only one figure—a solitary girl usherette in a brightly lighted and plush but entirely empty theater; a woman sitting alone by an upper window in a Victorian house at the shore in the deserted off-season; a lone person in a rocking chair on a porch not unlike the house in the small city in which my patient grew up. Hopper's paintings, indeed, give a poignant meaning to the quiet despair, the emptiness of human feeling and longing which is referred to by that cliché "alienation."

It is touching that her first pregnancy came in a relation with a human being who was *blind*. We are impressed here by her elemental generosity in wanting to give him something and to prove something also to herself, but most of all we are struck by the aura of "blindness" surrounding the whole event of getting pregnant. She was one of the many persons in our world of affluence and technological power who moved, humanly speaking, in a world of the blind, where nobody can see another and where our touching is at best a sightless fumbling, moving our fingers over the body of another trying to recognize him or her, but unable in our own self-enclosing darkness to do so.

We could conclude that she became pregnant (1) to establish her own self-esteem by proving somebody wants her—as her husband did not; (2) to compensate for her feelings of emotional poverty—which pregnancy does quite literally by filling up the womb if we take the womb ("hystera") as a symbol of vacuum of emotions; (3) to express her aggression against her mother and father and their suffocating and hypocritical middle-class background. All of which goes without saying.

But what of the deeper defiance required by, and indeed built into, the self-contradictions in her and in our society which belie our rational, well-meaning intentions? It is absurd to think that this girl, or any girl, gets pregnant simply because she doesn't know better. This woman lives in an age where, for upper-class and middle-class girls like her, contraceptives and sex knowledge were never more available, and her society proclaims on all sides that anxiety about sex is archaic and encourages her to be free of all conflict about love. What of' the *anxiety which comes precisely from this new freedom?* Anxiety which places a burden on individual consciousness and capacity for personal choice which, if not insoluble, is great indeed; anxiety which in our sophisticated and enlightened day cannot be acted out like the hysterical woman of Victorian times (for everyone nowadays *ought* to be free and uninhibited) and therefore turns inward and results in inhibiting *feelings,* suffocating *passion* in place of the inhibition of actions of the nineteenth-century woman.

I am proposing, in short, that girls and women in this predicament are partial victims of a gigantic repression in themselves and in our society—the repression of eros and passion and the over-availability of sex as a technique for the repression. A corollary is that our "dogmatic enlightenment" contains elements within it which rob us of the very means of meeting this new and inner anxiety. We are experiencing a "return of the repressed," a return of an eros which will not be denied no matter how much it is bribed on all sides by sex; a return of the repressed in a primitive way precisely designed to mock our withdrawal of feelings.

The same is found in our work with men. A young

psychiatrist, in his training analysis, was preoccupied mainly with the fear that he was homosexual. Now in his middle twenties, he had never had sexual relations with a woman, and though he had not been a practicing homosexual, he had been approached by enough men to make him think that he emanated that "aura." During his therapy, he became acquainted with a woman and in due course they began having sexual relations. At least half the time they did not use contraceptives. Several times I brought to his attention the fact that the woman was fairly sure to get pregnant; he—knowing all about this from his medical training—would agree and thank me. But when he still had intercourse without contraception and once was very anxious when the woman missed her period, I found myself vaguely anxious, too, and irritated at how stupid he seemed to be. I then caught myself up with the realization that, in my naïveté, I was missing the whole point of what was going on. So I broke in, "It seems you *want* to make this woman pregnant." He at first emphatically contradicted me, but then he paused to ponder the truth of my statement.

All talk of methods and what they *ought* to do was of course irrelevant. In this man, who had never been able to feel himself masculine, some vital need was pushing him not just to prove himself a man—of which impregnating a woman is much more decisive than merely the capacity to have intercourse—but to get some hold on nature, experience a fundamental procreative process, give himself over to some primitive and powerful biological process, partake of some deeper pulsations in the cosmos. We shall not understand these problems except when we see that our patients have been robbed of precisely these deeper sources of human experience.[3]

We observe in many of these illegitimate pregnancies —or their equivalent—a defiance of the very socially-ordered system which takes away affect, where technology is felt to be a substitute for feeling, a society which calls persons forth to an arid and meaningless existence and gives them, particularly the younger generation, an experience of depersonalization which is more painful than illegal abortion. No one who has worked with patients for a long period of time can fail to learn that the psychological and spiritual agony of depersonalization is harder to bear than physical pain. And, indeed, they often clutch at physical pain (or social ostracism or violence or delinquency) as a welcome relief. Have we become so "civilized" that we have forgotten that a girl can *yearn* to procreate, and can do so not just for psychobiological reasons but to break up the arid desert of feelingless existence, to destroy for once if not for all the repetitive pattern of fucking-to-avoid-the-emptiness-of-despair ("What shall we do tomorrow?" as T. S. Eliot has his rich courtesan cry, "What shall we ever do?"). Or that she can yearn to become pregnant because the heart is never fully converted to passionlessness, and she is driven to an expression of that which is denied her and which she herself consciously denies in our age of the "cool millennium." At least being pregnant is something *real*, and it proves to the girl and to the man that *they* are real.

Alienation is felt as a loss of the capacity to be intimately personal. As I hear these people, they are crying, We yearn to talk but "our dried voices" are "rats' feet over broken glass."[4] We go to bed because we cannot hear each other; we go to bed because we are too shy to look in each other's eyes, and in bed one can turn away one's head.[5]

It should not be surprising that a revolt is occurring against the mores which people think cause alienation; a defiance of social norms which promise virtue without trying, sex without risk, wisdom without struggle, luxury without effort—all provided that they agree to settle for love without passion, and soon even sex without feeling. The denial of the daimonic means only that the earth spirits will come back to haunt us in a new guise; Gaea will be heard, and when the darkness returns the black madonna will be present if there is no white.

The error into which we have fallen obviously consists not of our scientific advances and enlightenment as such, but the using of these for a blanket allaying of all anxiety about sex and love. Marcuse holds that in a nonrepressive society, as sex develops it tends to merge with eros. It is clear that our society has done just the opposite: we separated sex from eros and then tried to repress eros. The passion which is one element of the denied eros then comes back from its repression to upset the person's whole existence.

WHAT IS EROS?

Eros in our day is taken as a synonym for "eroticism" or sexual titillation. *Eros* was the name given to a journal of sexy arcana, containing "Aphrodisiac Recipes" and posing such weighty question-and-answer articles as, "Q: How Do the Porcupines Do It? A: Carefully." One wonders whether everyone has forgotten the fact that eros, according to no less an authority than St. Augustine, is the power which drives men toward God. Such gross misunderstandings would tend to make the demise of eros unavoidable: for in our overstimulated age we have no need for titillation which no longer titillates. It is essential, therefore, that we clarify the meaning of this crucial term.

Eros created life on the earth, the early Greek mythology tells us. When the world was barren and lifeless, it was Eros who "seized his life-giving arrows and pierced the cold bosom of the Earth," and "immediately the brown surface was covered with luxuriant verdure." This is an appealing symbolic picture of how Eros *incorporates* sex—those phallic arrows which pierce—as the instrument by which he creates life. Eros then breathed into the nostrils of the clay forms of man and woman and gave them the "spirit of life." Ever since, eros has been distinguished by the function of giving the spirit of life, in contrast to the function of sex as the release of tension. Eros was then one of the four original gods, the others being Chaos, Gaea (mother earth), and Tartarus (the dark pit of Hades below the earth). Eros, says Joseph Campbell, is always, regardless of guise, the progenitor, the original creator from which life comes.[6]

Sex can be defined fairly adequately in physiological terms as consisting of the building up of bodily tensions and their release. Eros, in contrast, is the experiencing of the personal intentions and meaning of the act. Whereas sex is a rhythm of stimulus and response, eros is a state of being. The pleasure in sex is described by Freud and others as the reduction of tension; in eros, on the contrary, we wish not to be released from the excitement but rather to hang on to it, to bask in it, and even to increase it. The end toward which sex points is gratification and relaxation, whereas eros is a desiring, longing, a forever reaching out, seeking to expand.

All this is in accord with the dictionary definitions. *Webster's* defines sex (coming from the Latin *sexus*, meaning "split") as referring to "physiological distinctions. . . . the character of being male or female, or . . . the distinctive functions of male or female."[7] Eros, in contrast, is defined with such terms as "ardent desire," "yearning," "aspiring self-fulfilling love often having a sensuous quality."[8] The Latins and Greeks had two different words for sex and love, as we do; but the curious thing to our ears is how rarely the Latins speak of *sexus*. Sex, to them, was no issue; it was *amor* they were concerned about. Similarly, everyone knows the Greek word *eros*, but practically no one has ever heard of their term for "sex." It is φυλον, the word from which we derive the zoological term "phylon," tribe or race. This is an entirely different stem from the Greek word *philia*, which means love in the sense of friendship.

Sex is thus a zoological term and is rightly applied to all animals as well as human beings. Kinsey was a zoologist, and appropriately to his profession, he studied human sexual behavior from a zoological point of view. Masters is a gynecologist and studies sex from the viewpoint of sexual organs and how you manage and manipulate them: sex, then, is a pattern of neurophysiological functions and the sexual problem consists of what you do with organs.

Eros, on the other hand, takes wings from human imagination and is forever transcending all techniques, giving the laugh to all the "how to" books by gaily swinging into orbit above our mechanical rules, making love rather than manipulating organs.

For eros is the power which *attracts* us. The essence of eros is that it draws us from ahead, whereas sex pushes us from behind. This is revealed in our day-to-day language when I say a person "allures" me or "entices" me, or the possibilities of a new job "invite" me. Something in me responds to the other person, or the job, and pulls me toward him or it. I participate in forms, possibilities, higher levels of meaning, on neurophysiological dimensions but also on aesthetic and ethical dimensions as well. As the Greeks believed, knowledge and even ethical goodness exercise such a pull. Eros is the drive toward union with what we belong to—union with our own possibilities, union with significant other persons in our world in relation to whom we discover our own self-fulfillment. Eros is the yearning in man which leads him to dedicate himself to seeking *arête,* the noble and good life.

Sex, in short, is the mode of relating characterized by tumescence of the organs (for which we seek the pleasurable relief) and filled gonads (for which we seek satisfying release). But eros is the mode of relating in which we do not seek release but rather to cultivate, procreate, and form the world. *In eros, we seek increase of stimulation.* Sex is a need, but eros is a desire; and it is this admixture of desire which complicates love. In regard to our preoccupation with the orgasm in American discussions of sex, it can be agreed that the aim of the sex act in its zoological and physiological sense is indeed the orgasm. But the aim of eros is not: eros seeks union with the other person in delight and passion, and the procreating of new dimensions of experience which broaden and deepen the being of both persons. It is common experience, backed up by folklore as well as the testimony of Freud and others, that after sexual release we tend to go to sleep—or, as the joke puts it, to get dressed, go home, and *then* go to sleep. But in eros, we want just the opposite: to stay awake thinking of the beloved, remembering, savoring, discovering ever-new facets of the prism of what the Chinese call the "many-splendored" experience.

It is this urge for union with the partner that is the occasion for human tenderness. For eros—not sex as such—is the source of tenderness. Eros is the longing to establish union, full relationship. This may be, first, a union with abstract forms. The philosopher Charles S. Peirce sat alone in his house in Milford, Connecticut working out his mathematical logic, but this did not prevent his experiencing eros; the thinker must be "animated by a true eros," he wrote, "for the task of scientific investigation." Or it may be a union with aesthetic or philosophical forms, or a union with new ethical forms. But it is most obvious as the pull toward the union of two individuals sexually. The two persons, longing, as all individuals do, to overcome the separateness and isolation to which we all are heir as individuals, can participate in a relationship that, for the moment, is not made up of two isolated, individual experiences, but a genuine union. A sharing takes place which is a new *Gestalt,* a new being, a new field of magnetic force.

We have been led astray by our economic and biological models to think that the aim of the love act is the orgasm. The French have a saying which, referring to eros, carries more truth: "The aim of desire is not its satisfaction but its prolongation." André Maurois, speaking of his preference for love-making to which the orgasm is not the goal but an incidental conclusion, quotes another French saying, "Every beginning is lovely."

The moment of greatest significance in love-making, as judged by what people remember in the experience and what patients dream about, is not the moment of orgasm. It is rather the moment of entrance, the moment of penetration of the erection of the man into the vagina of the woman. This is the moment that shakes us, that has within it the great wonder, tremendous and tremulous as it may be—or disappointing and despairing, which says the same thing from the opposite point of view. This is the moment when the persons' reactions to the love-making experience are most original, most individual, most truly their own. This, and not the orgasm, is the moment of union and the realization that we have won the other.

The ancients made Eros a "god," or more specifically, a daimon. This is a symbolic way of communicating a basic truth of human experience, that eros always drives us to transcend ourselves. When Goethe wrote, "Woman draws us upward," his line may be more accurately read, "Eros, in relation with a woman, draws us upward." Such a truth is both inner, personal, and *subjective* on one hand, and external, social, and *objective* on the other—that is, it is a truth which obtains in our relationships in the objective world. The ancients, taking sex for granted simply as a natural bodily function, saw no need to make it into a god. Antony presumably had all his sexual needs taken care of by the concubines accompanying the Roman army; it was only when he met Cleopatra that *eros* entered the picture and he became transported into a whole new world, ecstatic and destructive at the same time.

The artists have always instinctively known the difference between sex and eros. In Shakespeare's play, Romeo's friend Mercutio teases him about his previous sweetheart, describing her in good modern anatomical style:

> I conjure thee by Rosaline's bright eyes,
> By her high forehead, and her scarlet lip,
> By her fine foot, straight leg, quivering thigh,
> And the desmesnes that there adjacent lie.
>
> (Act II, Scene i)

It reads like a contemporary realistic novel, the bodily description of the heroine ending with the expected "quivering thigh" and allusion to the adjacent parts. For Mercutio is not in love; from his external view the phenomenon appears to be sex and to be used as any vital young Veronese man would use feminine pulchritude.

But does Romeo use that language? Absurd question! He is in the state of *eros* with Juliet:

> O! she doth teach the torches to burn bright.
> It seems she hangs upon the cheek of night
> Like a rich jewel in an Ethiop's ear;
> Beauty too rich for use, for earth too dear!
>
> (Act I, Scene v)

It is interesting to recall that Romeo and Juliet were members of feuding families. Eros leaps the barriers between enemies. Indeed, I often wonder whether the eros in us is not excited and challenged *especially* by the "enemy." Eros is strangely fascinated by the "outlander," the person of the forbidden class, the foreign color or race. Shakespeare is true to the meaning of eros when he has the love of Romeo and Juliet, tragic as it was, bind together the previously warring Montagues and Capulets, and unite the whole city of Verona.

EROS IN PLATO

There is good basis in man's ancient wisdom for the urge we all feel in eros to unite with the beloved, to prolong the delight, to deepen the meaning and treasure it. This holds in our relationships not only with persons but with objects, like a machine we are making or a house we are building or a vocation to which we are devoted.

To find the roots of our understanding of eros, we turn to *The Symposium*, which still surprises and delights readers with the contemporaneousness of its insights into love.[9] Plato's dialogue describing this banquet—aptly called the most famous drinking party in history—is given over entirely to the discussion of eros. The setting is Agathon's home, where Socrates, Aristophanes, Alcibiades, and others have been invited to celebrate Agathon's winning of the prize the previous day for tragic drama. The evening is passed by each one in turn giving his thoughts and experience of eros.

"What is love?" asks Socrates in a crucial summary passage. He quotes the answer from Diotima, the celebrated teacher of love: "He is neither mortal nor immortal, but a mean between the two. . . . He is a great spirit (daimon) and like all spirits he is intermediate between the divine and the mortal. . . . He is the mediator who spans the chasm which divides men and gods, and therefore in him all is bound together. . . ."[10]

Eros is not a god in the sense of being above man, but the power that binds all things and all men together, the power *informing* all things. I do not use "in-form" loosely—it means to give inward form, to seek out by the devotion of love the unique form of the beloved person or object and to unite one's self with that form. Eros is the god or demiurge, Plato continues, who constitutes man's creative spirit. Eros is the drive which impels man not only toward union with another person in sexual or other forms of love, but incites in man the yearning for knowledge and drives him passionately to seek union with the truth. Through eros, we not only become poets and inventors but also achieve ethical goodness. Love, in the form of eros, is the power which generates, and this generation is "a kind of eternity and immortality"— which is to say that such creativity is as close as men ever get to becoming immortal.

Eros is the drive for union and reproduction in the biological realm. Even in the birds and animals, says Diotima, we see the "desire of procreation," and they are "in agony when they take the infection of love, which begins with the desire of union. . . ."[11] Human beings are changing all the time—

> hair, flesh, bones, blood, and the whole body are always changing. Which is true not only of the body, but also of the soul, whose habits, tempers, opinions, desires, pleasures, pains, fears, never remain the same in any one of us, but are always coming and going; and equally true of knowledge, and what is still more surprising to mortals, not only do the sciences in general spring up and decay, so that in respect of them we are never the same. . . .[12]

Now in all this change, what binds the diversity together? It is eros, the power in us yearning for wholeness, the drive to give meaning and pattern to our variegation, form to our otherwise impoverishing formlessness, integration to counter our disintegrative trends. Here we must have a dimension of experience which is psychological and emotional as well as biological. This is eros.

It is eros which impels people toward health in psychotherapy. In contrast to our contemporary doctrines of adjustment or homeostasis or release of tension, there is in eros an eternal reaching out, a stretching of the self, a continuously replenished urge which impels the individual to dedicate himself to seek forever higher forms of truth, beauty, and goodness. The Greeks believed that this continuous regeneration of the self is inherent in eros.

The Greeks also knew that there always is a tendency for eros to be reduced simply to sexual desire—*epithymia* or lust in their terms. But they insisted that the biological is not denied but *incorporated* and *transcended* in eros:

> Those who are pregnant in the body only, betake

themselves to women and beget children—this is the character of their love; their offspring, as they hope, will preserve their memory and give them the blessedness and immortality which they desire in the future. But souls which are pregnant—for there certainly are men who are more creative in their souls than in their bodies—conceive that which is proper for the soul to conceive or contain. And what are these conceptions?—wisdom and virtue in general. And such creators are poets and all artists who are deserving of the name inventor.[13]

We are in eros not only when we experience our biological, lustful energies but also when we are able to open ourselves and participate, via imagination and emotional and spiritual sensitivity, in forms and meanings beyond ourselves in the interpersonal world and the world of nature around us.

Eros is the binding element par excellence. It is the bridge between being and becoming, and it binds fact and value together. Eros, in short, is the original creative force of Hesiod now transmuted into power which is both "inside" and "outside" the person. We see that eros has much in common with the concept of intentionality proposed in this book: both presuppose that man pushes toward uniting himself with the object not only of his love but his knowledge. And this very process implies that a man already participates to some extent in the knowledge he seeks and the person he loves.

Later, in St. Augustine, eros was seen as the power which drives men toward God. Eros is the yearning for mystic union which comes out in the religious experience of union with God, or in Freud's "oceanic" experience.[14] There is also an element of eros in the love of one's fate —"*amor fati*" as Nietzsche called it. By fate I do not mean the specific or accidental misfortunes which befall us, but rather fate as the acceptance and affirmation of the finite state of man, limited as we are in intelligence and strength, faced everlastingly with weakness and death. The myth of Sisyphus presents man's fate in as stark a form as could be imagined; yet Camus finds in that fate, for the man who has courage to accept the consciousness of it, something which calls forth his eros, something to love:

> I leave Sisyphus at the foot of the mountain! . . . This universe without a master seems to him neither sterile nor futile. Each atom of that stone, each mineral flake of that night-filled mountain, in itself forms a world. The struggle itself toward the heights is enough to fill a man's heart. One must imagine Sisyphus happy.[15]

Eros pushes toward self-fulfillment, but it is not at all the ego-centric assertion of one's subjective whims and wishes on a passive world. The idea of "mastering" nature or reality would have horrified the Greeks and would promptly have been labelled *hubris*, or inordinate pride which is an affront to the gods and a sure invitation for a man's doom. The Greeks always showed a respect which amounted to a reverence for the objective, given world. They delighted in their world—its beauty, its form, its endless challenges to their curiosity, its mysteries to be explored; and they were everlastingly attracted by this world. Not that they would have had any truck with the modern sentimental belief that life by *itself* is good or bad; it all depends on what a man dedicates himself to. Their tragic view itself enabled them to delight in life. You can't outwit death anyway by "progress" or accumulating wealth; so why not accept your fate, choose values which *are* authentic, and let yourself delight and believe in the being you are and the Being you are part of?

"Shall not loveliness be loved forever?" sings Euripides. The question is rhetorical, but the answer is not. Loveliness shall be loved not because of infantile needs, or because it stands for the breast, or because it is aim-inhibited sex, or because it aids adjustment or because it will make us happy—but simply because it is lovely. Loveliness exercises a pull upon us, we are drawn to life by love.

What does all this have to do with psychotherapy? I believe a great deal. When Socrates remarks, with a deceptive simplicity, "Human nature will not easily find a helper better than eros," we can take his words as apply-

ing to the process of psychotherapy as well as the drive
within a person toward psychic health. Socrates himself,
as we see and listen to him in the Dialogues, is perhaps
history's greatest model of the psychotherapist. His pray-
er at the end of *Phaedo* could well be inscribed on the
wall of every therapist's office:

> Beloved Pan, and all ye other gods who haunt this
> place, give me beauty in the inward soul; and may
> the outward and inward man be at one. May I reckon
> the wise to be the wealthy, and may I have such a
> quantity of gold as none but the temperate can carry.

FREUD AND EROS

But the ancient Greeks knew, as every society and almost
every individual learns, that responding as a total person
in one's encounters with life requires an intensity and dis-
ciplined openness of consciousness which is not easy to
sustain. A tendency to desiccate eros, to reduce it to sheer
sexual gratification or lust then occurs. In our day, we
see several groups which seek to deny eros. There are
the idealists, who, like Denis de Rougement, identify eros
with sexual passion as part of their dubious and rejecting
attitude toward eros. For eros is always an inescapable
embarrassment to any purely mental or religious category.

There are also the naturalists, like the early Freud. He
struggled valiantly to reduce love to libido, a quantitative
concept which fitted the nineteenth-century Helmholtzian
model in physics to which he was devoted. So great was
his need to deny eros, that the term is not in the index to
his *General Introduction to Psychoanalysis*. In the first
two volumes of Ernest Jones's *Life and Work of Freud*,
the term is also not mentioned in the index, whereas
there are roughly thirty discussions of libido in the second volume alone. In the third volume Jones writes,
"There are only a few earlier [before *Beyond the Pleasure Principle*, 1920] allusions to Eros in Freud's writings." Jones gives only two references, and they are very
minor, using "erotic" as a simple synonym for "sexual."
It is only in this last volume that Freud discovers eros in
its own right. He finds it as an aspect of human experi-

ence that must not only be distinguished from libido but is in important ways *opposed* to libido. And here a remarkable event occurs: *Freud recognizes that fully gratified libido leads, via the death instinct, to self-destruction. Then eros—the spirit of life—is brought in to rescue libido from demise in its own self-contradictions.*

But we are ahead of our story.

We have to distinguish three levels when discussing Freud on this topic. First, there is his popular influence, which has obviously been great indeed. When his concepts of "drive" and "libido" in the popular sense are taken literally, Freudianism in the popular sense plays directly into the banalization of sex and love, however contrary the real intentions of its author were.[16]

Freud sought to enrich and extend the concept of sex to include everything from fondling and nursing to creativity and religion. "We use the word 'sexuality' in the same comprehensive sense as that in which the German language uses the word 'lieben.' "[17] This wide extension of the term sex refers specifically to Viennese Victorian culture, for when any important human function is repressed as sex then was, it seeps out to color every other human activity.

There is, second of all, Freud's own use of the terms sexual instinct, drive, and libido. As in any thinker with such richness of mind, we find Freud boldly ambiguous in employing these terms, cheerfully changing their meaning from stage to stage in the development of his thought. His concepts of libido and sexual drive have within them elements of the daimonic which transcend the physiological definition of sex, as we shall indicate below. Early in his career, his friends urged him to use the term "eros" because it was more urbane and would avoid some of the opprobrium aroused by the term sex; but he steadfastly—and rightly, if seen in his light—refused to accommodate himself by doing this. He seemed to be assuming in this period that eros means the same thing as sex. He held here to a model of sexual love (libido) which consists of a fixed economic quantity in every person and makes any kind of love other than sexual union merely the expression of sexuality which is "aim-inhibited."

Freud's belief that we have only a given quantity of

love leads him to argue that when a person loves someone else there is a depletion of the love he has for himself.

> We see . . . an antithesis between ego-libido and
> object-libido. The more the one is employed, the
> more the other becomes depleted. The highest phase
> of development of which object-libido is capable is
> seen in the state of being in love, when the subject
> seems to give up his own personality in favor of an
> objective-cathexis.[18]

There is an analogy here to what I have called the fear
of the loss of one's own being in falling in love. But on
the basis of my own clinical experience, I believe expressing this on the hydraulic model of sex destroys the
critical values at stake. The threat of the loss of one's
own being in falling in love comes from the dizziness and
shock of being hurled into a new continent of experience.
The world is suddenly vastly widened and confronts us
with new regions we never dreamed existed. Are we capable of giving ourselves to our beloved and still preserving what center of autonomy we have? Understandably,
this experience scares us; but anxiety about the vastness
and dangers of the new continent—accompanied by delight and anxiety simultaneously—should not be confused with loss of self-esteem.

Actually, anyone's normal day-to-day observation demonstrates just the opposite to Freud's view. When I fall
in love, I feel *more* valuable and I treat myself with
more care. We have all observed the hesitant adolescent,
uncertain of himself, who, when he or she falls in love,
suddenly walks with a certain inner assuredness and confidence, a mien which seems to say, "You are looking at
somebody now." And we cannot subsume this under the
rubric of "returned libido cathexis" from the loved one;
for this inner sense of worth that comes with being in
love does not seem to depend essentially on whether the
love is returned or not. The now generally accepted formulation of this problem was made best by Harry Stack
Sullivan, who gave abundant evidence that we love others
to the extent that we are able to love ourselves, and if

we cannot esteem ourselves, we cannot esteem or love others.

Now the fact that Freud does not mention eros during the first two-thirds of his life and work does not mean that he would have agreed with our contemporary gospel of "free expression." He would have looked askance at all the talk in our society about simply "doing what comes naturally," the setting up of Rousseau's happy primitive in a South Sea isle as the ideal. In 1912 he wrote:

> . . . It can easily be shown that the psychical value of erotic [sexual] needs is reduced as their satisfaction becomes easy. An obstacle is required in order to heighten libido; and where natural resistances to satisfaction have not been sufficient men have at all times erected conventional ones so as to be able to enjoy love. This is true of both individuals and of nations. In times in which there were no difficulties standing in the way of sexual satisfaction, such as perhaps during the decline of the ancient civilizations, love became worthless and life empty, and strong reaction-formations were required to restore indispensable affective values . . . the ascetic current in Christianity created psychical values for love which pagan antiquity was never able to confer on it.[19]

Freud wrote the above paragraph two years before World War I. It was directly after the war that he realized the implications of this problem for the individual person. Certain radical reflections were forced on him by his seeing that patients afflicted with war neuroses did not behave according to the pleasure principle. That is, they did not seek to get rid of the painful trauma—indeed, they behaved in just the opposite way; they relived the painful trauma again and again, in their dreams and in real life. They seemed to be struggling to do something with the remembered trauma, to re-experience the anxiety so that something could be assuaged, or to reform themselves in relation to their world in such a way that the trauma could have meaning. However one de-

scribes it, something was occurring that was infinitely
more complex than the mere reduction of tension and increase of pleasure. This specifically led Freud to the clinical problems of masochism and the repetition compulsion. He saw that love, more complex than his previous
theories implied, always exists in polarity with hate. It
was not a far step from there to his formulation of the
theory that life exists always in polarity with death.

We now come to the third level in Freud's view of sex
and eros, appearing in his middle and later writings,
which is, for our purposes, the most interesting and important of all. He began to see that the gratifying of the
sexual drive itself—the full satisfaction of libido with its
reduction of tension—has an ultimately self-defeating
character and tends toward death.

In this period directly after the war, when he was six-
ty-four, Freud wrote *Beyond the Pleasure Principle,* a
book about which there has been, and still is, endless
controversy even within the psychoanalytic movement itself. He begins by summarizing his previous beliefs that
"the course of mental events automatically regulated by
the pleasure principle . . . is inwardly set in motion by an
unpleasurable tension, and it takes a direction such that
its final outcome coincides with a lowering of tension."[20]
The sexual instincts (which, he whimsically remarks, are
so hard to "educate") were the prime example of the
goal of pleasure by means of reduction of tension. An
instinct, Freud emphasizes, has as its goal the restoring
of an earlier state. He borrows here from the second law
of thermodynamics, that the energy of the universe is
constantly running down. Since ". . . *an instinct is an
urge inherent in organic life to restore an earlier state of
things . . .*"and *"inanimate things existed before living
ones,"*[21] so our instincts push us back to the inanimate.
The instincts move toward nirvana, which is complete
absence of excitation. The "aim of all life is death."[22]
And here we find ourselves at Freud's most controversial
theory termed the death instinct, or Thanatos. Our instincts, which seem to propel us onward, are now only
moving us in a great circle which is doomed to come
back to death. Man, this creature so "noble in faculty,"
moves step by step in a pilgrimage that is destined to
bring him only back again to the inanimate state of the

stone. From dust we are, and to dust we ultimately return.[23]

Then a remarkable event occurred, the importance of which I do not believe is recognized by students of Freud. For the first time in Freud's work, eros comes into its own as a central and necessary concept. It is perhaps not surprising that this man, who as a boy in a gymnasium in Vienna had kept his diary in Greek, should now, at the point of his greatest dilemma, find in the wisdom of the ancients a way to meet his perplexity. *Eros comes in to rescue sex and libido from extinction.*

Eros enters as the opposite to Thanatos, the death instinct. Eros fights for life against the death tendencies. Eros is the "uniting and binding, the building and blending, the increase of tension within us."[24] Eros introduces "fresh tensions," writes Freud.[25] Eros is given a character not only greater than, but in significant ways different from, libido. Eros, "builder of cities," as Auden calls it, standing against the pleasure principle with its reduction of tension, enables man to create cultures. "Eros operates from the beginning of life, and appears as a 'life instinct' in opposition to the 'death instinct.'" Human existence now consists of a new form of the battle of the giants, Eros against Thanatos.

How Freud himself must have experienced the contradiction going on in his thinking as this birth-process went on is shown in the way he himself writes about it: ". . . the death instincts are by their nature mute and . . . the clamor of life proceeds for the most part from Eros. And from the struggle against Eros!"[26] This is the bold inconsistency of genius! And one of the most serious inconsistencies is the endeavor in Freud still to identify this Eros with the sexual instincts. He speaks of the "libido of Eros," the "libido of the Id," and the "libido of the Ego," and about "desexualized libido" and "non-desexualized libido"—until the reader feels that Freud is laboring under the necessity of forcing all his insights, even a great one like this rediscovery of eros, onto the procrustean bed of his old energy system.

We can cut through this confusion if we keep clearly in mind the dynamic point that Freud did not bring eros into his work at all until he had to face the fact that the sexual instincts operating on the pleasure principle were

self-defeating. Eros, thus, *does* represent something genuinely new. Freud ends one essay by affectionately calling
"Eros, the mischief maker," and we are left with the impression that this Eros is not easily going to let the
death instinct establish peace in the id "prompted by the
pleasure principle" and bought at the price of apathy.
When "satisfaction triumphs," writes Freud, "then Eros
is eliminated, and the death instinct has a free hand for
accomplishing its purposes."[27]

The dilemma we face in our society is similar to the
one Freud faced—the assumption that the ultimate goal
of existence is the satisfaction of impulses has led sex
into the cul-de-sac of tedium and banality. Eros, drawing
us ahead, refers to the realms of possibilities; it is the
reach of human imagination and intentionality. Several
authorities,[28] in refutation of the literal form of the
death instinct, point out that reasoning from the second
law of thermodynamics is false, since plants and animals
draw renewed power from their environments. Thus, eros
is our capacity to participate in a constant dialogue with
our environment, the world of nature as well as persons.

Freud himself took pride in relating his concept of
eros to that of the ancient Greeks. He writes, ". . . anyone who looks down with contempt upon psychoanalysis
from a superior vantage-point should remember how
closely the enlarged sexuality of psychoanalysis coincides
with the Eros of the divine Plato."[29] When Freud's fol-
lowers wrote papers arguing the close relation of his eros
to Plato's, the master affirmed their views with enthusiasm: "In its origin, function, and relation to sexual love,
the Eros of the philosopher Plato coincides exactly with
the love-force, the libido, of psychoanalysis, as has been
shown in detail by Nachmansohn (1915) and Pfister
(1921)."[30] Not only is Freud's concept of eros radically
different from Plato's, but, as Professor Douglas Morgan
states, after appreciative and lengthy studies of both
Platonic and Freudian love,

> The truth is that Freudian love is very nearly the
> obverse of Platonic love. In their metaphysical bases,
> and in their dynamic directions, they not merely dif-
> fer, but in effect contradict one another. So far are
> the   two   interpretations   from   being   (as   Freud

thought) coincident, that neither could be true if the other were even meaningful.[31]

Phillip Rieff agrees with this, ". . . the psychoanalytic Eros is basically unlike the Platonic."[32]

What Freud does have in common with Plato is that both believed love is fundamental in human experience, love pervades all actions, and is a deep, broad, motivating force. "Within the meaning of 'Eros' in both, are encompassed genital-sexual love, fraternal and civic love, the loves of science and art and perfection."[33] But when we ask what that love is, we find entirely different answers. Even after introducing eros, Freud defined it as a push from behind, a force coming out of "chaotic, undifferentiated, instinctive energy-sources along predictable and prescribable paths toward mature life and only partially, painfully civilized love."[34] Whereas for Plato, eros is entirely bound up with the possibilities ahead which "pull" one; it is the yearning for union, the capacity to relate to new forms of human experience. It is "wholly telic, goal-directed, and moves toward the more-than-nature."[35] The culture in which Freud studied, thought, and worked was an alienated one, and that alienation is already revealed in his definitions of love and sex—as it reveals even more in ours a half century later. This may partly account for his confusion of his eros with Plato's.[36]

But on my part, I value Freud's intuition, or "hope" if I may say so, that his eros would have something of Plato's in it. This is another example of what we find so often in Freud—which underlies his frequent and important use of myths—that the ethos and meaning of his concepts went way beyond his methodology and beyond the logic of the strict application of the concept. My disagreement with Professor Morgan is his statement above —that the Freudian and Platonic concepts of love are incompatible. On the basis of my clinical work with patients, I believe that not only are the two compatible, but that they represent two halves both of which, in a human being's psychological development, are required.

THE UNION OF EROS: A CASE STUDY

I shall give as an example a psychoanalytic session that took place while I was writing this chapter, which I believe demonstrates not only the contrast between the Freudian and Platonic views of eros in therapy but also their interrelationship.

A woman in her late twenties had come for treatment because of severe lack of feeling, blockage in spontaneity —both of which made sexual relations a difficult problem for her husband and herself—and a self-consciousness which at times paralyzed her. She was the daughter of one of the old aristocratic American families of considerable stature, a family in which her masochistic mother and prestigious father and three older brothers constituted a rigid structure in which she had to grow up. In therapy, she learned—with her rational temperament— to inquire of herself the "reason why" she was emotionally paralyzed in this or that situation, what was occurring when she felt nothing sexually, and she became able to experience and express her anger, sexual passion, and other feelings with considerable freedom. This was aided by a good deal of useful inquiry into her childhood and the difficult traumas she had sustained in this overly-structured family, and it was accompanied by a positive effect on her practical living.

But at a certain stage, we hit a stalemate. She kept asking the "reason why," but it no longer made any change in her; her emotions seemed to be their own reason when she was working on the possibilities of a genuine love with her husband.

She reported that the previous night she had felt flirtatious with her husband and in that mood had asked him to reach down the back of her dress and take out a bug or whatever was there. Later in the evening when she was writing checks at her desk, he unexpectedly threw his arms around her. She, furious at being interrupted, scratched a line across his face with her pen. In telling me about this, she tossed off some ready-at-hand explanations of her anger as due to her brothers' having taken advantage of her as a child no matter what she was doing. When I questioned this by asking what she was using her feelings *for* in the incident, she flared up in anger: I was taking away her "free spontaneity." Didn't I see she must "trust her instincts"? Hadn't we spent a good deal of time helping her learn to feel, and so what did I mean by asking her what she was *doing* with her feelings? And what is more, the question sounded just like her family's telling her to be responsible. She finished the attack with the expostulation, "Feelings are feelings!"

We can readily see the contradiction she is caught in. She had effectively ruined the evening with her husband. Ostensibly seeking the possibilities of a genuine love between them, she had accomplished exactly the opposite. She pulls her husband toward her with one hand and as quickly drives him away with the other. She justifies this contradictory behavior by an assumption which is very common in our day, namely, that feeling is a subjective push from inside you, emotions (the term coming from *e-movere*, to move out) are forces which put you into motion, and so are to be "emoted" in whatever way you happen to feel at the moment. This is probably the most prevalent unanalyzed assumption about emotions in our society. It takes its model from a kind of glandular hydraulics we have an inner secretion of adrenalin and need to let off our anger, or gonadal excitement and must find a sexual object. (Whatever Freud actually meant, his name is brought in to halo this assumption.) It fits the popularly accepted mechanical model of the body as well as the more sophisticated deterministic models that many of us were exposed to in our first courses in psychology and physiology.

What we were *not* told—because practically nobody saw it—is that this is a radically solipsistic, schizoid system. It leaves us separated like monads, alienated, with no bridge to any persons around us. We can "emote" and have sexual relations from now till doomsday and never experience any real relationship with another person, only literally a doomsday. It does not decrease the horror of the situation to realize that a great many people, if not most in our society, experience their emotions in just this lonely way. To feel, then, makes their loneliness more painful rather than decreasing it, so they stop feeling.

What is omitted in my patient's (and our society's)

view is that emotions are not just a push from the rear
but a *pointing toward* something, an impetus for forming
something, a call to mold the situation. Feelings are not
just a chance state of the moment, but a pointing toward
the future, a way I *want* something to be. Except in the
most severe pathology, feelings always occur in a personal field, an experience of one's self as personal and an
imagining of others even if no one else is literally present. Feelings are rightfully a way of communicating with
the significant people in our world, a reaching out to
mold the relationship with them; they are a language by
which we interpersonally construct and build. That is to
say, feelings are *intentional*.

The first aspect of emotions, as forces which "push,"
has to do with the past and is correlated with causality
and the determinism of one's past experience, including
the infantile and archaic. This is the *regressive* side of
emotions about which Freud has taught us so much of
lasting importance. In this respect, the investigation
of the childhood of the patient, and the re-experiencing
of it, has a sound and essential role in enduring psychotherapy.

The second view, in contrast, starts in the present and
points toward the future. It is the *progressive* aspect of
emotions. Our feelings, like the artist's paints and brush,
are ways of communicating and sharing something meaningful from us to the world. Our feelings not only take
into consideration the other person but are in a real sense
partially *formed by the feelings of the other persons
present*. We *feel* in a magnetic field. A sensitive person
learns, often without being conscious of doing so, to pick
up the feelings of the persons around him, as a violin
string resonates to the vibration of every other musical
string in the room, although in such infinitessimally small
degrees that it may not be detectable to the ear. Every
successful lover knows this by "instinct." It is an essential
—if not *the* essential—quality of the good therapist.

In dealing with the first aspect of emotions it is entirely sound and accurate to ask the "reason why." But
the second aspect requires asking the "purpose for."
Freud's approach is roughly correlated with the former,
and he would, no doubt, have denied my use of "purpose"
here. Plato's and the Greek concept of eros is correlated

with the second: emotion is attraction, a pulling toward; my feelings are aroused by virtue of goals, ideals, possibilities in the future which grasp me. This distinction is also made in modern logic; the *reason* is the consideration in the past which explains why you are doing this or that, and *purpose,* in contrast, is what you want to get out of doing it. The first concept is correlated with determinism. The second refers to your opening up to new possibilities of experience. It is thus correlated with freedom. *We participate in the forming of the future by virtue of our capacity to conceive of and respond to new possibilities, and to bring them out of imagination and try them in actuality.* This is the process of active loving. It is the eros in us responding to the eros in others and in the world of nature.

To return to my patient: she experienced a hopelessness in the above session, arising out of her dim awareness of the trap she was caught in. Two sessions later she was to say, "I've always looked for reasons I feel such and such toward George. I believed that was what was important—that process would lead to a nirvana. Now I've run out of reasons. Maybe there aren't any." It is interesting that her last phrase is more brilliant than she realized. For it is true, both in therapy and in life, when we get to the stage where our essential needs are mostly met and we are not need-driven, that "there aren't any reasons" in the sense that reasons lose their relevancy.[37] The conflict becomes stalemate and boredom on one hand, or on the other, the opening of one's self to new possibilities, the deepening of consciousness, the choosing and committing of one's self to new ways of life.

The distinction between "reason why" and "purpose" clicked strongly with my patient and released in her several important insights. To her considerable surprise, one of these was a radical shift in the meaning she gave to responsibility. Now she saw it not as merely the external and passively-received expectations from her family, but as an active responsibility to *herself* in being aware of the power she was exerting that evening with her husband. Responsibility now consisted of her choosing what she wanted of her life with him and elsewhere.

It is no doubt safe to say—again excepting severely pathological individuals—that *all* emotions, no matter

how contradictory they appear on the surface, have some
kind of unity in the *Gestalt* which constitutes the self.
The clinical problem—as in the case of the anxious child
who is forced to act lovingly toward parents who are
actually hostile and destructive toward him—is that the
person cannot or will not let himself be aware of what
he feels or is doing with his feelings. When my patient
was able to analyze her two contradictory acts that evening toward her husband, it turned out that both were
motivated by anger toward him and men in general, she
setting up the situation to prove the man is the villain.
Both actions presupposed the man as the authority figure
(which she was doing with me in the "nirvana process"
of therapy). And, in the meantime, she remains the
whim-directed, willful child. She could cope with men on
the basis of the childhood pattern, but—as came out in
pronounced anxiety in subsequent sessions—could she
cope with them as an adult?

We have arrived on the wings of eros, if I may put it
so, at a new concept of causality. No longer are we
forced to understand the human being in terms of a bil-
liard-ball cause-and-effect, based solely on the explanations of "reason why" and susceptible to rigid prediction.
Indeed, Aristotle believed that the motivation of eros
was so different from the determinism of the past that he
would not even call it causality. "In Aristotle we find the
doctrine of the universal *eros*," writes Tillich, "which
drives everything towards the highest form, the pure actuality which moves the world not as a cause (*kinou-
menon*) but as the object of love (*eromenon*). And the
movement he describes is a movement from the potential
to the actual, from *dynamis* to *energeia*. . . ."[38]

I am proposing a description of human beings as given
motivation by the new possibilities, the goals and ideals,
which attract and pull them toward the future. This does
not omit the fact that we are all partially pushed from
behind and determined by the past, but it unites this
force with its other half. Eros gives us a causality in
which "reason why" and "purpose" are united. The former is part of all human experience since we all participate in the finite, natural world; in this respect, each of
us, in making any important decision, needs to find out
as much as he can about the objective facts of the situa-

tion. This realm is particularly relevant in problems of neurosis in which past events *do* exercise a compulsive, repetitive, chainlike, predictable effect upon the person's actions. Freud was right in the respect that rigid, deterministic causality does work in neurosis and sickness.

But he was wrong in trying to carry this over to apply to *all* human experience. The aspect of purpose, which comes into the process when the individual can become conscious of what he is doing, opens him to new and different possibilities in the future, and introduces the elements of personal responsibility and freedom.

EROS SICKENING

The Eros we have been discussing is that of the classical age, when he was still the creative power and the bridge between men and gods. But this "healthy" Eros deteriorated. Plato's understanding of Eros is a middle form of the concept, standing between Hesiod's view of Eros as the powerful and original creator and the later deteriorated form in which Eros becomes a sickly child. These three aspects of Eros are also accurate reflections of psychological archetypes of human experience: each of us at different times has the experience of Eros as creator, as mediator, and as banal playboy. Our age is by no means the first to experience the banalization of love, and to find that without passion, love sickens.

In the charming story quoted at the beginning of this chapter, we saw that the ancient Greeks had put into the quintessential language of myth the insights which spring from the archetypes of the human psyche. Eros, the child of Ares and Aphrodite, "did not grow as other children, but remained a small, rosy, chubby child, with gauzy wings and rougish, dimpled face." After telling us that the alarmed mother was informed, "Love cannot grow without Passion," the myth goes on:

> In vain the goddess strove to catch the concealed meaning of this answer. It was only revealed to her when Anteros, god of passion, was born. When with his brother, Eros grew and flourished, until he became a handsome slender youth; but when separated

from him, he invariably resumed his childish form
and mischievous habits.[39]

Within these disarmingly naïve sentences, with which
the Greeks were wont to clothe their most profound wisdom, lie several points which are crucial for our problems now. One is that Eros is the child of *Ares* as well
as Aphrodite. This is to say that love is inseparably connected with aggression.

Another is that the Eros which had been the powerful
creator in Hesiod's time, causing the barren earth to spring
up with green trees and breathing the spirit of life into
man, has now deteriorated into a child, a rosy, chubby,
playful creature, sometimes a mere fat infant playing with
his bow and arrows. We see him represented as an effete
Cupid in so many of the paintings of the seventeenth and
eighteenth centuries as well as in ancient times. "In archaic art Eros is represented as a beautiful winged youth and
tends to be made younger and younger until by the Hellenistic period he is an infant." In Alexandrine poetry,
he degenerates into a mischievous child.[40] There must be
something within Eros' own nature to cause this deterioration, for it is present already in the myth which, while
later than the Hesiod version, still dates from long before
Greek civilization disintegrated.

This brings us to the very heart of what has also gone
wrong in our day: eros has lost passion, and has become
insipid, childish, banal.

As is so often the case, the myth reveals a critical conflict in the roots of human experience, true for the Greeks
and true for us: we engage in a flight from eros, the once
powerful, original source of being, to sex, the mischievous
plaything. Eros is demoted to the function of a pretty
bartender, serving grapes and wine, a stimulator for dalliance whose task is to keep life endlessly sensuous on a
bank of soft clouds. He stands not for the creative use of
power—sexual, procreative, and other—but for the immediacy of gratification. And, *mirabile dictu*, we discover
that the myth proclaims exactly what we have seen happening in our own day: *eros, then, even loses interest in
sex.* In one version of the myth, Aphrodite tries to find
him to get him up and about his business of spreading
love with his bow and arrows. And, teen-age loafer that

he has become, he is off gambling with Ganymede and cheating at the cards.

Gone is the spirit of the life-giving arrows, gone the creature who could breathe spirit into man and woman, gone the powerful Dionysian festivals, gone the frenzied dancing and the mysteries that moved the initiates more than the vaunted drugs of our mechanical age, gone even the bucolic intoxication. Eros now playboy indeed! Bacchanal with Pepsi-Cola.

Is this what civilization always does—tames Eros to make him fit the needs of the society to perpetuate itself? Changes him from the power that brings to birth new being and ideas and passion, weakens him till he is no longer the creative force that breaks old forms asunder to make new ones? Tames him until he stands for the goal of perpetual ease, dalliance, affluence, and, ultimately, apathy?[41]

In this respect we confront a new and specific problem in our Western world—*the war between eros and technology.* There is no war between *sex* and technology: our technical inventions help sex to be safe, available, and efficient as demonstrated from birth-control pills all the way to the how-to-do-it books. Sex and technology join together to achieve "adjustment"; with the full release of tension over the weekend, you can work better in the buttondown world on Monday. Sensual needs and their gratification are not at war with technology, at least in any immediate sense (whether they are in the long run is another question).

But it is not at all clear that technology and *eros* are compatible, or can even live without perpetual warfare. The lover, like the poet, is a menace on the assembly line. Eros breaks existing forms and creates new ones and that, naturally, is a threat to technology. Technology requires regularity, predictability, and runs by the clock. The untamed eros fights against all concepts and confines of time.

Eros is the impetus in building civilizations. But the civilization then turns on its progenitor and disciplines the erotic impulses. This can still work toward the increase and expansion of consciousness. The erotic impulses can and should have some discipline: the gospel of the free expression of every impulse disperses experience like a river with no banks, its water spilled and wasted as it flows in every direction. The discipline of eros provides *forms* in which we can develop and which protect us from unbearable anxiety. Freud believed that the disciplining of eros was necessary for a culture, and that it was from the repression and sublimation of erotic impulses that the power came out of which civilizations were built. De Rougement, for one of the few times, here agrees with Freud; he does not forget

> that without the sexual discipline which the so-called puritanical tendencies have imposed on us since Europe first existed, there would be nothing more in our civilization than in those nations known as underdeveloped, and no doubt less: there would be neither work, organized effort nor the technology which has created the present world. There would also not be the problem of eroticism! The erotic authors forget this fact quite naively, committed as they are to their poetic or moralizing passion, which too often alienates them from the true nature of the "facts of life," and their complex links with economy, society, and culture.[42]

But there comes a point (and this is the challenge facing modern technological Western man) when the cult of technique destroys feeling, undermines passion, and blots out individual identity. The technologically efficient lover, defeated in the contradiction which is copulation without eros, is ultimately the impotent one. He has lost the power to be carried away; he knows only too well what he is doing. At this point, technology diminishes consciousness and demolishes eros. Tools are no longer an enlargement of consciousness but a substitute for it and, indeed, tend to repress and truncate it.

Must civilization always tame eros to keep the society from breaking up again? Hesiod lived in the strongly fomenting, archaic sixth century, closer to the sources of culture and the moments of gestation and birth, when the procreative powers were at work, and man *had* to live with chaos and form it into something new. But then, with the growing need for stabilization, the daimonic and tragic elements tended to be buried. Insight into the downfall of civilizations is revealed here. We see effete Athens set up for the more primitive Macedonians, they in turn for the Romans, and the Romans in turn for the Huns. And we for the yellow and black races?

Eros is the center of the vitality of a culture—its heart and soul. And when release of tension takes the place of creative eros, the downfall of the civilization is assured.

FOUR

LOVE AND DEATH

The confrontation with death—and the reprieve from it—makes everything look so precious, so sacred, so beautiful that I feel more strongly than ever the impulse to love it, to embrace it, and to let myself be overwhelmed by it. My river has never looked so beautiful. . . . Death, and its ever present possibility makes love, passionate love, more possible. I wonder if we could love passionately, if ecstasy would be possible at all, if we knew we'd never die.

—FROM A LETTER BY ABRAHAM MASLOW,
WRITTEN WHILE RECUPERATING FROM A
HEART ATTACK.

We now confront one of the most profound and meaningful paradoxes of love. This is the intensified openness to love which the awareness of death gives us and, simultaneously, the increased sense of death which love brings with it. We recall that even the arrows with which Eros creates—these life-giving shafts he shoots into the cold bosom of the earth to make the arid surface spring up with luxuriant green verdure—are *poisoned*. Here lie the anxiety-creating elements of human love. For the shafts in Eros' bow pierce "brutal as well as gentle hearts, to their death or to their healing in delight."[1] Death and delight, anguish and joy, anxiety and the wonder of birth—these are the warp and woof of which the fabric of human love is woven.

It is Eros who "breaks the limbs' strength," who, "in all gods, in all human beings, overpowers the intelligence in the breast and all their shrewd planning."[2] Thus speaks Hesiod in his *Theogony*. He was writing in that powerfully creative archaic period (c. 750 B.C.) when Greece was filled with the ferment which marked the birth of the city-states and the new Greek individual of self-consciousness and dignity. The "overpowering" of the rational functions is thus directly connected with the power of Eros to create. How could we be told more eloquently that the act of creating form and life out of chaos and bringing vitality to man requires a passion which transcends the intelligence and "calculated planning": Eros *"breaks the limbs' strength . . . in all gods, in all human beings!"* Eros destroys as he creates.[3]

LOVE AS THE INTIMATION OF MORTALITY

To love means to open ourselves to the negative as well as the positive—to grief, sorrow, and disappointment as well as to joy, fulfillment, and an intensity of consciousness we did not know was possible before. I shall first describe this phenomenologically, in its ideal form as a paradigm.

When we "fall" in love, as the expressive verb puts it, the world shakes and changes around us, not only in the way it looks but in our whole experience of what we are doing in the world. Generally, the shaking is consciously felt in its positive aspects—as the wonderful new heaven and earth which love with its miracle and mystery has suddenly produced. Love is the answer, we sing. Aside from the banality of such reassurances, our Western culture seems to be engaged in a romantic—albeit desperate —conspiracy to enforce the illusion that that is *all* there is to eros. The very strength of the effort to support that illusion betrays the presence of the repressed, opposing pole.

This opposing element is the consciousness of death. For death is always in the shadow of the delight of love. In faint adumbration there is present the dread, haunting question, Will this new relationship destroy us? When we love, we give up the center of ourselves. We are thrown from our previous state of existence into a void; and though we hope to attain a new world, a new existence, we can never be sure. Nothing looks the same, and may well never look the same again. The world is annihilated; how can we know whether it will ever be built up again? We give, and give *up*, our own center; how shall we know that we will get it back? We wake up to find the whole world shaking: where or when will it come to rest?

The most excruciating joy is accompanied by the consciousness of the imminence of death—and with the same intensity. And it seems that one is not possible without the other.

This experience of annihilation is an inward one and, as the myth rightly puts it, is essentially what *eros* does to us. It is not simply what the other person does to us. To love completely carries with it the threat of the annihilation of everything. This intensity of consciousness has something in common with the ecstasy of the mystic in his union with God: just as he can never be *sure* God is there, so love carries us to that intensity of consciousness in which we no longer have any guarantee of security.

This razor's edge, this dizzy balance of anxiety and joy, has much to do with the exciting quality of love. The dread joy is not just the question of whether the love will be returned in kind. Indeed, the real dialectic is within the person himself and the anxiety is not essentially quieted if the loved one *does* respond. Paradoxically, the lover is sometimes *more* anxious when the love is returned than when not. For if one loves unrequitedly, which is even an aim in some love writing, or from a safe distance, like Dante and the whole Stylist movement in Italian literature, he can at least go on about his customary daily tasks, writing his *Divine Comedy* or his sonnets or novels. It is when the love *is* realized that eros may literally "break the limb's strength," as with Antony and Cleopatra, or Paris and Helen, or Héloïse and Abelard. Hence, human beings are afraid of love. And, all the saccharine books to the contrary, there is reason to be afraid.

In common human experience, this relationship between death and love is perhaps most clear to people when they have children. A man may have thought very little about death—and prided himself on his "bravery" —until he becomes a father. Then he finds in his love for his child an experience of vulnerability to death: the Cruel Imposter can at any time take away the child, the object of his love. In this sense love is an experience of greater vulnerability.

Love is also a reminder of our own mortality. When a friend or member of our family dies, we are vividly impressed by the fact that life is evanescent and irretrievable. But there is also a deeper sense of its meaningful possibilities and an impetus to risk ourselves in taking the leap. Some—perhaps most—human beings never know deep love until they experience, at someone's death, the preciousness of friendship, devotion, loyalty. Abraham Maslow is profoundly right when he wonders whether we could love passionately if we knew we'd never die.

This is one of the reasons, mythologically speaking, why the love affairs among the immortal gods on Mt. Olympus are so insipid and boring. The loves of Zeus and Juno are completely uninteresting until they involve a mortal. Love has the power to change the course of history only when Zeus comes down to Leda or Io and falls in love with this mortal woman who can yearn to have a child because she knows she will not live forever. *Love is not only enriched by our sense of mortality but constituted by it.* Love is the cross-fertilization of mortality and immortality. This is why the daimon Eros is described as midway between gods and men and partakes of the nature of both.

I have been speaking, to some degree, in ideal terms. I am fully aware that this degree of involvement will be called neurotic by many of my colleagues. This is the day of "cool" relationships—one should never become involved to a degree which prevents his moving out at any moment! But I submit that this involvement is neurotic only if "frozen," or fixated; only if the partners demand that they live always on this level. While none of us lives on the level I am describing for very long, it remains a kind of backdrop, an ideal situation which ought to be somewhere in the relation lending meaning to the drab and dull days which also come.[4]

The relation between death and love has an impressive history in literature. In Italian writing, there was the frequent play upon the words *amore,* love, with *morte,* death. The connection also has its biological analogies in nature. The male bee dies after inseminating the Queen. More vivid is the case of the praying mantis: the female bites off the head of the male as he copulates, and his death throes unite with his copulatory spasms to make the thrusts stronger. Inseminated, the female proceeds to eat him to store up food for the new offspring.

Freud associated this threat of death with the depletion of Eros.

> This accounts for the likeness of the condition of that following complete sexual satisfaction to dying, and for the fact that death coincides with the act of copulation in lower animals. These creatures die in the act of reproduction because, after Eros has been eliminated through the process of satisfaction, the death instinct has a free hand for accomplishing its purpose.[5]

My viewpoint is that, in human beings, it is not merely the depletion of eros which causes the fear of death—or, as I call it above, the experience of mortality—but that in all stages of human development the experiences of love and death are interwoven.

The relationship between death and love is surely clear in the sex act. Every kind of mythology relates the sex act itself to dying, and every therapist comes to see the relationship ever more clearly through his patients. A patient, whose problem was sexual frigidity and who had never experienced an orgasm in intercourse, told me of a dream which dramatically illustrates this sex and death theme. In her dream, she experienced herself for the first time in her own identity as a woman. Then, still in the dream, she had the strange conviction that she would have to jump into the river and drown. The dream ended in great anxiety. That night, in sexual intercourse, she had an orgasm for the first time. The capacity for surrender, for giving one's self up, must exist in love-making if there is to be the spontaneity required for orgasm.

Something very basic had taken place in this woman's dream—the capacity to confront death, a capacity which is a prerequisite to growth, a prerequisite to self-consciousness. I take the orgasm here as a psychophysical symbol of the capacity to abandon one's self, to give up present security in favor of the leap toward deeper experience. It is not by accident that the orgasm often appears symbolically as death and rebirth. The myth of going under water, of being drowned and born again has been passed down through history in different religious and different cultures as the myth of *baptism*—the being immersed in the river to be drowned, to die, in order to be born again. This is a daring to leap into non-being with the prospect of achieving new being.

Hence, the *virginal* quality of every genuine love experience. It seems that each time is new; we feel convinced that nobody ever experienced this before, though in our conceit we are sure that we shall remember it forever. When I was lecturing on this theme at a university, two different young men came up to tell me privately that they understood me because they were in love, but they expressed genuine concern that the other students wouldn't understand. Such presumption—that nobody has ever been in love but me and I never before! —is, I fear, par for the course.

Mythology, that treasure house of the revelations of man's self-interpretation of his inner experience and his world down through the ages, has been clear and eloquent about the relationships of love to anxiety and death. We do not need to resort to Tristan and Iseult, though that is the clearest myth. Joseph Campbell points out, on the basis of the whole Aegean prehistoric mythology, that the goddess Aphrodite and her son Eros are "exactly the great cosmic mother and her son—the ever-dying, ever-living god." All myths on the parentage of Eros point to such a background, Campbell says.

> He is hatched from the egg of Night. He is the son, now of Gaea and Uranus, now of Artemis and Hermes, now again of Iris and Zephyrus: all transformations of the same mythological background, pointing without exception to the timeless catalogue of themes with which we are now familiar—of that willing victim in whose death is our life, whose flesh is our meat and blood our drink; the victim present in the young embracing couple of the primitive ritual of the love-death, who in the moment of ecstacy are killed, to be sacramentally roasted and consumed; the victim present in Attis or Adonis slain by a boar, Osiris slain by Seth, Dionysus torn apart, roasted, and consumed by the Titans. In the charming later allegories of Eros (Cupid) and his victim, *the god*

is in the role of the dark enemy—the rushing boar,
the dark brother Seth, the Titan band—and *the lover
is the incarnate, dying god.*[6]

In the mythology of old Egypt, Campbell relates, the
lover and the loved one are the slayer and the victim
which, though on the stage they appear to be in conflict,
are behind the scenes of one mind, "in the life-consum-
ing, life-redeeming, -creating and -justifying dark mystery
of love."[7]

What a different light this throws on the human problems in love than all our glib talk about the art of loving, about love as the answer to all our needs, love as
instant self-actualization, love as contentment, or love as
a mail-order technique! No wonder we try to reduce eros
to purely physiological sex or try to avoid the whole
dilemma by playing it cool, by using sex to drug and
vaccinate ourselves against the anxiety-creating effects of
eros.

It is possible to have sexual intercourse without any
particular anxiety. But by doing this in casual encounters,
we shut out, by definition, our eros—that is, we relinquish passion in favor of mere sensation; we shut out
our participation in the imaginative, personal significance
of the act. If we can have sex without love, we assume
that we escape the daimonic anxiety known throughout
the ages as an inseparable part of human love. And if,
further, we even use sexual activity itself as an escape
from the commitments eros demands of us, we may hope
to have thus gained an airtight defense against anxiety.
And the motive for sex, no longer being sensual pleasure
or passion, becomes displaced by the artificial one of providing identity and gaining security; and sex has been
reduced to an anxiety-allaying strategy. Thus we set the
stage for the development of impotence and affectlessness
later on.

DEATH AND THE OBSESSION WITH SEX

There is another side to the relationship between death
and love. The obsession with sex serves to cover up contemporary man's fear of death. We in the twentieth cen-

tury have fewer defenses against this universal fear, such as the belief in immortality which armored our ancestors, and we also lack any widely agreed-upon purpose of life. Consequently, the awareness of death is widely repressed in our day. But none of us can fail to be aware at the same time of the tremendous preoccupation with sex: in our humor, our drama, and our economic life, even down to the commercials on television. An obsession drains off anxiety from some other area and prevents the person from having to confront something distasteful. What would we have to see if we could cut through our obsession about sex? That we must die. The clamor of sex all about us drowns out the ever-waiting presence of death.

When I strive to prove my potency in order to cover up and silence my inner fears of impotence, I am engaging in a pattern as ancient as man himself. Death is the symbol of ultimate impotence and finiteness, and anxiety arising from this inescapable experience calls forth the struggle to make ourselves infinite by way of sex. Sexual activity is the most ready way to silence the inner dread of death and, through the symbol of procreation, to triumph over it.

Note that the ways we repress death and its symbolism are amazingly like the ways the Victorians repressed sex.[8] Death is obscene, unmentionable, pornographic; if sex was nasty, death is a nasty mistake. Death is not to be talked of in front of the children, nor talked about at all if we can help it. We dress death up in grotesquely colorful caskets in the same way Victorian women camouflaged their bodies by means of voluminous dresses. We throw flowers on the casket to make death smell better. With make-believe funerals and burial ceremonies and fancy tombs we act as though the deceased had somehow not died; and we preach a psychoreligious gospel that says the less grief the better.[9] Even our economy joins in the same promise of physical comfort, with everything arranged as though the deceased had not died.[10] Protecting the children, camouflaging smell and dress, the make-believe ceremonies, ending up in the inward pretense—all of this bears a striking parallel to the Victorian's repression of sex.

But human beings cannot block off any important bio-

logical or emotional aspect of experience without developing an equivalent amount of inner anxiety. Where there
is an obsession, we can assume some equivalent repression. Where does the anxiety engendered by this repression of death and its symbols go? Into our compulsive
preoccupation with sex. Repression of death equals obsession with sex. Sex is .the easiest way to prove our
vitality, to demonstrate we are still "young," attractive,
and virile, to prove we are not dead yet. This carries
the weight of asserting our potency in ultimate form over
nature. This hope has an understandable biological base
in that sexuality and procreation *are* the only way of insuring the carrying on of our name and our genes in our
children who live beyond our own death.

Contemporary concern with sexuality reaches far beyond this biological fact which man has always known.
The compulsive preoccupation with sexuality drugs the
individual so that he does not need to admit the fact
that *he* dies and, indeed, that death—the one experience
which is inexorable—may occur at any moment. The
greater our alienation from nature—alienation's ultimate
symbol being the atom bomb and radiation—the closer
we actually are to death. The rape of nature in the form
of the splitting of the atom is thus related to our fear of
death, our guilt (which always increases fear), and our
consequently redoubled need to repress the consciousness
of death.[11] And here the mother symbol enters; we speak
of *mother* nature. It is not a far cry from experiencing
the achievement of the splitting of the atom as gaining
power over the "eternal feminine." The atom bomb sets
us into conflict with the symbolic mother. This is why
the construction of the bomb carries such a personal
symbolic power for almost everyone. No wonder Western
man shows signs of bearing—in some buried depth—a
great quantity of guilt!

The drive to repress the awareness of death falls with
particular weight on Western man because of his reliance
on the "myth of potency." (I use the term "myth" not in
its deteriorated popular sense of "falsehood," but in its
historically accurate sense of a psychobiological pattern
which gives meaning and direction to experience.) The
myth of potency has played a central role in Western

man's struggle for identity since the Renaissance, and has been particularly crucial in forming his psychological and spiritual character. Western man's preoccupation with manipulating nature, which led to such astonishing success in the physical sciences and industrialism, was extended, in the late nineteenth and the twentieth centuries, to human beings. I gain potency, then, by manipulating myself. But to the extent that I do this successfully, I am not genuinely potent; I am caught in an insoluble dilemma. My self is this inert hunk of living matter which submits to manipulation. Self-manipulating, like the manipulation of another, never increases potency but, on the contrary, undermines it. We always presuppose some potent person or standard behind ourselves, the manipulator. But as the system is extended, the identity of this "behind the scenes" person or standard becomes lost in an infinite regression. This control of the controllers is a real issue, confused as it may be; and is always shifted back until it becomes daimonic in the negative sense.

The myth of individual potency became particularly overemphasized for those of us in America who grew up on an actual frontier, be it an economic, social, or geographical one. On the frontier of the West, which I take for our example, it was crucial that a man be able to defend himself by the strength of his own hand, that he cultivate a rough and active type of physical strength, and that he not let tenderness or sentimental emotions slow his movement in drawing his gun. Indeed, the gun as a symbol for the penis, useful when stiff and erect, first remarked by Freud, has greater relevancy in America than in Vienna; this is one of the few specific cultural symbols which still seems cogent in spite of social change. The life and legend of Ernest Hemingway provide vivid pictures of the masculine virtues of potency carried over from the frontier—physical strength, hunting, sexual prowess (partially compensating for his real struggle with and fear of sexual impotence), and the active themes and style in his writing. But death, and the insupportable anxiety of his living on in the face of a death coming no one knows when, became too pressing a threat as he became sexually impotent in his middle sixties, and led to the ultimate act a man can make as assertion of his potency, namely taking his own life in suicide. As long as you can hang on to the virtue of individual potency, you can laugh in the face of death. But once you lose this advantage, your choice is to accept death and its gradual and often ignominious victory, or rush headlong to meet it as Hemingway did.

Sex and death have in common the fact that they are the two biological aspects of the *mysterium tremendum*. Mystery—defined here as a situation in which the data impinge on the problem—has its ultimate meaning in these two human experiences. Both are related to creation and destruction; and it is, therefore, scarcely surprising that in human experience, they are interwoven in such complex ways. In both, we are taken over by an event; we cannot stand outside either love or death—and, if we try to, we destroy whatever value the experience can have.

THE TRAGIC SENSE IN LOVE

I recall a discussion with a highly-respected psychotherapist colleague and friend on the significance of the tragedy of Romeo and Juliet. My friend stated that the trouble with Romeo and Juliet was that they hadn't had adequate counseling. If they had had, they would not have committed suicide. Taken aback, I protested that I didn't think that was Shakespeare's point at all, and that Shakespeare, as well as the other classical writers who have created and molded the literature which speaks to us age after age, is in this drama picturing how sexual love can grasp a man and woman and hurl them into heights and depths—the simultaneous presence of which we call tragic.

But my friend insisted that tragedy was a negative state and we, with our scientific enlightenment, had superseded it—or at least ought to at the earliest possible moment. I argued with him, as I do here, that to see the tragic in merely negative terms is a profound misunderstanding. Far from being a negation of life and love, the tragic is an ennobling and deepening aspect of our experience of sexuality and love. An appreciation of the tragic not only can help us avoid some egregious over-simplifications in life, but it can specifically protect us against the danger that sex and love will be banalized also in psychotherapy.

I am, of course, not using tragedy in its popular sense of "catastrophe," but as the self-conscious, personal realization that love brings both joy and destruction. I mean in this context a fact which has been known all through man's history but which our own age has accomplished the remarkable feat of forgetting, namely, that sexual love has the power to propel human beings into situations which can destroy not only themselves but many other people at the same time. We have only to call to mind Helen and Paris, or Tristan and Iseult, which are mythic presentations, whether based on historical personages or not, of the power of sexual love to seize man and woman and lift them up into a whirlwind which defies and destroys rational control. It is not by accident that these myths are presented over and over again in Western classic literature and passed down from generation to generation. For the stories come from a mythic depth of human experience in sexual love that is to be neglected only at the price of the impoverishment of our talk and writing about sex and love.

The tragic is an expression of a dimension of consciousness which gives richness, value, and dignity to human life. Thus the tragic not only makes possible the most humane emotions—like pity in the ancient Greek sense, sympathy for one's fellow man, and understanding —but without it, love becomes saccharine and insipid and eros sickens into the child who never grows up.

But the reader may raise an objection. Whatever the classical meaning of tragedy may be, are not the so-called tragic presentations in today's art, on the stage or in the pages of the novel, a portrayal of meaninglessness? Is not what we see in O'Neill's *The Iceman Cometh* the lack of the greatness and dignity in man, and is not *Waiting for Godot* a presentation of emptiness?

To this, I would make a double response. First, in presenting the *ostensible* lack of the greatness in man and his actions, or the lack of meaning, these works are doing infinitely more. They are confronting exactly what *is* tragic in our day, namely the complete confusion, banality, ambiguity, and vacuum of ethical standards and the consequent inability to act or, in *Who's Afraid of Virginia Woolf?*, the paralyzing fear of one's own tenderness. True, what we see in *The Iceman Cometh* is that greatness has fled from man, but this already presupposes a greatness, a dignity, a meaning. No one would ever think of reminding a Greek audience that it means something when Orestes kills his mother. But Willy Loman's wife in *Death of a Salesman* pleads, "Attention must be paid," and she was entirely right. It *does* mean something if a man is destroyed even if he is only a traveling salesman. (Nowadays, we would perhaps have to explain to an audience why Orestes' killing his mother is so meaningful: for we are the generation which has learned that such killing is not at all a problem requiring a terrible struggle with the Furies and later a trial concerning guilt, responsibility, and forgiveness, but an acted-out, psychological, counter-Oedipal mechanism which temporarily got out of hand!) In my judgment, the best of the novels and dramas and paintings in our day are those which present to us the tremendous meaning in the fact of meaninglessness. The most tragic thing of all, in the long run, is the ultimate attitude, "It doesn't matter." The ultimately tragic condition in a negative sense is the apathy, the adamant, rigid "cool," which refuses to admit the genuinely tragic.

But I would also ask, in rebuttal, Do not these works we are citing profoundly reveal what is wrong with love and will in our day? Take the contradiction in acting so vividly portrayed in *Waiting for Godot*. Didi says, "Let us go," and the stage direction in the play states, "They do not move." There could be no more telling vignette of modern man's problem with will, his inability to make significant acts. They wait for Godot: but in this waiting there is *expectation:* the waiting itself implies hope and belief. And they wait together. Or take the rabid denial of love in the savage in-fighting of the married couples in *Who's Afraid of Virginia Woolf?*. This presentation of the inability to come to terms with whatever love and tenderness they do have shows more vividly and convincingly than reams of research what modern man's problem in love is.

THE TRAGIC AND SEPARATION

There is another source of the tragic aspect of love. This is the fact that we are created as male and female, which leads to perpetual yearning for each other, a thirst for completion which is doomed to be temporary. This is another source of joy and disappointment, ecstasy and despair.

I need to introduce here a difficult concept—ontology. The term literally means the "science of being." But that definition is not very helpful, especially since we post-nineteenth-century Americans are not accustomed to ontological thinking. I shall never forget Paul Tillich describing to a class his shock when, as a student of philosophy, he was confronted with the question, "Why is there something and not nothing?" This is the question which puts one on the ontological level. Why is there such a thing as sex? And why not no-sex; why don't we propogate the way the paramecium and earthworm do, by lopping off part of ourselves for the new being? We cannot take the easy road here with the answer "evolution"—it just developed that way. Nor can we use the likewise easy answer "divine purpose"—there is some teleological "reason" we are made this way. Both of these answers—though in opposite ways—beg the question. No, we must ask the ontological question directly, examining the *being* of the thing at hand—in this case, sex—to find a convincing answer. If "sex is the human counterpart of the cosmic process," we obviously cannot come to a conclusion on the basis of how boys and girls wear their hair in this decade. Ontology seeks to discover the basic structures of existence—the structures which are given to everyone at every moment.

The existence of maleness and femaleness, seen ontologically, is one expression of this fundamental polarity of all reality. The smallest molecular particle gets its dynamic movement from the fact that it consists of a negative and positive charge, with tension—and therefore movement—between them. Using this analogy of

the molecular particles of matter and energy, Alfred
North Whitehead and Paul Tillich both believe that reality has the ontological character of negative-positive
polarity. Whitehead and the many contemporary thinkers
for whom his work has become important see reality
not as consisting of substances in fixed states but as a
process of dynamic movement between polarities. This
is why Whitehead could develop a *process* philosophy.
Indeed, it could be argued that all of reality has a male-
female character—surely Hegel's theory of thesis, antithesis, and synthesis can be seen in this light. Paul Tillich
points out that "it is well known to the students of Hegel
that he started in his early fragments as a philosopher
of love, and it can be said without exaggeration that
Hegel's dialectical scheme is an abstraction from his concrete intuition into the nature of love as separation and
reunion."[12]

In sexual intercourse, we directly and intimately experience this polar rhythm. The sex act is the most powerful enactment of relatedness imaginable, for it is the
drama of approach and entrance and full union, then
partial separation (as though the lovers could not believe
it were true and yearned to look at each other), then
a complete reunion again. It cannot be an accident of
nature that in sex we thus enact the sacrament of intimacy and withdrawal, union and distance, separating
ourselves and giving ourselves in full union again. For
this eternally repeated participation in each other, the
touch and the withdrawal, is present even in the hesitant
beginnings of acquaintanceship and is the essence of
courtship in birds and animals as well as men and wom-
en. In the rhythm of participation in a union in a dual
being and the eventual separation into individual autonomy are contained the two necessary poles of human
existence itself, shown in their fullness in sexual intercourse.

It is likely that these differences underlie the myths,
rising spontaneously in many different cultures, of sex
being a reunion with the other half of one's self. The
most famous of these is given by Aristophanes in Plato's
Symposium—the myth of the androgyne. But the crucial
point is made in the counterpart of this myth in the
Upanishads when it relates regarding man on his crea-

tion, "But he felt no delight. Therefore a man who is lonely feels no delight." Thereupon "was created the wife to fill the void."[13]

But we do not need to go to the myths to appreciate the value of the polarity. I once spent a week on Mt. Athos, a little country in northern Greece extending 12 miles down into the Aegean Sea and populated only by monks living in fifteen or twenty monasteries. No woman, supposedly, had stepped off the boat at Athos since the twelfth century. But the monks themselves had taken on the gestures, the ways of talking, walking, and carrying themselves of women. I would find myself thinking, as I saw a monk walking away from me down the village street, that there was a *woman*. The same was true of another very different masculine group, the Foreign Legion, the soldiers of which would dance with each other on the decks of the French ship in the Mediterranean. The incidence of homosexuality is not the point here and, in any case, does not explain this phenomenon. I propose, rather, that when there are no women present, there is no accent on acting male and vice versa; we become more masculine when there are women around, and they more feminine. *The two sexes have the function of accentuating the characteristics of the opposite one.*

It is the common experience of all of us that when you put a bunch of men together—as in the army, fraternities, or a monastery—you may be able to get them to devote themselves single-mindedly to the task at hand. But there is a curious lack of vitality in other realms. We see a deadening, a lack of variety of response; and they will accept authoritarian procedures without any tendency to rebel. But introduce a woman, as in the Garden of Eden, and consciousness sharpens, a moral sense develops, and even rebellion begins to sprout. In a genuine sense, sexes seem to ignite each other, offering a vitality and power—and even better ideas.

By virtue of the fact of two sexes, reproduction can produce greater diversity. The polarity of male and female, the intermingling and combining of genes, gives infinitely increased variety; originality and new combinations of possibilities emerge. It is only the lowest forms of nature, such as paramecia, which reproduce by offshoots from the same organism (although George Bernard Shaw, in one of his acerbic warnings to the human race, predicted that this is the fate to which the human race may succumb if we continue to place efficiency above all else!). In studies of sections of America where persons grow taller than in other areas, it is believed that one of the causes is the intermingling with a new group of people migrating into the area and intermarrying with the previous stock. It is also well-known that while incest is not *biologically* harmful, the intermarrying of brother and sister and members of the same family is nevertheless prohibited in almost every society because of social impoverishment, the loss of differentiation which would block the development of the race.

We are fitted for this rhythmic process by the differing masculine and feminine musculature, so the Dutch psychologist Buytendijk concludes. He points out that in bones and muscles, the male is built essentially on straight lines, approaching right angles—the better to thrust, to strike by poking, punching, and other assertive aspects of the male's role. The woman is built on curves and rounded lines—the better to open herself, to carry and nurse the offspring, to give and receive the peculiarly feminine kind of pleasure. The thrusting mechanism of the penis is present already in the little boy, who makes motions of wishing to poke his penis into things. The little girl has her counterpart, the desire to harmonize, to conserve, to inform things not by overpowering, head-on attacks, but by approaching in a curve. Our society associates the masculine virtues with action and the feminine with passivity—which, below the obvious level, is as wrong as it is misleading. It is as accurate (though it also has the error of all generalizations) to say that women are for preserving the arts of peace as that men are for the arts of war. Actually, both masculine and feminine are active *and* passive in their own way.[14]

The fact that these characteristics have been exaggerated grossly and unfairly in our society is no reason for forgetting the real differences. It is true that the so-called masculine virtues in the nineteenth century were such that a man, to prove his potency, had to conquer not only nature but himself and all the women who came within his path. And a sterotype was made of the female as gentle and sweet-smelling, unable to take care of herself, unable to survive hearing profanity, and ready to swoon at the slightest excuse. As a reaction to this came the movement to wipe away the distinctions; no longer was *vive la différence* the rallying cry but "everybody feels the same"; and both sexes were to react the same way to the same things. But we found, to our horror, that we had thrown out the delight-giving differences along with the unfair suppression.

For in our egalitarian crusade, we overlooked the fact which Dr. Helena Deutsch has pointed out, that the woman has a vaginal "drawing in" response which may actually give her more pleasure than experiencing the apocalyptic orgasm. Language mirrors these differences: there is in English the word "invaginate" for the drawing in response, and we have no counterpart for the male. The closest parallels are the various forms of "phallic," which refer essentially to thrusting, asserting, conquering behavior, and which may or may not have a hostile connotation. The male experiences not only the assertive response but also a response to this being drawn in; and while the woman's orgasm is complex and diffuse, the male has a built-in neurological and physiological mechanism which trips off the orgasm and, when excited beyond a certain point, becomes impossible to withhold.

A final ontological fact we observe in sexuality is simple and elemental. This is that sexual intercourse is procreative; it can make a new being, a baby. This fact creates profound changes in the female's body and life for at least nine months whether the male stays or leaves; and, except in pathological cases, it makes a radical difference to the female for a much longer time than that. The primitive words of an Abyssinian noblewoman put this excellently:

. . . The day when a woman enjoys her first love cuts her in two. . . . The man is the same after his first love as he was before. The woman is from the day of her first love another. That continues so all through life. The man spends a night by a woman and goes away. His life and body are always the same. The woman conceives. As a mother she is another person than the woman without child. She carries the fruit of the night nine months long in her body. Something grows. Something grows into her life that never again departs from it. She is a mother. She is and remains a mother even though her child die, though all her children die. For at one time she carried the child under her heart. And it does not go out of her heart ever again. Not even when it is dead. All this a man does not know. . . . He does not know the difference before love and after love, before motherhood and after motherhood. Only a woman can know that and speak of that. . . . She must always be maiden and always be mother. Before every love she is maiden, after every love she is mother. . . .[15]

It is argued, by Karen Horney for one, that the fact that women can bear children and men cannot sets up the jealousy in men which makes them strive so hard, struggling to prove *their* creativity in cultural activities and building civilizations. Often in psychoanalysis, this jealousy erupts in men with personal humiliation and despair. One South American patient cried out from the couch again and again that he could never forgive his mother that she bore him and he had to suck at her breasts—and he firmly believed every man carried within him that same angry envy. The archetypal roots of this conflict go infinitely deeper than the modern age or our "western" problems and are lodged in the roots of man's history and existence itself.

But the opposite side of the matter is as pressing. When I said in an earlier chapter that the "new sophisticate is afraid of his procreative powers," I meant it literally in the sense that his anxiety arises from his profound ambivalence about his power to create another human being. A patient of mine experienced periodic impotence each month at the time of his wife's fertility, despite the fact that consciously both he and his wife wished to have a baby. It turned out in his fantasies, however, that he did not wish to father a child which could be his rival for her affection but wished himself to remain her baby as well as her husband.

This ambivalence is present in Freud's term "castration," the original fear to which he believed all anxiety can be traced. For castration does not mean what Freud and most people take it to mean, a cutting off of the male member—the term for that is "mutilation." Castration, rather, refers to the severing of the testicles, becoming a eunuch; it consists of the *loss of the power to procreate*. The eunuchs in the Sultan's court were able to have erections and perform intercourse; but they could not father a baby. The line of blood was kept clear, despite peccadillos in the harem. I think Freud here was wiser than he seemed to be aware of, for this anxiety about procreative power—birth control notwithstanding —is truly fundamental.

CONTRACEPTIVES AND THE TRAGIC

We take as our illustration a young woman of thirty who came to consult with me some years ago and was my patient for a brief period. A graduate of one of the best New England girls' colleges, she had grown up in a well-to-do suburb, was intelligent and attractive, and seemed in every way a typically nice girl. In college, she had absorbed what had then been, in the mid-40's, the generally accepted belief in togetherness and the family, and had chosen as her goal to get married on graduation and immediately raise a large family. She had admirably lived up to her plan by marrying her boy friend from a neighboring college on commencement day, and then had five children, spaced one every two years just as she had planned.

But when she came to me at the age of thirty, she revealed that she was "in love" and having an affair with a garage mechanic, with whom, for the first time in her life, she was experiencing strong passion. She reported that she now knew that she had never loved her husband but had contempt for him. By the time she considered psychotherapy (on the urging of friends), she had gone home with her five children to live with her parents in the suburbs—a curious and pathetic denouement to what had once been such brave plans.

She and I were not able to do much effective therapy because she felt the love with the garage mechanic to be "sacred" and she did not wish to go into it. When I happened to see her some years later, she seemed a faded middle-aged woman working dutifully to support her children. This daughter of upper middle-class suburbia had gotten herself into a situation which was as little susceptible of solution, if not less so, than the old-time prototype of the "lost girl" who has a child out of wedlock. The reason was certainly not lack of information or lack of planning and responsibility. A modern, intelligent woman, my patient with her five children seemed in many ways as trapped as her forebears in Victorian times before the emancipation of women and the invention of contraceptives.

I cite this case to illustrate that the mere capacity for family planning is not an obviation of the tragic. The psychological meaning of contraception is the expanding of the realm of personal responsibility and commitment. But far from being easier, this personal relationship may have to carry more weight and may, therefore, be harder.

Since contraception allays anxiety about pregnancy in a given act of intercourse, it seems to be used in our culture as a symbol that we have left behind us once and for all the tragic aspect of sexual love. Now I am certainly in favor of contraceptives and the planning of procreation—a point so obvious it ought not need to be made. But this almost universally accepted principle of birth control should not blind us to the fact that contraception, great boon to sexuality as it is, does not change one whit the basic issue about which we are talking. Although it frees the individual from the immediate biological enchainment of pregnancy, it may well increase his psychological ambivalence.

The tragic dimension of sex and love is just as prevalent as it always was, even with contraception, but is raised out of the automatic, biological realm to the psychological realm. This is where tragedy should be anyway; it is not the biological facts of life itself, such as death and procreation, that give the tragic dimension, but how we as human beings *relate* to these inescapable necessities of human fate. The tragic is always a psychological and spiritual issue.

There is also the dilemma of personal responsibility which comes from the freedom to choose to have a baby or not. It has been possible to plan babies for the last four decades, and though we have acted upon that power, we have never accepted the psychological and personal responsibility for it. Our blithe evasion of that issue comes out in the guilt we feel as a whole society toward our children. We do everything for them, we cater to their development and their whims, we count it a sign of our broadmindedness and virtue that we give in to them on every moral issue (and now on marijuana) so that the poor children have an impossible time trying to find something about these always-giving-in parents against which they can revolt. When they go away, we say, "Have a good time," and we get worried if they don't have a good time and worried if they have *too* good a time. And all the while we are secretly envious of them and their youth and resentful at how good they have it as compared with how hard we had it. Through all of this treating our young like little royalty, heirs apparent to heaven knows what, we are the maids-in-waiting, chauffeurs, cooks, nurses, bottomless money-bags, home teachers, camp leaders—until it is no wonder our children stand up and scream, "For heaven's sake, leave us *alone!*" And that is the biggest threat of all to us—for we are filled with some nameless, pervasive guilt about our children and can't let go. And the guilt we are expiating is not about some specific thing we did or didn't do in rearing them; it is about the basic fact of having children in the first place. For no longer does "God" decide we are to have children; we do. And who has even begun to comprehend the meaning of that tremendous fact?

Or imagine the couples—and, with the need for population control, there will perforce be many—who will plan to have only one baby: consider the tremendous psychic weight this poor infant will have to carry. As we see in our therapy, particularly with professional people who have had their one child, there is great temptation to overprotect the infant. When he calls, the parents run; when he whimpers, they are abashed; when he is sick, they are guilty; when he doesn't sleep, they look as though *they* are going to have nervous breakdowns. The infant becomes a little dictator by virtue of the situation he is born into, and couldn't be anything else if he wanted to. And there is, of course, the always complicating and contradictory fact that all this attention actually amounts to a considerable *curtailing* of the child's freedom, and he must, like a prince born into a royal family, carry a weight for which children were never made.

Contraception, like all devices and machines, can increase our range of freedom and choice. But the new freedom and power thus given to us also increases our ambivalence and anxiety, an ambivalence which now expresses itself in the banalization of sex and love. As the girls who, in these days of the pill, are promiscuous say, according to Dr. Seymour Halleck, director of psychiatry in the student health service at the University of Wisconsin, "It's just too much trouble to say no."[16] To make something banal, to undercut its significance, to say it "doesn't matter," is the method par excellence of avoiding anxiety. Is not the upshot of the situation that contraception is misused to serve a detached, indiscriminate, here-today-and-gone-tomorrow attitude toward sexuality? Surely an act which carries as much power as the sexual act, and power in the critical area of passing on one's name and species, cannot be taken as banal and insignificant except by doing violence to our natures, if not to "nature" itself.

With contraception, sex can become, at least in some instances, a *purely personal* relationship. And the challenge this presents to us is no less than finding the meaning of this personal relationship.

FIVE

LOVE AND THE DAIMONIC

If my devils are to leave me, I am afraid my angels
will take flight as well.

> —RILKE, ON WITHDRAWING FROM
> PSYCHOTHERAPY AFTER LEARNING
> THE GOALS TO WHICH IT ASPIRED.
> LETTER 74, *Briefe aus den
> Jahren 1907 bis 1914.*

"Eros is a daimon." So simply and directly Plato informs
us and his banqueting friends in *The Symposium* of the
depth-dimension of love. This identification of Eros with
the daimonic, so natural for the Greeks, is the stumbling
block over which practically all modern theories of love
fall. It is surely not surprising that contemporary man
seeks to bypass, if not to deny and repress outright, the
whole realm of the daimonic. But doing so means "castrating" Eros—robbing ourselves of the very sources of
fecundity in love. For the polar opposite to the daimonic
is not rational security and calm happiness, but the "return to the inanimate"—in Freud's terms, the death instinct. The antidaimon is apathy.

DEFINING THE DAIMONIC

The daimonic is *any natural function which has the power to take over the whole person*. Sex and eros, anger
and rage, and the craving for power are examples. The
daimonic can be either creative or destructive and is
normally both. When this power goes awry and one element usurps control over the total personality, we have
"daimon possession," the traditional name through history for psychosis.[1] The daimonic is obviously not an en-

tity but refers to a fundamental, archetypal function of human experience—an existential reality in modern man and, so far as we know, in all men.

The daimonic is the urge in every being to affirm itself, assert itself, perpetuate and increase itself. The daimonic becomes evil when it usurps the total self without regard to the integration of that self, or to the unique forms and desires of others and their need for integration. It then appears as excessive aggression, hostility, cruelty—the things about ourselves which horrify us most, and which we repress whenever we can or, more likely, project on others. But these are the reverse side of the same assertion which empowers our creativity. All life is a flux between these two aspects of the daimonic. We can repress the daimonic, but we cannot avoid the toll of apathy and the tendency toward later explosion which such repression brings in its wake.

The Greek concept of "daimon"—the origin of our modern concept—included the creativity of the poet and artist as well as that of the ethical and religious leader, and is the contagious power which the lover has. Plato argued that ecstasy, a "divine madness," seizes the creative person. This is an early form of the puzzling and never-solved problem of the intimate relationship between the genius and madman.

In *The Apologia,* when he was being tried for teaching false *"daimonia"* to the youth, Socrates describes his own "daimon": "This sign, which is a kind of voice, first began to come to me when I was a child." After he is found guilty and a break in the court proceedings is declared so that he can decide whether to choose exile or death, he comes back and tells the court he has chosen to die. He explains his choice in these words:

> O my judges—for you I may truly call judges—I should like to tell you of a wonderful circumstance. Hitherto the divine faculty of which the internal oracle is the source has constantly been in the habit of opposing me even about trifles, if I was going to make a slip or error in any matter. But the oracle made no sign of opposition, either when I was leaving my house in the morning or while I was speaking. . . . It is an intimation that what has happened

to me is a good, and that those of us who think that death is an evil are in error. For the customary sign would surely have opposed me had I been going to evil and not to good.[2]

Thus his "daimon," which he believed every man possessed, acted as a kind of guardian.

The daimonic is not conscience; for conscience is largely a social product, related to the cultural mores and, in psychoanalytic terms, to the power of the superego. The daimonic refers to the power of nature rather than the superego, and is beyond good and evil. Nor is it man's "recall to himself," as Heidegger and, later, Fromm have argued, for its source lies in those realms where the self is rooted in natural forces which go beyond the self and are felt as the grasp of fate upon us. The daimonic arises from the ground of being rather than the self as such. It is shown particularly in creativity. We never could apply to conscience Yeats's definition of the daimonic—that "other Will," "that dazzling, unforeseen wing-footed wanderer . . . of our own being but as water with fire."[3] Nor could Goethe's words about the daimonic be applied to conscience. Speaking of the "tremendous power" emanating from daimonic persons, he states, "All united moral powers do not prevail against them. . . . And they cannot be overcome except by the Universe itself which they have challenged to combat."[4]

Aristotle comes the closest to "taming" the daimon in his concept of "eudaimonistic" ethics. Happiness—or eudaimonism—in the Greek language was the result of "being blessed with a good genius."[5] Happiness is to live in harmony with one's daimon. Nowadays, we would relate "eudaimonism" to the state of integration of potentialities and other aspects of one's being, with behavior.

The daimon gives individual guidance in particular situations. The daimonic was translated into Latin as *genii* (or *jinni*). This is a concept in Roman religion from which our word "genius" comes and which originally meant a tutelar diety, a spirit presiding over the destiny of a person, and later became a particular mental endowment or talent. As "genius" (its root being the Latin *genere*) means to generate, to beget, so the daimonic is the voice of the generative processes within the individual. The daimonic is the unique pattern of sensibilities and powers which constitutes the individual as a self in relation to his world. It can speak in dreams and to the sensitive person in conscious meditation and self-questioning. Aristotle believed that dreams might be called daimonic, and echoes our statement when he says, "for Nature is daimonic." Freud quotes this remark and adds that it contains "deep meaning if it be correctly interpreted."[6]

The deteriorated form of this concept, consisting of the belief that we are taken over by little demons flying around equipped with horns, is a projection of inner experience outward, reified into an objective reality. It was entirely right that the Enlightenment and Age of Reason, in the flush of their success in making all life reasonable, should have thrown this out, and have regarded it as a deteriorated and unproductive approach to mental illness. But only during the last couple of decades has it been clearly impressed upon us that in discarding the false "demonology," we accepted, against our intention, a banality and a shallowness in our whole approach to mental disease. This banality was specifically damaging to our experience of love and will. For the destructive activities of the daimonic are only the reverse side of its constructive motivation. If we throw out our devils, as Rilke aptly observes, we had better be prepared to bid goodbye to our angels as well. In the daimonic lies our vitality, our capacity to open ourselves to the power of eros. We must rediscover the daimonic in a new form which will be adequate to our own predicament and fructifying for our own day. And this will not be a rediscovery alone but a recreation of the reality of the daimonic.

The daimonic needs to be directed and channeled. Here is where human consciousness becomes so important. We initially experience the daimonic as a blind push. It is *impersonal* in the sense that it makes us nature's tool. It pushes us toward the blind assertion of ourselves, as in rage, or toward the triumph of the species by impregnating the female, as in sex. When I am in a rage, it couldn't matter to me less who I am or who you are; I want only to strike out and destroy you. When a man is in a state of intense sexual excitement, he loses his personal sense and wants only to "make" or "lay" (as the verbs of forcing so clearly put it) the woman, regardless of who she is. But consciousness can integrate the daimonic, make it personal. This is the purpose of psychotherapy.

The daimonic always has its biological base. Indeed, Goethe, who knew modern man's daimonic urges intimately, as shown so eloquently in Faust, and who was forever fascinated by the daimonic, states, echoing Aristotle, "The daimonic is the power of nature." But the crucial question always involves the breakdown of integration: one element in the personality usurps command and drives the person into disintegrative behavior. The erotic-sexual urge, for example, pushes the person toward physical union with the partner; but it may, when it takes command of the total self, drive the person in many diverse directions and into all kinds of relationships without regard for the integration of himself, the self of his partner, or the community. The Karamazoff father, coming home one night with his drunken companions, is dared to have coitus with the idiot woman in the ditch, and in doing so he spawns his own murderer. For Dostoevsky, with the true instinct of the artist in the matter of the daimonic, has the son born of this copulation later kill the father.

"Eros is a daimon," said Diotima, the authority on love among Plato's banqueting friends. The daimonic is correlated with *eros* rather than libido or sex as such. Anthony presumably had all his sexual needs well taken care of by concubines ("regular release of sexual tension" as Masters and Johnson infelicitously put it). But the daimonic power which seized him in his meeting with Cleopatra was a very different thing. When Freud introduced eros as the opposite to and adversary of libido, i.e., as the force which stood against the death instinct and fought for life, he was using it in this way which includes the daimonic. The daimonic fights against death, fights always to assert its own vitality, accepts no "threescore and ten" or other timetable of life. It is this daimonic which is referred to when we adjure someone who is seriously ill not to give up the "fight," or when we sadly acknowledge some indication that a friend will die as the fact that he has given up the fight. The daimonic will never take a rational "no" for an answer. In this respect the daimonic is the enemy of technology. It will accept no clock time or nine-to-five schedules or assembly lines to which we surrender ourselves as robots.

If the daimonic is shown particularly in creativity, we should find the clearest testimonies to its presence in poets and artists. Poets often have a conscious awareness that they are struggling with the daimonic, and that the issue is their working something through from the depths which push the self to a new plane. Said William Blake, "Every poet is of the Devil's party."[7] Ibsen gave a copy of *Peer Gynt* to a friend, writing in the flyleaf,

> To live is to war with trolls in heart and soul.
> To write is to sit in judgment on oneself.[8]

William Butler Yeats could have been writing for all poets when he proclaimed,

> And in my heart the daemons and the gods
> Wage an eternal battle. . . .[9]

In his essays, Yeats goes so far as to specifically define the daimonic as the "other Will," which he believed was both a force outside himself which was at the same time oriented to his personal being. The following is the complete quotation which has already been alluded to:

> Only when we have seen and foreseen what we dread shall we be rewarded by that dazzling, unforeseen wing-footed wanderer. We could not find him if he were not in some sense of our being, and yet of our being but as water with fire, a noise with silence. He is of all things the most difficult, for that only which comes easily can never be a portion of our being.[10]

Even more obvious in the arts of paint and canvas and the carver's stone, the daimonic is the daily companion—and if the truth were known, the inspiration—of artists of all kinds. It seems that our technological society will permit art to "invite the daimonic" and to live with it, while it looks askance at other professions when they attempt to do so. Art is the only way modern man will · allow himself to be shown the unflattering, cruel, and hideous aspects of himself which are part of the daimonic. Art can, indeed, be defined from one side as a specific method of coming to terms with the depths of the daimonic. Picasso lives and paints within the daimonic and is rewarded handsomely for it; his *Guernica,* showing the dismembered men, women, children, and bulls in the defenseless Spanish village which the Luftwaffe bombed, presents the daimonic with unforgetable vividness—and transcends it by giving it significant form. Paul Klee is quite conscious that his paintings are a dialectic between children's play on the one hand and daimonic forces on the other, and writes in his diaries about the daimonic. Indeed, the daimonic has a special place in the conscious center of the modern art movement. One has only to look at the all-too-obvious demonstration of this in surrealism of the second and third decades of our century, with its witches, demons, and grotesque figures. But it is more subtly and more powerfully shown in contemporary nonobjective art in the broken spaces which often give the effect of an arresting nihilism, the grating tensions of color, and the desperate grasping, by dedication or tour de force, at new forms of communication.

We note, furthermore, the West's great interest in the twentieth century in *primitive* art, whether the art comes from Africa or China or the peasants of Central Europe. The painters in the past who confront the daimonic directly, such as Hieronymus Bosch and Matthias Grünewald, are the ones by whom many people seem especially grasped these days. Though painted four centuries ago, their canvasses have a rare and penetrating relevance to our needs, and serve as mirrors for our self-interpretation even in contemporary times. Understandably, the daimonic is unleashed and comes to the fore in times of transition in a society, when the customary psychic defenses are weak or broken down entirely. Like artists in our day, Bosch and Grünewald lived and painted in such a chaotic time of psychological and spiritual upheaval when the medieval period was dying and the modern not yet born. It was a time of actual fear among people of

witchcraft, sorcerers, and others who claimed to know
how to consort with the demons.

Before going further into the meanings of the concept, it
may be valuable to take account of the contemporary objection to the word. The concept of the daimonic seems
so unacceptable not for intrinsic reasons, but because of
our own struggle to deny what it stands for. It constitutes a profound blow to our narcissism. We are the
"nice" people and, like the cultivated citizens of Athens
in Socrates' time, we don't like to be publicly reminded,
whether we secretly admit it to ourselves or not, that we
are motivated even in our love by lust for power, anger,
and revenge. While the daimonic cannot be said to be
evil in itself, it confronts us with the troublesome dilemma of whether it is to be used with awareness, a sense of
responsibility and the significance of life, or blindly and
rashly. When the daimonic is repressed, it tends to *erupt*
in some form—its extreme forms being assassination,
the psychopathological tortures of the murders on the
moors and other horrors we know only too well in this
century. "Although we may recoil in horror," writes Anthony Storr, "when we read in newspapers or history
books of the atrocities committed by man upon man, we
know in our hearts that each one of us harbors within
himself those same savage impulses which lead to murder, to torture and to war."[11] In a repressive society, individual members, representatives of the daimonic of
their times, express vicariously these atrocities for the society as a whole.

True, we try to forget the daimonic. When in the
course of his State of the Union address in January,
1968, President Johnson mentioned as one of his goals
getting crime and violence off the streets, there was enthusiastic applause, far and away the longest applause of
any point in the hour long speech. But when the President cited such goals as new and fair housing and im-
provement of race relations, there was not a clap to be
heard in all of Congress. Thus the destructive side of

the daimonic is deplored; but we turn a deaf ear, indeed play ostrich, to the fact that *the destructive side can be met only by transforming that very power into constructive activities.*

For in all this passion to get gangs off the streets, what homes are they to go to? The daimonic is all about us in our cities—frightening us in the form of individual violence while we walk on the streets of New York, shocking us in the fiercer racial violence of the riots in Newark and Detroit. No matter how much citizens and congressmen alike deplore the violence of the black-power movement, we can be certain that the boxed-up and suppressed power will come out violently if it cannot come out constructively.

Violence is the daimonic gone awry. It is "demon possession" in its starkest form. Our age is one of transition, in which the normal channels for utilizing the daimonic are denied; and such ages tend to be times when the daimonic is expressed in its most destructive form.

An outstanding example of the self-defeating effects of forgetting the daimonic can be seen in the rise of Hitler. The inability of America and the nations of western Europe to recognize the daimonic made it impossible for us to assess the significance of Hitler and the Nazi movement realistically. How well I recall those years in the early 1930's when Hitler was coming into power. I had just graduated from college and had gone to teach in Europe. My fellow liberals and I in America, and in Europe to a lesser extent, believed so strongly in peace and world brotherhood in those days that we could not even *see* Hitler or the destructively daimonic reality he represented. Human beings just couldn't be that cruel in our civilized twentieth century—the accounts in the papers must be wrong. Our error was that we let our convictions limit our perceptions. We had no place for the daimonic; we believed that the world must somehow fit *our* convictions, and the whole daimonic dimension was ruled out of our perception. *Not to recognize the daimonic itself turns out to be daimonic; it makes us accomplices on the side of the destructive possession.*

The denial of the daimonic is, in effect, a self-castration in love and a self-nullification in will. And the denial leads to the perverted forms of aggression we have seen in our day in which the repressed comes back to haunt us.

THE DAIMONIC IN PRIMITIVE PSYCHOTHERAPY

Native psychotherapy shows exceedingly interesting and revealing ways of dealing with the diamonic. Dr. Raymond Prince, a psychiatrist who lived with and studied the natives of Yorubaland for a number of years, filmed a fascinating ceremony which I present here as an illustration.[12]

When the tribe's mental healer is to treat some members of the community for what we would call psychological ailments, the whole village participates. After the usual rituals of the casting of bones and a ceremony which is believed to transfer the problem—be it sexual impotence or depression or what not—to a goat who then (as the "scapegoat") is ceremonially slaughtered, everybody in the village joins together for several hours of frenzied dancing. This dance constitutes the main part of the healing. In this dance, the significant point is that *the native who wants to be cured identifies with the figure he believes has demonic possession of him.*

A man in Dr. Prince's film, whose problem was sexual impotence, put on the clothes of his mother and danced around at length *as though he were she.* This reveals to us that the natives had enough insight to know that such a man's impotence is connected with his relationship with his mother—ostensibly an overdependence on her which he, in his own self-system, has denied. What is necessary for the "cure," thus, is that he confront and come to terms with this daimonic in himself. Now needing and clinging to one's mother are a normal part of the experience of everyone, absolutely essential for our survival when we are infants, and the source of much of our tenderness and sensitivity in later years. If this clinging is felt by the person to be too great, or if he feels that he must repress it for some other reason, he *projects it outside: it is the woman he goes to bed with who is the evil one, the devil who would castrate him.* So he is, therefore, impotent, castrating himself.

Assumedly, such a man has become preoccupied with women—"possessed" by them—and has found himself fighting off this obsession to no avail. Whether he visualizes his mother specifically as the demon or not, I do not know—usually we would expect some symbolic expression of the "demon." Accurately speaking, the daimonic is his own inner morbid relationship to his mother. In the frenzied dance, he then "invites the daimonic," welcomes it. He not only confronts the devil toe to toe, but accepts her, welcomes her, identifies with her, assimilates and hopefully integrates her as a constructive part of himself—and becomes both more gentle and sensitive as a man as well as sexually assertive and potent.

In Dr. Prince's film of this healing dance, we also see a village girl in her late teens who had a problem with male authority and had felt herself "possessed." In the ceremony, she danced wearing the hat and coat of the British census taker of the region, apparently the symbol of her daimonic problem with authority. We would hope and expect that, after the healing trance of the ceremony, she would be more assertive in her own right, less "mousy," more able to deal with authorities and able to give herself with less ambivalence to a man in sexual love.

Both the man and the girl boldly identified with what they feared, with what they had been previously struggling so hard to deny. The principle this implies is *identify with that which haunts you, not in order to fight it off, but to take it into your self; for it must represent some rejected element in you.* The man identifies with his feminine component; he does not become homosexual but heterosexually potent. As he dances wearing the hat and dress of a woman, and the girl the officer's hat and jacket, you would think you are seeing a film of a masquerade. But not at all: none of the villagers who are dancing smiles a bit; they are there to perform a significant ceremony for members of their community, and they partly share the trancelike quality in which the patients are caught up. The girl and man were emboldened to "invite" the daimonic by the support of their community.

Particular emphasis should be placed, indeed, on the importance of the backing of the neighbors, friends, and fellow townsmen of the individual as he faces his "demons." It is hard to see how this man or girl would have been able to muster up the courage to encounter the daimonic if they had not had the participation and tacit encouragement of their group. The community gives a humanly trustworthy, interpersonal world in which one can struggle against the negative forces.

We note that both of these persons happen to be identifying with someone of the opposite sex. This reminds us of Jung's idea that the shadow side of the self which is denied represents the opposite sex, the *anima* in the case of men and, in the case of women, the *animus*. Now what is especially interesting is that this term *animus* means both a feeling of hostility, a violent, malevolent intention (animosity), and also to *animate,* to give spirit to, to enliven. All of these terms have their root in the Latin *anima,* soul or spirit. Thus, the wisdom of the words, distilled through man's history, is that the denied part of you is the source of hostility and aggression, but when you can, through consciousness, integrate it into your self-system, it becomes the source of energy and spirit which enlivens you.

You take in the daimonic which would possess you if you didn't. The one way to get over daimonic possession is to possess it, by frankly confronting it, coming to terms with it, integrating it into the self-system. This process yields several benefits. It strengthens the self because it integrates what had been left out. It overcomes the "split," the paralyzing ambivalence in the self. And it renders the person more "human" by breaking down the self-righteousness and aloof detachment which are the usual defenses of the human being who denies the daimonic.

In such therapy we notice that there is a *freeing* of the patient from morbid ties to the past, and specifically in the case of the man, the ties to mother. This is related to the fact that, as is the case so often in mythology, legend, and psychotherapy, the devils are conceived as *female.* The Furies of ancient Greece were female; the Gorgon is female. In his comprehensive studies of world mythology, Joseph Campbell gives a lengthy list of the female deities and figures in mythology in all cultures who are seen as daimonic. He believes these figures are earth goddesses and have to do with fertility; they represent "mother earth." From a different viewpoint, I believe, the female is so often seen as daimonic because every individual, male or female, begins life with a tie to the mother. This "biological imbeddedness" to the woman who bears him is an attachment that the human being, simply by being born at the end of an umbilical cord, must fight if he is to develop his own consciousness and autonomy of action—if he is, in other words, to possess himself. But having fought the imbeddedness and declared his own autonomy, he must welcome the daimonic back again on a conscious plane. This is the healthy dependence of the mature man.

We observe, finally, that there is a remarkable parallel in the experience of these two patients with the theme of this book. One of the patients begins with the problem of sexual love—he cannot get an erection. He ends up with his will aided: he overcomes the passive dependency on mother and is able to assert himself, be potent. The other, the girl, begins ostensibly with a problem of will—she cannot assert herself in relation to authorities; and ends up, hopefully, able to love a man with greater abandon. Thus love and will are reciprocally related: to help one is to strengthen the other.

SOME HISTORICAL SOUNDINGS

We shall now explore more deeply the meaning of the daimonic. In archaic Greece, the term *daimon* was used interchangeably with *theos* and also had a meaning very similar to fate. Like fate, it was never used in the plural by Homer and the authors before Plato.[13] I have a "fate" just as I have a "daimon"—it reflects a condition of life to which we all are heir. The crucial questions are always, To what extent is this condition an external force which acts *upon* us (which is what the archaic writers tended to believe) and, To what extent is it a force within the individual man's own psychology (which was the view of the later Greek rationalists)? Heraclitus, siding with the latter, proclaimed that "Man's character is his daimon."[14]

It was Aeschylus, that reinterpreter par excellence of

the ancient myths and religion making them adequate
for the emerging self-conscious Greek, who cut the Gordian knot. He formed the concept of the daimonic for
the individual Greek citizen who was to achieve a remarkable pinnacle of development in responsibility for
civilization and for himself. In his play, *The Persians,*
Aeschylus has the Queen describe the delusions of Xerxes
which have ruined Persia, and she ascribes these delusions to a "daimon." This is an illustration of man as
simply the passive victim of the daimon. But the ghost
of Darius, hearing that Xerxes tried to put chains on the
sacred Bosphorus (an act of overbearing pride), states
that "a powerful daimon *took away his judgment.*" This
is something different. Now the daimonic power does not
merely take the individual over as its victim, but works
through him *psychologically;* it clouds his judgment,
makes it harder for him to see reality, but still leaves
him with the responsibility for the act. This is the age-
old dilemma of my own personal responsibility even
though I am moved by fate. It is the ultimate statement
that truth and reality can be psychologized only to a
limited extent. Aeschylus is not impersonal but *transpersonal,* a believer in fate and moral responsibility at the
same time.

The tragic hero in Aeschylus asserts himself autono-
mously without regard to the nature of things; and
hence comes to destruction. Death, infirmity, time—these
are the natural realities which encompass us and, at their
appointed times, bring us low.

Already in Aeschylus, the daimonic is both *subjective*
and *objective*—which is the sense in which I use it in
this book. The problem is always to see both sides of the
daimonic, to see phenomena of the inner experience of
the individual without psychologizing away our relation
to nature, to fate, and to the ground of our being. If the
daimonic is purely objective, you run the danger of slid-
ing into superstition in which man is simply the victim of
external powers. If, on the other hand, you take it purely subjectively, you psychologize the daimonic; everything tends to be a projection and to become more and
more superficial; you end up without the strength of nature, and you ignore the objective conditions of existence,
such as infirmity and death. This latter way leads to a

solipsistic oversimplification. Caught in such a solipsism, we lose even our ultimate hope. The greatness of Aeschylus is that he sees and preserves both sides so clearly. He has Athena recommend to the people near the end of the *Oresteia:*

> From anarchy
> And slavish masterdom alike . . .
> Preserve my people! Cast not from your walls
> All high authority; for where no fear
> Awful remains, what mortal will be just?[15]

But by the end of that splendid fifth century B.C., the daimonic had become the protector of man's rational autonomy. It was man's helper toward self-realization; it would warn him when he was about to lose his autonomy. Socrates—who is the best examplar of this viewpoint—was by no means a simple rationalist, but he could preserve his rational autonomy because he accepted its base in a realm which is transrational. This is why he triumphed over Protagoras. Socrates believed in the daimonic; he took both dreams and the oracle of Delphi seriously. He did not close his eyes or wilt before daimonic phenomena like the plague in Athens in 431 B.C. and the war with Sparta. Socrates' philosophy had dynamic sources which saved it from the aridity of rationalism, while Protagoras' beliefs were wanting because they omitted the dynamic, irrational forces in human nature. Protagoras' philosophy, based on the concept that "man is the measure of all things," became "pathetically" optimistic, writes Dodds, and he must have died an unhappy man at the beginning of the war between Athens and Sparta.[16]

The later men of the modern Enlightenment were to be considerably troubled by Socrates' daimon. It is fascinating to watch Thomas Jefferson, fresh in his faith from the Age of Reason, ponder the fact that Socrates was under the "care and admonition of a guardian Daemon." Jefferson writes regretfully, if, from our vantage point, absurdly: "How many of our wisest men still believe in the reality of these inspirations, while perfectly sane in all other subjects" (!)[17] And John Quincy Adams was also genuinely puzzled: "It is not easy to say whether this [Socrates' daimon] was the effect of superstition or whether he spoke in figure. . . . The instances which he gives of the occasions when he heard the voice, make it hardly possible to consider him as having intended only Prudence or conscience."[18]

No, Socrates did not mean Prudence or conscience, and Jefferson and Adams could not ignore the fact that he was the least superstitious man imaginable. Though he did not speak in figure in the sense of metaphor, he did speak in symbol. For the language of symbol and myth is the only way such fundamentally archetypal experiences affecting the whole man can be expressed. The daimonic belongs to that dimension of experience where discursive, rational language can never tell more than part of the story; if we stop with discursive language, we impoverish ourselves. Thus Plato, who also spoke in the language of symbol and myth in areas where only this language could express his meaning, could write that God has given every man a daimon, and that this is man's tie with the divine. What Socrates did mean is easier to understand in our post-Enlightenment and post-Freudian age when we explore the id and know the "dark" and irrational springs not only of inspiration and creativity but of all human actions.

Now we note the *union of good and evil* the Greeks achieved in their concept of the daimon. It is the bridge between the divine and the human, and shares in both. To live in accord with one's daimon (eudaimonism) is difficult but profoundly rewarding. It is natural drive in its starkest form but a drive which man, being conscious of, can to some extent assimilate and direct. The daimonic destroys purely rationalistic plans and opens the person to creative possibilities he did not know he possessed. It is illustrated by the powerful, snorting horses in Plato's metaphor which require all of a man's strength to control. And though man is never free from this conflict, the struggle gives him a never-failing source of forms and potentialities to awe and to delight him.

In the Hellenistic and Christian eras, the dualistic split between the good and evil side of the daimon became more pronounced. We now have a celestial population separated into two camps—devils and angels, the former on the side of their leader Satan, and the latter allied to

God. Though such developments are never fully rationalized, there must have existed in those days the expectation that, with this split, it would be easier for man to
face and conquer the devils.

But if something is gained in moral dynamism for the
Hellenistic Greeks and early Christians by this splitting
of the struggle of good and evil into devils and angels,
much is also lost. And what is lost is important; namely,
the classical organismic concept of *being* as combining
both good and destructive possibilities. We see the beginning of Rilke's problem—if his devils are driven away,
his angels will take flight as well.

Satan, or the devil, comes from the Greek word
diabolos; "diabolic" is the term in contemporary English.
Diabolos, interestingly enough, literally means "to tear
apart" (*dia-bollein*).[19] Now it is fascinating to note that
this diabolic is the antonym to "symbolic." The latter
comes from *sym-bollein,* and means "to throw together,"
to unite. There lie in these words tremendous implications with respect to an ontology of good and evil. The
symbolic is that which draws together, ties, integrates the
individual in himself and with his group; the *diabolic,* in
contrast, is that which disintegrates and tears apart. Both
of these are present in the daimonic.

Originally an archangel, Satan is given the specific
name "adversary." He is the one who tempts Eve in the
Garden and Jesus on the mountain. But when we look
more closely, we see that Satan is much more than a
mere adversary; Satan enlisted the aid of the snake in
the garden, which is clearly a daimonic element of nature. In Eden, Satan is the embodiment of the daimonic
of lust and the desire for power by means of knowledge
which will make man immortal, "like god." The Lord rebuked Adam and Eve for eating of "the tree of the knowledge of good and evil" and was concerned lest they would
now try to eat of the tree of eternal life. This drama in
the Garden and Jesus' temptations on the mountain are
symbolic representations of the daimonic urges of lust
and power, and Satan is the symbol who embodies these
daimonic urges.

Satan, Lucifer, and the other daimonic figures who were
all at one time archangels, are psychologically necessary.
They *had* to be invented, *had* to be created, in order to

make human action and freedom possible. Otherwise, there would be no consciousness. For every thought destroys as it creates: to think this thing, I have to cut out something else; to say "yes" to this is to say "no" to that and to have a "no" in the very ambivalence of the "yes." To perceive this thing I have to shut out other things. For consciousness works by way of either/or: it is destructive as well as constructive. Without rebellion, no consciousness.

Thus, the hope that Satan or the other "adversaries" can be gotten rid of by gradual progress toward perfection, would not be a constructive idea even if it were possible. And it is patently not possible. The saints were not talking nonsense when they called themselves the greatest sinners. The goal of perfectibility is a bastardized concept smuggled into ethics from technology, and results from a confusion between the two.

One trouble with the devils-and-angels cosmic scheme —and it is a formidable difficulty—is that angels are such bland and uninteresting creatures. They are, by definition, sexless; they often look like Cupid, which is Eros in his most deteriorated form. They seem to have the function chiefly of flying about delivering announcements and messages—a sort of celestial Western Union. They are relatively powerless creatures, except for a few archangels like Michael. I, for one, have never been able to get much interested in angels except as decorative appurtenances to a larger drama like the Christmas epic.

Angels boring? Yes—until they fall! Then the angel takes on fascination and interest. Lucifer, an angel thrown out of heaven, becomes the dynamic hero of Milton's *Paradise Lost*. When an angel assumes independent self-assertion—call it pride or refusal to knuckle under or what not—he then takes on power and the capacity to grasp our attention and even admiration. He asserts his own being, his own choice, his individual lust. If we think of symbolic representations like Lucifer as exemplifying some significant urge in the human psyche—an urge toward growth, a new form born in the individual which he then sees in the world about him—then this assertion of independent choice is surely a positive aspect of growth. The child who is the "little angel" for too long a period is the one we should worry about; the growing youngster who is a "little devil" at least at times gives us more hope of potentialities for future development.

The fallen angel is one who takes on some of the power of the daimonic again, a power relinquished in the dualism needed to face the disintegrating mythology of the ancient pagan world. Rilke is right, then, in wanting to retain his angels *and* his devils, for both are necessary. *Both together make up the daimonic.* And who is to say that Rilke's devils do not contribute to his poetry as much as or more than his angels?

The dichotomy between devils and angels was carried on through the Middle Ages, and the word for the daimonic is now clearly "demon." The medieval citizens were enthralled by their "demons," even in the act of condemning them; why else all these gargoyles, beasts laughing and looking sinister, animals of every sort, scampering and climbing up the sides of their cathedrals, carved in stone by artisans who must have known the daimonic at first hand? In this passionate period, the people gloried in their "demonic" natures. But this did not stand in the way of their using this handy method of condemnation of their enemies as the devil's party in their wars of religion and particularly in the Albigensian uprising. It seems that it is always man's proclivity to define the outsider, the stranger, the one who differs from him, as the evil one and himself as on the side of the angels.

The rediscovery of the daimonic as a force which cannot be measured in terms of good and evil "was due to the anti-rational cult of genius at the end of the eighteenth century," writes Prof. Wolfgang Zucker.[20] This was the expression of a fundamental opposition to the Enlightenment and to the utilitarian, middle class concepts of order and a protest against the prevailing moralistic and intellectualistic theology. Prof. Zucker writes of this with special cogency,

> Such expression needed as its social precondition the breakdown of the old social orders and the emergence of a new marginal class of artists who were no longer merely skilled artisans. It is at this time that the designations "artiste" and "Kuenstler"

came into use, designations which did not mean simply specific occupations, but a way of life outside of the hierarchy of social and economic values. . . . According to this viewpoint, the artist was no longer a man who simply had learned the use of brush or chisel or could play different musical instruments because of diligent study and practice, but he was now gifted with some supernatural power: he had genius, or even he himself was "a genius." . . . His acts do not conform to the norms of accepted behavior, but also his work has a superhuman quality that makes it incomparable with the work of other men. . . . Therefore the usual categories of good and evil, of useful and useless, do not apply to the genius. What he does and what he suffers is his fate. He is not a genius because he is an extraordinary artist, but conversely, he is an artist because he is possessed by genius.[21]

The elderly Goethe was continuously enthralled by the daimonic and discussed it at length. It is not *merely* nature, he believed, but also fate; it guides one to significant meetings—as his own friendship with Schiller—and it produces great men. To see the experiential justification for this point we have only to recall that greatness consists of being in "the right place at the right time"; it is an encounter between a man of particular qualities and the particular needs of an age. Men of talent are seized by the historical situation (*vide* Tolstoy's thesis in *War and Peace*) and hurled to greatness. They are used by a history which has the same function as nature at this point. Goethe describes himself as having discovered the daimonic very early in his career, and it was responsible for his particular destiny. The daimonic was:

. . . discovered in Nature, animate and inanimate, with soul and without soul, something which was only manifested in contradictions, and therefore could not be grasped under one conception, still less under one word. . . . Only in the impossible did it seem to find pleasure, and the possible it seemed to thrust from itself with contempt.

This principle, which seemed to step in between

all other principles, to separate them and to unite them, I named Daemonic, after the example of the ancients, and of those who had become aware of something similar.[22]

The great men come crashing down to destruction when they have performed their acts. For Goethe, "poetry and music, religion and patriotic enthusiasm of the wars of liberation, Napoleon and Lord Byron, were all daimonic." He writes also at the end of his autobiography:

> Although the demonic can manifest itself in the most remarkable way even in some animals, it primarily is connected with man. It represents a power which is, if not opposed to the moral order of the world, yet at cross-purposes to it; such that one could compare the one to the warp, and the other to the woof. . . . In the most awesome form the demonic appears when it manifests itself in some human beings. In the course of my life I have had the opportunity of observing several cases either from near or from afar. They are not always men superior in mind or talents, seldom do they recommend themselves by the goodness of their heart. Yet a tremendous power emanates from them, they possess an incredible force over all other creatures and even over the elements; nobody can say how far their influence will reach.[23]

Goethe, in his fascination with the daimonic, neither blindly admires it, as do the romantics, nor condemns it, as do the rationalists. He has developed a kind of aristocracy of the daimonic: some men are chosen to bear it in great degree and some are not. It is nonrational in its resembling the "Dionysian" of Nietzsche and the *élan vital* of Bergson. Great men who are especially characterized by the daimonic are invincible until, driven by their *hubris* as they inevitably must be, they attack nature itself. This proves to be their undoing. Napoleon is brought low not by the Russians as such, but by the Russians cooperating with their own winter. We see here an example of *willing according to the daimonic:* what the Russians cannot do by their own power they can accomplish by setting their will in accord with nature, the size of their land, and other aspects of that no-man's realm of cooperation between men and nature and between men and their fate. This is then personified in an interesting combination of man-nature elements into "General Winter."

Paul Tillich is the contemporary thinker who has been chiefly responsible for bringing the daimonic to our attention today. This accounts for his great attraction to psychiatrists and psychologists, who turned out by the hundreds to hear him whenever he spoke. They were not listening simply to a wise and learned man; they were listening to a man who "invited" the daimonic as they, in their work, needed to invite it. I was once consulted by a schizophrenic woman who had been on the edge of psychotic breakdown a year earlier. She had gone to Paul Tillich and had explained the "demons" as she experienced them. Unperturbed, he had remarked, "Every morning between seven and ten, I live with the demons." This had helped her greatly, and I believe had been chiefly responsible for her survival. Tillich's statement had said that she was not strange and "foreign" to the race of man because of what she experienced. Hers was a human problem differing only in degree from the problems of others; she was restored to some communion and communication with her world and the people around her.

But it was not always so. When Tillich came to this country in 1933 after being exiled from Hitler's Germany, he spoke often of the wave of pseudoromanticism sweeping Germany and told how the students in his classes had found him "too rationalistic and logical." After a trip back to Germany in the summer of 1936, he related his experiences before a group in New York. He had been so gripped by the ominousness of the future of Germany that he had gone into a woods near Berlin and experienced there the threat of the daimonic to come. ("I see ruins, ruins, ruins. Sheep will be grazing in Potzendammer Platz.") Now these mid-1930's were liberal times in America; hardly anyone in the audience agreed with Tillich that day. One theologian from Chicago remarked while walking out, "We've at last gotten rid of the de-

mons, and now Tillich brings them back from behind
every tree!" Well, the worst of Tillich's predictions turned
out to be too mild for what actually occurred in the
civilized barbarism of Hitler's Germany. Indeed, the age
which began after World War I with the promise of being an age of "technological reason" is now often referred to in retrospect as the age of the daimonic.

Freud took us into the Dantean purgatory of daimonic
forces and gave us plenty of empirical demonstrations of
how serious the daimonic urges are, and how perversions,
neurosis, psychosis, and madness are the results of this
power gone awry. "No one who, like me," as Freud
wrote, "conjures up the most evil of those half-tamed
demons that inhabit the human breast, and seeks to wres-
tle with them, can expect to come through the struggle
unscathed."[24] That word "half-tamed," seemingly used
lightly, is an accurate description of the human form of
the daimonic; fully-tamed is applicable to the angels, untamed to the devils—and we are both. In psychotherapy,
it is clear that it is not constructive to give in to the
temptation to flee *from* the daimonic simply because it
is dangerous; that way, the healing of psychological
problems leads to the blandness of "adjustment." Curing
people is then the royal road to their boredom. No wonder patients prefer neurosis and psychosis to "normality,"
for at least their deviate existence had vitality and force.

Freud's sense of the relentlessness of life, his humility
in the face of destiny side by side with his pride in his
own intellect, his refusal to pander to man's need to be
reassured about himself—these characteristics stem not
from pessimism, of which he is often accused, but from
a sense of the portentous quality of human existence and
the finality of death. They bespeak a genuine sense of the
daimonic.

In Freud's writings, we find the daimonic implicit in
his emphasis on "fate" and "destiny," and in many of
his concepts such as libido, Thanatos, and *Trieb*. There
is in each of them the implication that powers reside in
us that can seize us, can render us "nature's tool," can
whirl us up in functions greater than ourselves. Libido, or
lust, is the natural drive which works in man's imagination, can lay all kinds of traps for him, and just when
he lies back assuring himself that he has withstood the

temptation this time, it can seize him against his judgment and use him for the impersonal purposes of the race. Not to come to terms with such inescapable psychobiological phenomena leads to pathology. This is an emphasis of Freud's which is realistic, sharp, and constructive, especially when it is seen against the background of the Victorian separation of the self from nature. I say the daimonic is "implicit" in these concepts; libido, for example, has its say and dies. It is eros which is then introduced as the force to stand as our ally against the death instinct and for the fight for life. It is required that eros come in in the form of the daimonic which saves the day. This is Freud's clear calling upon eros as a daimon.

Prof. Morgan contrasts Freud's rigorous and tough-minded view of love with those of the positive thinkers which carry illusory promises to modern man. "No Frommesque 'art of loving,' no calisthenic healthy-mindedness, no liberal-utilitarian technology . . . will bring peace on earth, good will toward men [in Freud's view]. The reason is blunt and basic: We humans carry within us the seeds of our own destruction, and we nourish them continuously. We must hate as well as love. We will to destroy ourselves and our fellowmen, as well as to create and protect them."[25]

LOVE AND THE DAIMONIC

Every person, experiencing as he does his own solitariness and aloneness, longs for union with another. He yearns to participate in a relationship greater than himself. Normally, he strives to overcome his aloneness through some form of love.

The psychotherapist Otto Rank once remarked that all the women who came to him had problems because their husbands were not aggressive enough. Despite the oversimplified sound of that sentence, it contains a telling point: our effete cultivation of sex can make us so arbitrary and detached that the simple power of the sexual act evaporates and the woman loses the vital, elemental pleasure of being taken, carried away, transported. The "love bite"—that moment of hostility and aggression, usually occurring at the point of orgasm but which may be an obligato all through love-making—has a constructive psychophysical function, as pleasurable, or more so, for the woman as it is expressive for the man.

There is required a self-assertion, a capacity to stand on one's own feet, an affirmation of one's self in order to have the power to put one's self into the relationship. One must have something to give and be able to give it. The danger, of course, is that he will overassert himself—which is the source of the experience shown in the notion of being taken over by a demon. But this negative side is not to be escaped by giving up self-assertion. For if one is unable to assert oneself, one is unable to participate in a genuine relationship. A dynamic dialectical relationship—I am tempted to call it a balance, but it is not a balance—is a continuous give-and-take in which one asserts himself, finds an answer in the other, then possibly asserts too far, senses a "no" in the other, backs up but does not give up, shifts the participation to a new form, and finds the way that is adequate for the wholeness of the other. This is the constructive use of the daimonic. It is an assertion of one's own individuality in relation to another person. It always skates on the edge of exploitation of the partner; but without it, there is no vital relationship.

In its right proportion, the daimonic is the urge to reach out toward others, to increase life by way of sex, to create, to civilize; it is the joy and rapture, or the simple security of knowing that we matter, that we can affect others, can form them, can exert power which is demonstrably significant. It is a way of making certain that we are valued.

When the daimonic takes over completely, the unity of the self and the relationship is broken down; a fact confessed by the person when he or she says, "I had no control, I acted as if in a dream, I did not know it was I." The daimonic is the elementary power by which one is saved from the horror of not being one's self on one hand, and the horror, on the other hand, of feeling no connection and no vital drive toward the other person.

The woman we described in a previous chapter, who had fallen in love with the garage mechanic, reported to me that her husband had always "cringed around the house in the evening with a hangdog expression waiting for me to come up to bed." Though we can understand why the husband was in this scarcely proud state, we can also understand that it was a great relief to the wife and a boon to her own need for abandon that the erotic aggressiveness of the mechanic was inhibited by no such ambivalence.

Biologically, a vivid expression of the daimonic in the male is in the erection—a phenomenon which in itself has bewitching, erotic seductiveness for the woman as she realizes it is occurring, if she is already interested. (If she is not, she is repulsed, which simply proves in reverse that the phallic erection exerts emotional power.) The erection itself is such a rich daimonic symbol that the ancient Greeks were led to decorate their vases with paintings of dancing satyrs, each with a proud phallic erection, performing in a Dionysian religious festival. Men have only to remember their own fascination as little boys in experiencing the magical quality of their penis becoming erect, possibly without apparent conscious cause, and giving them such wonderful sensations. A similar daimonic assertion, though perhaps less biologically obvious than in the human male, is present and necessary in the woman in her capacity to have outright desire for her man, to want him and to let it be subtly known to him that she wants him. Both man and woman need this self-assertion to bridge their separateness and to achieve union with each other.

Not in the slightest am I arguing here for a return to primitive sexuality. Nor do I want to comfort the still infantile man or woman who interprets aggression as blunt insistence upon his or her demands of the sexual partner. I am using aggression in its healthy sense as assertion of the self rooted in strength not weakness, and inseparably allied to the capacities for sensitivity and tenderness. But I am also arguing that we have amputated significant aspects of our sexuality in overcultivation of sexual love, and so we run the risk of losing exactly what we set out to gain.

A curious thing which never fails to surprise persons in therapy is that after admitting their anger, animosity, and even hatred for a spouse and berating him or her during the hour, they end up with feelings of love toward this partner. A patient may have come in smoldering with negative feelings but resolved, partly unconsciously, to keep these, as a good gentleman does, to himself; but he finds that he represses the love for the partner at the same time as he suppresses his aggression. This is so clear that it becomes all but a rule of treatment. Dr. Ludwig Lefebre calls this the "inclusion of the negative" —which is essential if the positive is likewise to come out.

What is occurring here is more than the fact that human consciousness works in polarity: the positive cannot come out until the negative does also. This is why in analysis, the negative is analyzed, with the hope—which becomes true often enough to justify the rule—that the positive will then be able to come into its own. This is the constructive value in facing and admitting of the daimonic. For "eros is a daimon," we recall; eros has to do not simply with love but with hate also, it has to do with an energizing, a shocking of our normal existence— it is a gadfly that keeps us forever awake; eros is the enemy of nirvana, the breathless peace. Hate and love are not polar opposites; they go together, particularly in transitional ages like ours.

The most-discussed drama on Broadway and throughout the country in recent years consisted of a three-hour long, emotional butchering of one another by two couples, entitled *Who's Afraid of Virginia Woolf?*. That the audiences who saw this drama on the stage during its long run were uncomfortable was obvious in their nervous laughter or their hesitancy, not-knowing-whether-to-laugh; but that they were deeply affected was even more obvious. (We have to say, as has to be said so often, that the movie version of this drama was radically toned down. It gave the now mass audience much more assurance against the daimonic by emphasizing the love play between George and Martha at the outset of the movie story before the butchering started.)

Where did the play get its attracting power? I believe that it got this power from the fact that *it uncovered the daimonic wishes, thoughts, and feelings which go on in every marriage but are almost always denied in our bourgeois society*. What bewitched and gripped us, as when one of the actors in this play would coil like a

cobra to strike, was the laying bare on the stage of our
own daimonic tendencies, which appeared large and
clear. The lead couple, George and Martha, do have
some love for each other beneath the emotional savagery,
but they are afraid of it and afraid of their own tenderness. In this respect, the play penetratingly portrays modern Western man. For we are afraid of both our daimonic tendencies and our feelings of tenderness, which are,
of course, two aspects of the same thing. To be able to
experience and live out capacities for tender love requires the confronting of the daimonic. The two seem
opposites, but if one is denied, the other also is lost.

This drama, of course, *transcends* the daimonic by giving it significant *form,* as any good work of art must.
This is why we can permit ourselves to accept the daimonic when it is presented in art. The play also transcends the warfare in content in the last several lines
(though the subject matter is always less significant for
the transcendence of art than the art form itself). At the
very end, George and Martha are able to *will* something
with each other—hence, this has been called by its director an "existentialist" play. Ostensibly, they can will
because, in the process of the struggle, they have killed
off the illusion of their phantasmagoric son. But whether
they will really take the step, we don't know; we do
know that the disclosing of their struggles on the stage
strikes a powerful chord in the psyches of bourgeois,
civilized audiences.

We have only to call to mind the gruesome events of
ancient Greek dramas—Medea cutting up her children,
Oedipus gouging his eyes out, Clytemnestra murdering her
husband and being murdered by her own son—to see that
the daimonic, in utterly baldfaced terms, was at the very
heart of the great classical works which "cleansed the
audience with pity and terror," as Aristotle put it. But
the actual hair-raising event in the Greek dramas always
occurred off-stage, and was communicated by cries and
appropriate music. This has several benefits: it is accurate, in the sense that the daimonic does occur in our
lives generally slightly off-stage, i.e., in the subconscious
and unconscious. We don't murder the colleague with
whom we are arguing in a committee meeting; we only
fantasize his dropping dead of a heart attack. Also, the

Greeks weren't interested in barbarism and melodrama as such; they knew it destroyed the art of a work. The dramatist had to make his drama out of the *meaning* of the murder rather than out of the emotion as such.

I venture to propose that one of the central reasons the Greeks were able to rise to their unsurpassed height as a civilization was their courage and openness in facing the daimonic. They gloried in passion and eros and the daimonic which is connected unavoidably with these. They wept and made love and killed with zest. Nowadays, patients in therapy often remark at the strange spectacle in ancient Greece that it is the *strong* man, like Odysseus or Prometheus, who weeps. But because of their capacity to confront the daimonic directly, rather than resorting to modern man's self-castrating defense of denying and repressing it, the Greeks were able to achieve their belief that the essence of virtue (*arête*) for a man is that he responsibly choose his passions rather than be chosen by them.

What does it mean to confront the daimonic? Strange to say, William James, three quarters of a century ago, had an intuitive grasp of the daimonic and how to deal with it.

It is the very badness of the act that gives it then its vertiginous fascination. Remove the prohibition, and the attraction stops. In my university days a student threw himself from an upper entry window of one of the college buildings and was nearly killed. Another student, a friend of mine, had to pass the window daily in coming and going from his room, and experienced a dreadful temptation to imitate the deed. Being a Catholic, he told his director, who said, "All right! if you must, you must," and added, "go ahead and do it," thereby instantly quenching his desire. This director knew how to minister to a mind diseased.[26]

I shall give an example from psychotherapy of possession by a state not commonly considered daimonic—namely, loneliness. In this patient, attacks of acute loneliness, developing into panic, were not infrequent. He could not orient himself in the panics, could not hang on to his sense of time, and became, as long as the bout of loneliness lasted, numb in his reactions to the world. The ghostlike character of this loneliness was shown in the fact that it could vanish instantaneously with a ring on the phone or his hearing the step of someone coming down the hall. He tried desperately to fight off these attacks—as we all do, which is not surprising since acute loneliness seems to be the most painful kind of anxiety which a human being can suffer. Patients often tell us that the pain is a physical gnawing in their chests, or feels like the cutting of a razor in their heart region, as well as a mental state of feeling like an infant abandoned in a world where nobody exists.

The patient would try, when the loneliness began, to wrench his mind away to thoughts about something else, to get busy doing work or go out to a movie—but no matter what escape he tried, there remained the haunting, satanic menace hovering behind him like a hated presence waiting to plunge a rapier into his lungs.[27] If he were working, he could practically hear the Mephistophelean laugh behind him mocking him with the reminder that his stratagem would not succeed; sooner or later he would have to stop, more fatigued than ever— and immediately would come the rapier. Or, if he were in the movies, the awareness couldn't be suppressed every time the scene changed that his gnawing ache would come back again as soon as he stepped out on the street.

But one day, he came in reporting that he had made a surprising discovery. When an acute attack of loneliness was beginning, it occurred to him not to try to fight it off—running had never helped anyway. Why not accept it, breathe with it, turn toward it and not away? Amazingly, the loneliness did not overwhelm him when he confronted it directly. Then it seemed even to diminish. Emboldened, he began to invite it by imagining situations in the past when he was acutely lonely, the memories of which had, up to now, always been sure to cue off the panic. But strangely enough, the loneliness had lost its power. He couldn't feel the panic even when he tried. The more he turned on it and welcomed it, the more impossible it was even to imagine how he'd ever been lonely in that unbearably painful way before.

The patient had discovered—and was teaching me that day—that he felt the acute loneliness only as he ran; when he turned on the "devil," it vanished, to use metaphorical language. But it is not metaphorical to state that the very running is a response which assures the daimonic of its obsessive power. However much we agree or disagree with the James-Lange theory of emotions,[28] it is surely true that the anxiety (or loneliness) has the upper hand as long as we continue to run.

Anxiety (loneliness or "abandonment anxiety" being its most painful form) overcomes the person to the extent that he loses orientation in the objective world. To lose the world is to lose one's self, and vice versa; self and world are correlates. The function of anxiety is to destroy the self-world relationship, i.e., to disorient the victim in space and time and, so long as this disorientation lasts, the person remains in the state of anxiety. Anxiety overwhelms the person precisely because of the preservation of this disorientation. Now if the person can reorient himself—as happens, one hopes, in psychotherapy—and again relate himself to the world directly, experientially, with his senses alive, he overcomes the anxiety. My slightly anthropomorphic terminology comes out of my work as a therapist and is not out of place here. Though the patient and I are entirely aware of the symbolic nature of this (anxiety doesn't *do* anything, just as libido or sex drives don't), it is often helpful for the patient to see himself as struggling against an "adversary." For then, instead of waiting forever for the therapy to analyze away the anxiety, he can help in his own treatment by taking practical steps when he experiences anxiety such as stopping and asking just what it was that occurred in reality or in his fantasies that preceded the disorientation which cued off the anxiety. He is not only opening the doors of his closet where the ghosts hide, but he often can also then take steps to reorient himself in his practical life by making new human relationships and finding new work which interests him.

Still looking at my patient who had been obsessed with loneliness, let us ask, What was the constructive side of this daimonic which presumably had gone awry? Being a sensitive, gifted person, he had achieved notable success in practically all realms of human experience except

personal intimacy. His gifts included a capacity for interpersonal empathy and a good deal of tenderness—most of
which had been absorbed in his self-preoccupation. He
had failed to use his capacities for relationship; he had
been unable to open himself up to others, to reach out to
them, to share feelings and other aspects of personal experience, to identify with and affirm them in the ways
necessary to build durable relationship. In short, what he
had lacked, and now needed, was the exercise of his capacities to love in an active, outgoing concern for the
other's welfare, for the sharing of pleasure and delight
as an "I" with "Thou," for a communion of consciousness with his fellows. The daimon, in the constructive
sense in this case and put in the simplest terms, was his
potentiality for active loving.

SIX

THE DAIMONIC IN
DIALOGUE

> If he [the alcoholic] once gets able to pick out that
> way of conceiving, from all possible ways of conceiv-
> ing the various opportunities which occur, if through
> thick and thin he holds to it that this is being a
> drunkard and is nothing else, he is not likely to re-
> main one long. The effort by which he succeeds in
> keeping the right *name* unwaveringly present to his
> mind proves to be his saving moral act.
>
> —WILLIAM JAMES, *The Principles
> of Psychology*

We can no longer postpone the challenging question,
How does one know that among the bedlam of voices
which beset us all, one is really hearing his *daimon?* Inner "voices"—experienced as actual or metaphorical ones
—are notoriously untrustworthy; they can tell one anything. Many people hear voices, but there are few Joans
of Arc. How about our schizophrenic patients who are
instructed by their voices to bomb New York?

What keeps the theory of the daimonic from leading
to anarchism? And how is the individual saved from self-
righteous arrogance? What made that frenzied dance of
the Yoruba an *integrating* experience rather than simply
daimonic possession?

It is all very well for Socrates to proclaim that his
daimon tells him to be a gadfly to the state and then to
defy the court. This may indeed be integrity and honesty
—for him. But for many other not unworthy citizens of
Athens it must have seemed very different: the sheer arrogance of prying into everyone else's business! The
"good" citizens, experiencing him as the destroyer of
their peace, are speaking out of their own daimonic tendencies, just as he is speaking out of his daimon in defy-

ing them. And this seems to result in anarchy, with no principle of union. The daimonic disrupts the homeostasis of consciousness, giving Socrates a stand and requiring a stand from the "good" citizens. The disrupted homeostasis brings down the wrath of the people upon the disrupter, be he Socrates in Athens or a contemporary psychoanalyst. "Socrates, like all heroes who cause new worlds to rise and inescapably the old one to disintegrate," writes Hegel, "was experienced as a destroyer; what he stood for is a new form which breaks through and undermines the existing world."[1]

Observe that Hegel says it is a *new form* which Socrates stands for; we are not left simply with nihilism. Hegel adds with respect to the killing of Socrates by the Athenian people, "It was a force within themselves that they were punishing." Though much of this antagonism cannot be avoided, it makes our responsibility more compelling to have criteria to judge our own daimonic.

DIALOGUE AND INTEGRATION

The most important criterion which saves the daimonic from anarchy is *dialogue.* Here, the method of interpersonal dialogue—brought to its glory in Greece by Socrates and handed down for twenty-four centuries to be used in different forms by almost every contemporary psychotherapist—now gains in importance and becomes much more than a mere technique. For dialogue implies that man exists in relationship. The fact that dialogue is possible at all—that it is possible, in favorable circumstances, for us to understand each other, stand where the other is standing—is, in itself, a remarkable point. Communication presupposes community which, in turn, means a communion between the consciousness of the persons in the community. This is a meaningful interchange which is not dependent upon the individual's mere whim, but is a built-in aspect of the structure of human intercourse.

Buber has insisted that human life is life in dialogue; and although he makes of this point too extreme a theory —he says that we can know the self *only* in dialogue— he does present the crucial half of the truth. Sullivan's interpersonal emphasis on consensual validation also shows the central importance of dialogue, and has the merit of emphasizing the experiential side rather than mere discourse. The word *logos* (meaningful structure of reality) is the anchor of this term, *dia-logos*. If we can talk about the daimonic meaningfully, we already are in the process of integrating it into the structure of our lives.

Socrates was convinced that we find through dialogue the structure of experience and that each man is *not* cast adrift on his own. He demonstrates this to the Athenians on the street corner by getting Meno's completely uneducated slave boy to prove the Pythagorean theorem merely by asking him questions (the *Meno,* Dialogues of Plato). Socrates (or perhaps, more accurately, his interpreter Plato) believed that the truth of such a theorem already existed in the slave's mind, in line with the doctrine of "ideas" and reminiscence, and had only to be "awakened" and brought out. But even if we argue that Socrates put the theorem there by the suggestive questions he asked, we still end up with the same truth in a different form. That is that it is possible for the slave to hear the questions and to put them together meaningfully. Understanding is possible, specifically by *the structure of language,* and more generally by *the structure of human relationships.*

Truth exists in the individual as well as in universal structures, for we ourselves participate in these structures. *Logos* speaks not only in objective laws but subjectively, through the individual person. Socrates was, therefore, no relativist. "I do believe in the gods," he proclaims in his *Apologia,* "and in a sense deeper than my accusers do."

This is what makes the support of the whole community in the dance so important for our Yoruba natives. The dance welds the individual into deeper relatedness to his neighbors and friends, while daimon possession, on the other hand, increasingly isolates him from the community. The former makes the daimonic personal and conscious, whereas the latter not only leaves the daimonic unconscious but sets in motion a whole train of new repression. The integrated daimonic pushes the person toward some universal structure of meaning, as shown in dialogue. But daimon possession, in contrast, requires that the daimonic remain impersonal. The former is transrational, the latter—daimon possession—is irrational, and succeeds by virtue of blocking off rational processes. The former makes the vitality of the daimonic available for the use of the self; the latter *projects* the daimonic outside one's self on someone or something else.

Another important criterion by which the daimonic avoids anarchism is its own method of self-criticism. To be guided by your daimon requires a fundamental humility. Your own convictions will always have an element of blindness and self-distortion; the one ultimate illusion is to operate under the conceit that you are free from illusion. Indeed, some scholars believe the original Greek phrase "know thyself" means "Know that thou art only a man." This implies that what has to be surrendered or "worked through," as we say psychoanalytically, is the tendency arising in human infancy to play god and the omnipresent demand to be treated as though we were god.[2]

Freud's concepts of resistance and repression are descriptions of the profound difficulty of "knowing thyself." Sartre's concept of "bad faith" and "good faith" is also an illustration—the dilemma of honesty with one's self lying in the fact that there is always some element of self-distortion in our acts and beliefs. The man who thinks he is in "good faith" is at that point in "bad faith," and the only way to be in "good faith" is to know that you are in bad faith, i.e., to know that there is some element of distortion and illusion in your perception. The moral problem is not simply a matter of believing in one's convictions and acting on them, for people's convictions can be as dominating and destructive, if not more so, than mere pragmatic positions. The moral problem is the relentless endeavor *to find one's own convictions and at the same time to admit that there will always be in them an element of self-aggrandizement and distortion*. Here is where Socrates' principle of humility is essential, for psychotherapists and for any moral citizen.

A final criterion of validity of the guidance of the daimonic is the question implied in our definition of the daimonic at the start: Does the proposed way of acting make for the *integration* of the individual as a totality?

Does it—at least potentially—make for the expansion of *interpersonal meaning* in his life? And in the lives of those persons significant to him? A related criterion is one that is necessary for any value judgment, the criterion of universality: Would this way of acting, if adopted by other people (in principle, all of mankind), make for the increase of interpersonal meaning?

It may help to see what happens when the daimonic is *not* experienced in dialogue. Examples of this can be seen in every nation at war. Unfaced within one's self and one's group, the daimonic *is projected* on the enemy. It is no longer seen as a nation which has its own security and power needs, but as the Evil One, the personification of the devil; one's *own* daimonic tendencies are placed on it. (In America, this is abetted by our tendency to see ourselves as having left a Europe which was the seat of injustice, poverty, sin, and cruelty in order to construct a society on this side of the Atlantic which embodies justice, goodness, affluence, and brotherly love.) Thus our tendency to see in every communist a devil, to identify ourselves with God, and to fight no wars but only undertake crusades. In this country, we progressively saw the Russians, Japanese, and now Vietcong as the embodiment of evil; behind every rock, a communist or Jap. The enemy becomes the carrier of the elements we repress in ourselves. We fight our adversaries little realizing that we are fighting our own selves, denied though it be. This projection requires assertion of self-righteousness on the part of the "in" group, which is what makes it almost impossible to negotiate: to negotiate with the devil is to admit him in as an equal; you have, in principle then, already given in to him.

The next step in war psychology is that *imagination and vision are blocked*. There comes out of the capital —of whatever nation—cliché after cliché, each one thinner than its predecessor, which people do not believe on one level but join together in a conspiracy to believe on another. They become rigid in their daimonic obsession. It is impossible for them even to *conceive* of any solutions. Intentions become separated by a great gap from intentionality.

This process makes the daimonic *impersonal* again. It removes the whole area from our having control over it; the daimonic regresses to what it originally was—a blind, unconscious push unintegrated with consciousness. We now become not only nature's tools but her *blind* tools. This is abetted by the vicious-circle mechanism, present in nations as well as neurotics. We do not learn from experience; we make decisions patently against our own interest, and when they don't work we self-destructively make them all over again. Shrunken in vision and sensitivity, we move monolithically, straight ahead, like the ancient dinosaur who could not learn, blind even to our own dinosaurian movements.

STAGES OF THE DAIMONIC

We initially experience the daimonic as a blind push, driving us toward the assertion of ourselves as, say, in rage or sex. This blind push is original in two senses: first, it is the *original* way the infant experiences the daimonic, but it is also the way the daimonic instantaneously strikes each of us regardless of how old we are. The first yell that the infant lets out is a rich symbol indeed: it is in answer to the initial thing which life gives him —a spank administered by the good right arm of the doctor who delivers him. I not only begin life yelling but, for the first few weeks, my reaction to stimuli is indiscriminate. I may strike out in rage, thrashing my arms, needing and demanding to be fed—behaving like a "little dictator," as Auden puts it. But I shortly begin to experience that some demands work and some do not. My blind urges are now more and more sieved through the context of what gets me what I wish; I begin the long process of learning the gradual acculturation of daimonic urges. I am born into a social group, and I would not survive more than a few hours without this community—no longer than Oedipus would have lasted out on the hillside if he had not been found by the shepherd— though I cannot appreciate this fact for a number of months or even years. Regardless of how loud my protest is at the beginning, I need this mother and the others around me. The daimonic occurs within the context of this social group. To what extent will it be used against them, to attack them, or force them to bend to my needs and desires; and to what extent and when will it be used as a cooperative assertion?

Adults retain the propensity to experience the daimonic as a blind push, as sheer self-assertion. In lynch mobs and mass violence of all sorts, it is necessary to stir up the mob spirit before the act can be done. We experience security in the mob, a comfortable feeling of being completely protected. We surrender our individual consciousness to the "group mind"; we feel as though we were in the ecstatic state of a trance or under hypnosis. No matter how civilized an individual may pride himself on being, or how much he may deplore violence on the part of others, he must still admit that he is capable of this—or, if he is not, something important in his character has been suffocated. The attractiveness of giving one's self over to the mob lies in the excitement without individual consciousness—no more alienation, no sense of isolation, and none of that fatiguing burden of personal responsibility. All of this is taken over by the "group mind," a fictitious phrase which stands for the lowest common denominator. This is what constitutes the attraction—indeed, at times the horrendous joy—of war and of mass riots. They assume from us our individual personal responsibility for the daimonic; and the fact that my sentence begins with "they" indicates how we must assign the action to *anonymous* figures. In a society like ours, which represses the daimonic, these states are welcomed for the primitive security they give.

THE DAIMONIC AND THE ANONYMOUS

This brings us to the relation between the daimon and the special problem of modern Western man, namely, the tendency to get absorbed in the herd, lost in *das Mann*. "The daimonic is anonymity," states Paul Ricoeur.[3] The impersonal daimonic makes us all anonymous—nature draws no distinction between me and any illiterate peasant who also is its tool in its relentless drive toward self-increase, who copulates and begets offspring to perpetuate the race, and who can experience rage to keep himself alive long enough to serve as nature's pro-creator. Speaking psychoanalytically, this is the daimonic in the form of the id.

In our bourgeois, industrialized society, man's most effective way of evading the daimonic is by losing him-self in the herd. This is the particular reaction to the daimonic which *disperses* it. We look at the same pro-grams of murder and violence on television at the same time millions of other Americans do; or we join the army and kill not for ourselves but for our nation and for "freedom." This conformism and anonymity relieve us of the burden of the responsibility for our own dai-monic urges while insuring their satisfaction. But they also insure that *the daimonic will remain impersonal.* It makes the daimonic forces unavailable for individual integration; the price the person pays is the forfeiting of his chance to develop his own capacities in his own unique way.

The dispersion of the daimonic by means of imper-sonality has serious and destructive effects. In New York City, it is not regarded as strange that the anonymous human beings secluded in single-room occupancies are so often connected with violent crime and drug addiction. Not that the anonymous individual in New York is *alone:* he sees thousands of other people every day, and he knows all the famous personalities as they come, via TV, into his single room. He knows their names, their smiles, their idiosyncracies; they bandy about in a "we're-all-friends-together" mood on the screen which invites him to join them and subtly assumes that he does join them. He knows them all. *But he himself is never known.* His smile is unseen; his idiosyncracies are important to no-body; his name is unknown. He remains a foreigner pushed on and off the subway by tens of thousands of other anonymous foreigners. There is a deeply deperson-alizing tragedy involved in this. The most severe punish-ment Yahweh could inflict on his people was to blot out their name. "Their names," Yahweh proclaims, "shall be wiped out of the book of the living."[4]

This anonymous man's never being known, this alone-ness, is transformed into loneliness, which may then be-come daimonic possession. For his self-doubts—"I don't really exist since I can't affect anyone"—eat away at his innards; he lives and breathes and walks in a loneliness which is subtle and insidious. It is not surprising that he gets a gun and trains it on some passer-by—also anonymous to him. And it is not surprising that the young men in the streets, who are only anonymous digits in their society, should gang together in violent attacks to make sure their assertion is felt.

Loneliness and its stepchild, alienation, can become forms of demon possession. Surrendering ourselves to the impersonal daimonic pushes us into an anonymity which is also impersonal; we serve nature's gross purposes on the lowest common denominator, which often means with violence.

There is another form of the impersonal daimonic which is society's normal expression for at least part of this need. This is the curious phenomenon of masquerades and masked balls. Here is the *cultivation* of the fascination of the daimonic in anonymity—we do not know whose eyes are those of the person who seizes us or whom we seize to dance. We are freed, for the moment, from the perpetual responsibility—often wearisome indeed—of controlling our personal conduct. The masquerade, carnival, and *Fasching* are forms in which society permits us to temporarily go back to the freedom of the daimonic in anonymity. As I recall from my own experience while living in Mediterranean countries, the carnivals before Lent were a great and delightful relief in which one could let off steam; they performed a catharsis not unlike that which the Dionysian festivals must have provided for the ancient Athenians. This cultural form of the daimonic seems to draw off urges for violence. It is of the essence of the exciting pleasure of this abandon, however, that it is temporary, sanctioned by the community, and that everybody participates. Oases of free abandon to the daimonic, these masked balls can exist only in the larger context of community catharsis and social approval.

The next stage after the impersonal, both in the development of the infant and in each immediate experience of the adult, is to make the daimonic personal. To be human means to exist on the boundary between the anonymous and the personal. If we can channel the daimonic, we can become more individualized; if we let it disperse, we become anonymous. Man's task, by virtue of the deepening and widening of his consciousness, is to integrate the daimonic into himself. Making the anonymous personal requires standing up against the tendency of the daimonic to drive one into anonymity. This means enlarging our ability to break the automatic chain of stimulus and response; we can then, to some extent, choose what and what not to respond to. If the family training is rigid, or if there are traumatic experiences associated with it, the whole daimonic urge may be blocked off. *No* sexual feeling is to be experienced, or in some homes, *never* is any anger to be shown; the stage is then set for later daimonic possession—and ultimate explosion. For these urges do not sleep; and, if they cannot be expressed positively, they explode or are projected on whoever is the enemy of the person or the group. The trick here is that we learn not to let our wills "be sicklied o'er with the pale cast of thought and lose the name of action," but rather that we integrate the daimonic power wihout destroying our spontaneity. This is possible in the new dimension of consciousness of which I speak.

Thus, the daimonic becomes the personal daimon, the particular pattern of being which constitutes my own center, in this sense, individualizes. We can now understand how, in such a highly developed individual as Socrates, the daimon can be experienced as inner guidance: it is the voice of the relationship of the being, Socrates, to the Being as a whole in which he participates.

But having taken cognizance of the fact that there *are* rational criteria for judging the daimonic, we must not forget the central and most perplexing issue, that it is impossible ever to make the daimonic fully rational. The daimonic will always be characterized by the paradox inhering in the fact that it is potentially creative and destructive at the same time. This is the most important question facing modern psychotherapy, and the most fateful also—for on it hinges the lasting success and the survival of therapy. If we try to avoid the dilemma of the daimonic, as many therapists wittingly or unwittingly do, by helping the patient adjust to the society, by offering him certain "habits" which we think are better for him, or by making him over to fit the culture, we are then inevitably engaged in manipulating him. Rilke is then right: if he surrenders his devils, he will lose his angels too.

The daimonic, which is part of eros and underlies both love and will, acts as a gadfly to our consciousness by throwing us into continual dilemmas. The deepening and widening of consciousness we seek in psychotherapy consists not of the solution of these dilemmas—which is impossible anyway—but the confronting of them in such a way that we rise to a higher level of personal and interpersonal integration.

THE DAIMONIC AND KNOWLEDGE

Knowledge is another expression of the daimonic. The aura of mystical emanation which, in most people's minds, surrounds the physicist or the psychiatrist or psychologist, is composed of both veneration and suspicion. It is a contemporary form of an age-old phenomenon believed in not only by primitive men but by all people down through history; that acquiring knowledge gives one a daimonic weapon over other people. If I have some special knowledge of you or your world which you don't have, I have power over you. This may be as simple as the fact that I know how something works and you don't; but, basically, it is much more complex: it always skates on the edge of participation in the primitive belief that this knowledge gives me a special magical power. Some of the animosity against psychiatrists and psychologists and, specifically, against psychoanalysts (who, as Freud says, have to challenge the demons, and it would be a wonder if they did get off unscathed) arises from this deep-seated fear. Men in these professions, it is felt by many people, have a knowledge of life and death which others do not have. Thus, there is a tendency to cling to them as gods one day and fight them as hated devils the next.

Knowledge is also our source of freedom and security. "The truth shall set you free."[5] But in our emphasis on the gaining of knowledge, we have assumed that it was a one-way street—the more knowledge, the better; and we have forgotten this ambivalent, double characteristic of knowledge, that it is also dangerous. We hear so much these days about knowledge bringing power, security, financial success, and so on, that we overlook the fact that the very word which refers to the acquiring of knowledge, "apprehend," is also the word which means dread, "apprehension." Looking in *Webster's*, we find the definitions of apprehend, "to perceive, to recognize the meaning of, to lay hold of with understanding"; and the very next meaning is "to anticipate with anxiety, dread or fear." And the same with "apprehension": the first meaning, "a grasping of the mind," is followed by the second, "a distrust or fear of future evil."[6]

It cannot be an accident that woven into the very fabric of our language is this relationship between knowledge and the daimonic. "How dangerous it is to know," we can say with Oedipus, "But I must know, no less." It is dangerous to know, but it is more dangerous not to know.

It is the psychoanalyst who can afford to forget this least of all. Patients come for treatment ostensibly with open arms for revelations about themselves. But woe to the therapist who takes this at face value! The whole meaning of resistance and repression testifies to the anxiety and pain accompanying these disclosures about one's self. That is one reason why it is good that the patient pay for his sessions; if he won't take too much when he pays for it, he will take scarcely a thing given him gratis! This gives us a new approach to the concepts of resistance and repression—they reveal in a person an inescapable need to hide from the truth about himself. It is perpetually a moot question: *How much self-knowledge can a human being bear?*

Oedipus is the prototype of the man who gains knowledge about himself and pays the ultimate price for it. He is well aware of the threatening quality of knowledge: "Oh, I am in dread to hear," he cries, "but I must hear no less." Tiresias tries to persuade him *not* to search: "How terrible it is to know when no good comes from knowing." The issue in the drama is, Shall Oedipus know what he has done? Shall Oedipus know who he is and what his origins are? It does not take a Freud to point out that everyone commits these acts, in fantasy if not in reality—and in reality by the vicarious means of war and organized violence which his nation gives him. In actual fact, the only difference between Oedipus and the rest of mankind is that Oedipus faced and admitted what he had done despite all attempted persuasions to the contrary. Even Oedipus' wife, Jocasta, joins in the general consensus that it is best that he remain in darkness; to show that she means this as a general principle of life, she attacks all the soothsayers and those who deal in myths or take the daimonic seriously: "Have no part of this craft," she adjures her husband; dreams are not to be taken seriously and it is best to "live unthinking as a man may." When the truth finally dawns on her (and it is important to keep in mind that she did *not* know this when she advised Oedipus not to seek his origins), she cries out desperately to her husband, "God keep you from the knowledge of who you are!"

But Oedipus is a hero precisely because he will not let Tiresias or his wife or God or anyone else stand in the way of his knowledge about himself. He is the hero because he is man facing his own reality. Not that he does not cry out with the pain of it—he does, time and again. But he repeats, "I will not stop till I have known the whole." He also knows there are no false heroics "Curse on the man who took the cruel bonds from off my legs, as I lay in the field." Though he curses the childhood which brought him this fate, he confronts it directly, and destroys himself in the process: a relatively happy and successful king transformed into a blind, bad-tempered, old man exiled to Colonus. *But he knows.* And this courage to know, be it noted, with all its destructive possibilities, is found in the same person who can answer the riddle of the sphinx, the one *who knows what man is.*

Down through the ages, men have tried through their myths to tell each other of this connection between knowledge and the daimonic. In Goethe's *Faust,* the hero has such an all-encompassing drive to possess knowledge that he sells his soul to Mephistopheles and counts the price light—which was Goethe's, and the myth's, way of saying that to give in to such an infinite passion for knowledge is already to have become one of the devil's world. Adam and Eve are thrown out of Eden because they, having eaten of the tree of good and evil, now have *knowledge;* and this makes them like the gods, immortal. The myth portrays the birth of human consciousness and states that consciousness carries the daimonic with it. The myth of Prometheus has a parallel meaning: the god's disclosing of the cultural arts to men —central in which is language—amounts to the setting of himself against the other gods and incurring everlasting torment.

My point is that the more the daimonic is recognized, the more we shall be able to use the knowledge we acquire for our benefit and mankind's.

NAMING THE DAIMONIC

We come now to the positive, curative side of the role of knowledge in relation to the daimonic. "In the beginning was the Word," and the Word has always had a fascinating and complex relation to the daimonic. Referring to the alcoholic's proclivity for evading his problem by calling it everything else in the world except what it is, William James, in his pithy sentences quoted at the head of this chapter, speaks about the curing effect which occurs when he or any other patient dares to use the right name for his problem. "The effort by which he succeeds in keeping the right *name* unwaveringly present to his mind proves to be his saving moral act."[7]

Traditionally, the way man has overcome the daimonic is by naming it. In this way, the human being forms *personal meaning* out of what was previously a merely threatening *impersonal chaos*. We need only recall the crucial importance historically of knowing the particular *name* of the demon in order to expel him. In the New Testament, Jesus calls out "Beelzebub!" or "Legion!" or some other presumably accurate name, and the devil or devils leave the possessed unfortunate immediately. The priests who were successful at casting out devils in the Middle Ages were those who could divine the name of the demon, the pronouncing of which was sufficient to conjure the evil spirit out and away.

Names are holy. The naming gives one power over the other person or thing. In the book of Genesis, God entrusts man with the responsibility of naming the animals.

In ancient Israel, the Jews were not permitted to pronounce the name of God: Yahweh, or Jehovah, means "no name" and is a device used to refer to God without pronouncing his name.

I have come to the belief in my clinical work that this special power of words, as illustrated in the prohibition of naming, has something important to do with the clinical problem of writer's block. In all cultures, there is a basic ambivalence: words are what distinguish man from the rest of nature, and words also are dangerous to him who dares handle them. Writers in therapy may cry out, "If I write it, I'll be killed!" In Jewish tradition, as shown in Talmudic studies, there is an emphasis on words as carriers of special significance. It may be that writer's block tends more to threaten people who were brought up in the Jewish tradition.

One of the earliest and most fascinating accounts of the struggle with the daimonic and the importance of names, is Jacob's wresting with the "angel" in the 32nd chapter of the book of Genesis. The occasion for this was the enmity between Jacob and his brother Esau: Jacob had heard that his brother was coming with four hundred men. Within this, we find the problem of the love-hate ambivalence between the brothers. There is also the problem of will—certain that he would be defeated on the morrow, Jacob was tempted to capitulate. This problem of will was made more severe by feelings of guilt—he had, years before, craftily cheated Esau out of his birthright. The story illustrates how guilt and anxiety—Jacob was "greatly afraid and distressed"—can bring on the conflict with the daimonic. The conflict can also be thought of in terms of the light and dark man: Esau was "dark," hirsute, and the outlander, the hunter, the foreigner, as compared to Jacob, the farmer, the sower of seed.

So Jacob left his wives and children on one side of the river that night and went across to the other side to think, and to try to pull himself together for the crucial test which awaited him on the morrow. There, Genesis relates, he "wrestled all night with a man." The identity of the adversary, typical of all such occasions, is unclear. Is it some *subjective* prejudice of his own with which he wrestles; or a fantasy? a fear? Or is it—to make it more *objective*—an aspect of fate or an event like imminent death, something Jacob did not cause himself but life forced upon him and with which he must come to terms? Clearly, it is both.

But in the story, the identity of the adversary is charmingly ambiguous: though he is described at first as a "man," some commentators hold that he was Michael, the archangel. There is a passage later on in the book of Hosea which describes the same incident, and there two words are used in parallelism for this being, *Malak* and *Elohim*.[8] The first has its primary meaning as messenger and the second as God (or gods). In Hebrew, these early "daimons" (if I may substitute my own term) refer regularly to beings of indeterminate status, who owe their identity to their connection with some particular event. Which is as it should be—assuming the daimonic consists of a particular relationship of a human being to a significant event.

But about one thing there is no question: reading through the incident, we find the identity of the "man" becoming more and more that of a god until, in the latter part of the struggle, the adversary is called God himself. This man-god is a parallel to the "half-way between" stature of the Greek demiurge Eros, which participates in both mortality and immortality.

When this daimon found that he could not overcome Jacob in wrestling, he struck him in the thigh and maimed him. But Jacob still hung on. At length, the daimon implored, "Let me go for the day is breaking." Jacob responded, "I will not let you go unless you bless me"— Jacob, the insistent, the father of his race who does not ask whether God *deigns* to bless him, does not *implore* blessing; he *demands* it. And now we observe what an important role the names have! The daimon asks, "What is your name?" and on being told "Jacob," proclaims, "Your name shall no more be called Jacob, but Israel, for you have striven with God and with men, and have prevailed." Jacob, for whom politeness and decorum have no place when the issues are as critical as this moment, demands, "Tell me, I pray, your name." The daimonic character of the adversary comes to the fore in the fact that he only turns the question back, leaving his identity still ambiguous: "Wherefore is it you ask my name?" He then blessed Jacob. The new character Jacob forges in his struggle with the daimonic is sealed by the new name, Israel, literally meaning one-who-strives-with-God.[9]

Before Jacob leaves the spot, he gives us another illustration of the importance of names and the daimonic. He changes the *name* of the spot where the encounter had taken place: "And he called the name of the place Peniel, for I have seen God face to face, and my life is preserved" (Gen. 32:30). This again shows the assertion which the daimonic enforces upon us; the older Hebrew belief had been that for man to see God meant to die. Jacob breaks through that convention—through his own insistence, he not only sees God but wrestles with him. And he lives.

If we think of the daimonic as man's struggle with forces from within his own unconscious which, at the same time, are rooted in the objective world, we can understand how this conflict would be brought closer to the surface, made more demanding and available for Jacob, precisely at the moment when his struggle with Esau was imminent. The daimonic is more apt to come out when we are struggling with an inner problem; it is the conflict which brings the unconscious dimensions closer to the surface where they can be tapped. Conflict presupposes some need for a shift, some change in *Gestalt*, within the person; he struggles for a new life, as it were. This opens up the channels to creativity.

Jacob is the prototype of the religiously creative man; but the same is true for artists and writers. "The need to express one's self in writing," André Maurois tells us, "springs from a maladjustment to life, or from an inner conflict, which the . . . man cannot resolve in action."[10] No writer writes out of his having found the answer to the problem; he writes rather out of his having the problem and *wanting* a solution. The solution consists not of a resolution. It consists of the *deeper and wider dimension of consciousness to which the writer is carried by virtue of his wrestling with the problem*. We create out of a problem; the writer and the artist are not presenting answers but creating as an experience of something in themselves trying to work—"to seek, to find and not to yield." The contribution which is given to the world by the painting or the book is the process of the search.

But there is a final perplexing aspect to the story—Jacob is maimed. The account says that he limped away from the scene; he is now a cripple. The parallel to sexual intercourse is clear enough; Jacob has been struck in the thigh. In the orgasm, there is a combination of pain and ecstasy; a giving of one's self which is often experienced as something being ripped from the center of one's loins. But this refers more broadly to the creative experience as a whole. And to that curious and troublesome aspect of the creative moment, be it in art or thought or ethics or—as in Jacob's case—religion: that aspect of the creative experience which pulls all of the mans' self into it, calls forth an effort and level of consciousness which he did not know he could put forth, and leaves him crippled. The individual completes the creative work vastly relieved and more a person than before—but also *maimed*. We often hear the statement after a harrowing task which took years, "I'll never be the same again." It is the hurt after the struggle, the imminence of a neurotic or schizophrenic break, though the person may simultaneously be more a person after the wrestling. Van Gogh was maimed; Nietzsche was maimed; Kierkegaard was maimed. It is the danger of the razor-blade edge of heightened consciousness on which the creative person lives. No man shall see God and live; but Jacob did see God—and had to—and, though he lived, he was maimed. This is the paradox of consciousness. How much self-awareness can a man bear? Does not creativity take one to the frontiers of consciousness *and push one beyond* them? Does not this require an effort and courage beyond human capacities?; but doesn't it also push back the frontiers of consciousness so that those who follow, like the explorers in early America, may erect cities and live there? This is the mystery. The clearest explanation seems to be that in the creative act, the individual moves farther away from the innocence of the child, or from the virginal state of Adam and Eve. The gap between the "essential" and the "existential" now becomes greater. The wisdom of Thomas Wolfe's title, *You Can't Go Home Again*, is written more deeply in his (the creative man's) being.

In the heightened consciousness which is necessary for

the fully creative act—as in the case of Blake, Nietzsche, Kierkegaard, Ibsen, Tillich, and the few other men who have challenged the position of God—schizophrenia and the creative act go hand in hand. And the individual may move back and forth from one to the other. One can see the whole story in the eyes of the person who has "struggled with God and with man and prevailed." Assertion and dedication are necessary even to go to that frontier, and although a genuine self-realization may be achieved, he is also maimed in the process.

NAMING OF THE DAIMONIC IN THERAPY

In the naming of the daimonic, there is an obvious and interesting parallel to the power of naming in contemporary medical and psychological therapy. At some time, everyone must have been aware of how relieved he was when he went to the doctor with a troublesome illness and the doctor pronounced a *name* for it. A name for the virus or germ, a name for the disease process, and the doctor could then make a statement or two about the disease on the basis of this name.

Now something deeper is going on in this phenomenon than our relief at whether or not the doctor can predict a quick cure. Or any cure, for that matter. Some years ago, after weeks of undetermined illness, I heard from a specialist that my sickness was tuberculosis. I was, I recall, distinctly relieved, *even though I was fully aware that this meant, in those days, that medicine could do nothing to cure the disease.* A number of explanations will leap to the reader's mind. He will accuse me of being glad to be relieved from responsibility; that any patient is reassured when he has the authority of the doctor to which he can give himself up; and the naming of the disorder takes away the mystery of it. But these explanations are surely too simple. Even the last one— that the naming reduces the mystery—will be seen, on further thought, as an illusion: to me the bacillus or the virus or the germ is still as much a mystery as ever, and the tubercle bacillus was then still a mystery to the doctor.

The relief, rather, comes from the *act of confronting*

the daimonic world of illness by means of the names.
The doctor and I stand together, he knowing more names
in this purgatory than I and therefore technically my
guide into hell. Diagnosis (from *dia-gignoskein*, literally
"knowing through") may be thought of, on one side, as
our modern form of calling the name of the offending
demon. Not that the rational information about the disease is unimportant; but the rational data given to me
add up to something more significant than the information itself. It becomes, for me, a symbol of a change to
a new way of life. The names are symbols of a certain
attitude I must take toward this daimonic situation of illness; the disorder expresses a myth (a total pattern of
life) which communicates to me a way in which I must
now orient and order my life. This is so whether it is
for two weeks with a cold or twelve years with tuberculosis; the *quantity* of time is not the point. It is a
quality of life. In short, the image by which I identify
myself changes by its contact with the myth portraying
the daimonic in the natural processes of disease. If I
overcome the disease, I shall partly be a new being,
and I could rightly be initiated into a new community
and be given a new name.[11]

The parallel of this phenomenon to psychotherapy is
even closer than it is to medicine. Many therapists, like
Allen Wheelis, speak of their task as *"naming the unconscious."* Every therapist must be impressed almost every hour with the strange power which the names of psychological "complexes" or patterns have for the patient.
If the therapist proposes that the patient is afraid of his
memories of the "primal scene," or that he has an "in-
verted Oedipus," or that he is an "introvert" or "extro-
vert" or has an "inferiority complex," or that he is angry
at his boss because of "transference," or that the reason
he cannot talk this morning is "resistance"—if the therapist proposes any of these shibboleths, it is amazing how
the words themselves *seem* to help the patient. He re-
laxes and acts as though he has already gotten something
of great value. Indeed, one could burlesque psychoanalysis or therapy of any sort with the statement that the
patient pays money to hear certain seemingly magic
words; and he feels that he has received his money's
worth if he hears a few esoteric terms. This relief *does*

seem to have the characteristics of the "magic" of words. But this—such an easy straw man to be set up by the enemies of psychoanalysis—is a burlesque of therapy and not genuine therapy at all.

It has been argued that the relief the patient receives is due to the fact that the "naming" gets him off the hook; it relieves him of responsibility by making a technical process to blame; he is not doing it, but his "unconscious" is. There is some objective truth in this. Most patients take too much responsibility for the wrong things, and not enough responsibility for those things about which they can do something. Furthermore, on the positive side, the naming helps the patient feel allied with a vast movement which is "science"; and, also, he is not isolated any more since all kinds of other people have the same problem that he has. The naming assures him that the therapist has an interest in him and is willing to act as his guide through purgatory. Naming the problem is tantamount to the therapist's saying, "Your problem can be known, it has causes; you can stand outside and look at it."

But the greatest danger in the therapeutic process lies right here: that the naming for the patient will be used not as an aid for change, but as a substitute for it. He may stand off and get a temporary security by diagnoses, labels, talking about symptoms, and then be relieved of the necessity of using will in action and in loving. This plays into the hands of modern man's central defense, namely intellectualization—using words as substitutes for feelings and experience. The word skates always on the edge of the danger of *covering up* the daimonic as well as disclosing it.

Other forms of therapy, including lobotomy, may also "remove" the daimonic. Dr. Jan Frank, in his study of 300 patients before and after they underwent lobotomies, gives a poignant example. "One of my patients," he writes, "a schizophrenic doctor, complained before the operation about a recurring nightmare in which he was surrounded by wild animals in the arena. After the lobotomy the dream lions did not roar and were not frightening any longer but walked silently away."[12] When I read this, I was aware of a vague discomfort which I soon realized was the feeling that walking silently away was a potentiality precious to this man's life, and he was the poorer thereby.

It is the failure of therapy, rather than its success, when it drugs the daimonic, tranquillizes it, or in other ways fails to confront it head on. The Furies, or daimons, are called in Aeschylus' *Oresteia* the "disturbers of sleep." In the drama they drove Orestes into temporary insanity after he killed his mother. But when one stops to think about it, if Orestes had slept soundly that month after the killing, something tremendously important would have been lost. Sleep is possible only after the pattern of fate-guilt-personal-responsibility is worked through to new integration, as it is in the last drama of the trilogy, *The Eumenides.*

When Orestes is acquitted by the jury, Apollo demands the expurgation of the Furies—these daimons who are the symbolic spirits of anger, revenge, retaliation. Apollo speaks as the representative of highly respected rationality; he lives by logical balance, accepted forms, and civilized control. He argues that these primitive, archaic Furies—spokesmen for the irrational id if ever such existed—who torment men at night letting them neither sleep nor rest, be banished forever from the land.

But what Apollo does not see, and what Athena has to drive home to him, is that he can be as cruel and implacable in his intellectual detachment as the Furies can be in their primitive rage. Athena, who reconciles opposing poles in her own self (symbolized by the fact that "no mother . . . gave [her] birth"),[13] argues a greater wisdom as she refuses Apollo:

> Yet these, too [the Furies], have their work. We cannot brush them aside, and if this action so runs that they fail to win, the venom of their resolution will return to infect the soil, and sicken all my land to death. Here is dilemma. Whether I let them stay or drive them off, it is a hard course and will hurt.[14]

She is enunciating a psychotherapeutic insight demonstrated by Freud in the Victorian age, a lesson, alas, not yet learned in our time: if we repress the daimonic, we shall find these powers returning to "sicken" us; whereas, if we let them stay, we shall have to struggle to a new level of consciousness in order to integrate them and not be overwhelmed by impersonal power. And (what a refreshingly honest motto to put up in a psychotherapist's office!) *either way will hurt.*

But in this drama, the act of accepting the daimonic also opens the way for the development of human understanding and compassion, and even raises the level of ethical sensibility. Athena proceeds to persuade the Furies to remain in Athens and accept their role as respected guardians of the city. By accepting the daimonic Furies, welcoming them into Athens, the community is enriched.

Then our time-honored symbol comes home to us again, as at the birth of every new form of being—*the Furies have their name changed.* They are henceforth to be called *Eumenides,* literally meaning workers of grace. What a profound and eloquent way of proclaiming that the hated daimonic can be a guardian and a channel of grace!

We now arrive at the ultimate meaning of the daimonic in dialogue. What did the ancients mean by this "Word" which has power over the daimonic? They were referring to the logos, the meaningful structure of reality, which is man's capacity to construct form, and underlies his capacity for language as well as for dialogue. "In the beginning was the Word" is true experientially as well as theologically. For the beginning of man as man, in contrast to apes or the pre-self-conscious infant, is the potentiality for language. We find that some of the important functions of therapy rest on fundamental aspects of the structure of language; the Word discloses the daimonic, forces it out into the open where we can confront it directly. The Word gives man a power over the daimonic.

This Word is communicated, in its original, powerful forms, by symbols and myths. It is important not to forget that any healing process—even the question of what each of us with a common cold is to do about his virus—is a myth, a way of viewing and evaluating one's self and one's body in relation to the world. Unless my illness changes my image of myself, my *myth* of myself, I shall not have distilled from the trauma of illness the opportunity for new insight into myself and my possibilities of self-realization in life. And I shall not attain anything that can be rightly called "cure."

We have seen that the daimonic begins as *im*personal. I am pushed by the clamor of gonads and temper. The second stage consists of a deepening and widening of consciousness by which I make my daimonic urges *personal*. I transform this sexual appetite into the motivation to make love to, and be loved by, the woman I desire and choose. But we do not stop there. The third stage consists of the more sensitive understanding of bodies as body (to use a physical analogy) and of the meaning of love in human life (to use a psychological and ethical analogy). The daimonic thus pushes us toward the logos. The more I come to terms with my daimonic tendencies, the more I will find myself conceiving and living by a universal structure of reality. This movement toward the logos is *trans*personal. Thus we move from an impersonal through a personal to a transpersonal dimension of consciousness.

PART II

Will

SEVEN

THE WILL IN CRISIS

This is [our] true predicament: together with the fear
of man we have lost the love of man, the affirmation
of man, *the will to man*.   —NIETZSCHE

A friend of mine with whom I was having lunch seemed
depressed. The lunch was not far along when he told me
that he was preoccupied over some events of the weekend. His three children, aged twelve to twenty-three, had
devoted several pithy hours to pointing out how he had
been, if not responsible for, at least a prime contributor
to, their problems. The upshot of their attack was that
he hadn't made enough clear decisions in his relation to
them, hadn't taken a firm enough stand or set a strong
enough structure.

My friend, a sensitive, imaginative man who was a
considerable success in his own life and work, had been
brought up by strict "inner-directed" parents. But he had
known that he could never raise his children on that
Victorian "will-power" pattern. At the same time, he and
his wife had also never been devotees of the popular
overpermissiveness which filled the vacuum when Victorianism was routed. What struck me with poignancy
as he talked was my awareness that almost every parent
these days seems to express in some form the same pain
and perplexity that infused his question, "How *does* a
parent make decisions about his children? How should a
father assert his will?"

This crisis of will affects the "neurotic" and "normal"
alike—the patient on the couch as well as the psychiatrist
or psychologist in the chair listening to him. The man I
referred to was not in treatment for neurosis; yet he
was experiencing the same contradiction in will and decision that is an inescapable expression of the psycho-

logical upheaval of the transitional age in which we live. The inherited basis of our capacity for will and decision has been irrevocably destroyed. And, ironically if not tragically, it is exactly in this portentous age, when power has grown so tremendously and decisions are so necessary and so fateful, that we find ourselves lacking any new basis for will.

THE UNDERMINING OF PERSONAL RESPONSIBILITY

One of Sigmund Freud's great contributions—if not his greatest—lay in his cutting through the futility and self-deceit in Victorian "will power." That "will power" was conceived by our nineteenth-century forefathers as the faculty by which they made resolutions and then purportedly directed their lives down the rational and moral road that the culture said they should go. I say that this was possibly Freud's greatest discovery because it was this exploration of the ill effects of Victorian will power which led him to what he called the "unconscious." He uncovered the vast areas in which motives and behavior—whether in bringing up children or making love or running a business or planning a war—are determined by unconscious urges, anxieties, fears, and the endless host of bodily drives and instinctual forces. In describing how "wish" and "drive" move us rather than "will," Freud formulated a new image of man that shook to the very foundations Western man's emotional, moral, and intellectual self-image. Under his penetrating analysis, Victorian "will" did, indeed, turn out to be a web of rationalization and self-deceit. Now he was entirely accurate in his diagnosis of the morbid side of the vaunted Victorian "will power."

But along with this inevitably went an unavoidable undermining of will and decision and an undercutting of the individual's sense of responsibility. The image that emerged was of man as determined—not *driving* any more, but *driven*. Man is "lived by the unconscious," as Freud, agreeing with the words of Groddeck, put it. "The deeply rooted belief in psychic freedom and choice," wrote Freud, ". . . is quite unscientific and must give ground before the claims of a determinism which governs mental life."[1]

Now whatever the theoretical truth or falsehood of such a position is, it had very great practical significance. It reflected, rationalized, and played into the hands of modern man's most pervasive tendency—which has become almost an endemic disease in the middle of the twentieth century—to see himself as passive, the willy-nilly product of the powerful juggernaut of psychological drives. (And of economic forces, we may add, as Marx, on the socio-economic level, had demonstrated with an analysis parallel in brilliance to Freud's.)

I do not say that Freud and Marx "caused" this loss of individual will and responsibility. Great men, rather, *reflect* what is emerging from the depths of their culture and, having reflected, then interpret and mold what they find. We may disagree with their interpretations of their findings; we cannot disagree with the fact that they *found* it. We cannot ignore or slough over Freud's discoveries without cutting ourselves off from our own history, mutilating our own consciousness, and forfeiting the chance to push through this crisis to a new plane of consciousness and integration. Man's image of himself will never be the same again; our only choice is to retreat before this destruction of our vaunted "will power" or to push on to the integration of consciousness on new levels. I do not wish or "choose" to do the former, but we have not yet achieved the latter; and our crisis of will is that we are now paralyzed between the two.

The dilemma arising from the undermining of will has become a thorny problem in Freud's own field, psychoanalysis. The analyst Allen Wheelis is particularly perceptive of the problem as he writes:

> Among the sophisticated the use of the term "will power" has become perhaps the most unambiguous badge of naïveté. It has become unfashionable to try, by one's unaided efforts, to force one's way out of a condition of neurotic misery; for the stronger the will the more likely it is to be labeled a "counter-phobic maneuver." The unconscious is heir to the prestige of will. As one's fate formerly was determined by will, now it is determined by the re-

pressed mental life. Knowledgeable moderns put their backs to the couch and in so doing may fail to put their shoulders to the wheel. As will has been devalued, so has courage; for courage can exist only in the service of will, and can hardly be valued higher than that which it serves. In our understanding of human nature we have gained determinism, lost determination.[2]

The tendency to see ourselves as the spawns of determinism has spread, in late decades, to include contemporary man's conviction that he is the helpless object of scientific forces in the form of atomic power. The helplessness is, of course, vividly represented by the nuclear bomb, about which the typical citizen feels powerless to do anything. Many intellectuals saw this coming and asked in their own terms whether "modern man is obsolete."[3] But the important development in our present decade is that this is the common awareness of all who even watch TV or go to the movies: a recent film stated it baldly, "The nuclear age has killed man's faith in his ability to influence what happens to him."[4] Indeed, the central core of modern man's "neurosis," it may be fairly said, is the undermining of his experience of himself as responsible, the sapping of his will and ability to make decisions. The lack of will is much more than merely an ethical problem: the modern individual so often has the conviction that even if he *did* exert his "will,"—or whatever illusion passes for it—his actions wouldn't do any good anyway. It is this inner experience of impotence, this contradiction in will, which constitutes our critical problem.

CONTRADICTION IN WILL

Some readers will be countering with the assertion that man was never more powerful, both in respect to his individual opportunities and in his collective conquest of nature. To be sure, the emphasis on the human being's great power is exactly the other side of what I have referred to as the *contradiction* in will. Just as the individual is feeling powerless and plagued with self-doubts about his own decisions, he is, at the same time, assured that he, modern man, can do anything. God is dead and are we not gods—for have we not re-enacted Genesis by splitting the atom in our own laboratories and over Hiroshima? Of course, we did it in reverse: God made form out of chaos and we have made chaos out of form, and it is a rare human being who is not, in some secret place in his heart, scared to death that we shall not be able to turn chaos into form again before it is too late.

But our anxiety can be easily enough hushed up by all the excitement and glamor of standing on the brink of a new age, a Garden of Eden in which there never will be any snakes. We are bombarded with advertising which tells us that a new world lies at the end of every plane ticket and every endowment policy. We are promised every hour on the hour (in the commercial spot) our daily blessing, told of the tremendous power available in the harnessing of our computers, in the techniques of mass communication, in the new electronic age which will re-form our brain waves and make us see and hear in new ways, and in cybernetics, in the guaranteed income, in art for everyone, in new and ever-more amazing forms of automatic education, in LSD which "expands the mind" and releases the tremendous potential that was once hoped for from psychoanalysis but which now—thanks to an accidental discovery—can be achieved much more effortlessly and quickly in drugs, in chemical techniques which remake personality, in the developing of plastic organs which replace worn-out hearts and kidneys, and in the discovering of how to prevent nerve fatigue so that one can live on almost indefinitely, and so on ad infinitum. And it is not surprising that the listener is confused at times as to whether *he* is the anointed one, the recipient of all the blessings from these genii—or just the dumb fall-guy? And of course he is both.

In almost all of these promises of great power and freedom, a *passive* role is expected of the citizen who is to be recipient. Not only in the medium of advertising, but in matters of education, health, and drugs, things are done *to* and *for* us by the new inventions; our role, however subtly put, is to submit, accept the blessing, and be thankful. This is obvious in the area of atomic power and in the vast space explorations which may unite new planets to ours: you and I as individual persons have nothing whatever to do with the achievements except pay our taxes through anonymous, labyrinthine channels and watch the space flights on TV.

The phrase used, for example, for exploring new worlds through drugs or "happenings" is to "turn on." The positive side of this phrase lies in its undermining the delusion of Victorianism that "I am the captain of my soul," that nothing could occur unless *I* forced it to happen with my own Calvinistic effort and muscles—a voluntaristic arrogance which does, indeed, shrink our experience and all but suffocates our feelings. The phrase "to be turned on" points toward the spontaneity of letting ourselves be stimulated, be grasped, be opened. But it is no accident that it is also the phrase we use when we "turn on" our electricity, our motor cars, our TVs. The contradiction is clear: we move from the Victorian "will power" and rigid ego-control that produced the arid industrial civilization against which the hippies rightly revolt, to a "freedom" that may not be a new expansion of consciousness at all but a making of ourselves over into the image of the machine in a more powerful and subtle form. LSD is talked of as the remedy for a stiflingly nonpersonal civilization of mechanics. But the essence of the machine is that it does something for us by standing between us and nature. And does not the essence of the act of taking a drug have within it the same element as the using of the machine in that it too renders us passive? *Our curious predicament is that the same processes which make modern man so powerful—the magnificent development of atomic and other kinds of technical energy— are the very processes which render us powerless.* That our wills should be undermined is inescapable. And that we are told by many people "will is an illusion anyway" seems only a repetition of the obvious. We are caught, as Laing puts it, in a "hell of frenetic passivity."

The dilemma is sharpened, furthermore, by the fact that just when we feel most powerless in the face of the juggernaut of impersonal power that surrounds and molds us, we are called upon to take responsibility for much vaster and more portentous choices. Consider the matter of increased leisure. Choices will be necessary for the growing mass of people who will be working only four or six hours a day. There is already evidence that if people cannot fill the void with meaningful activities, they will be confronted with an endemic apathy that breeds impotence, addiction, and self-destructive hostility. Or take the birth control pills, particularly the retroactive one now being developed. The new freedom—principally, the complete freedom of choice about sexual relations—brings into the picture exactly that word "choice." If there is to be anything but anarchy, it rests now on the individual person to choose the values of sexual experience or at least the reasons for participating. But this new freedom occurs just at the time when the values which normally serve as a basis for choice (or rebellion, which also implies a structure) are most in chaos, when there is confusion approaching bankruptcy in outward guidance for sex by society, family, and church. The gift of freedom, yes; but the burden placed on the individual is tremendous indeed.

Or consider the contradiction in the area of physical health. The dramatic growth of medical techniques coupled with the increase of specialization tend inevitably to make the patient the *object* of cure, to send the patient hurrying to the phone to ask his doctor not for advice about his illness, but rather which specialist he should go to this morning, or which X-ray office, or which hospital clinic. As the process becomes more *impersonal* and Kafkaesque, the patient's responsibility is more and more reduced. But this all happens just at the time when the illnesses of the patient become *increasingly personal.* As in heart conditions and the infirmities of old age, the illnesses affect the total self rather than specific mechanisms in the body. How starkly this is true of old age, which requires accepting the limitations of the body, the finitude of one's self, and ultimately death! The "cure" or management of these illnesses can come only with a widening and deepening of the patient's own consciousness in relation to his body, and with his active participation in his own cure.

The kind of consciousness that enables a person to affirm, rather than to destructively fight against, the limitations of the body, as in heart conditions and the infirmities of old age and approaching death, used to be called "spiritual strength." It was, in its best form, a process of *acceptance* and *reconciliation*. This gave certain perspectives and values to the person which transcended the question of whether he lived or died, and made the necessary decisions possible for him. But the spiritual basis for this consciousness is not available in its old form for great segments of our modern secular society. And we have not yet found the new bases for such values and choices.

Particularly with the possibility of replacing bodily organs by artificial ones and the overcoming of nerve fatigue, the choice of how long you are to live may become a very real option. The ultimate decision based on the question. Do you *want* to live, and if so, how long?—which used to be posed as a metaphysical question on the theoretical basis that suicide is possible—now may become the practical choice of each one of us. How is the medical profession to decide how long to keep people living? Often the answer is that that question must be left to the philosophers and theologians. But where are these philosophers who are going to help us? Philosophy, in its academic sense, is reputed to be "dead" like God;[5] and in any case, philosophy in our day—with the emphatic exception of the existentialists—concerns itself with formal problems rather than with these critical life questions. Now that we have bid goodbye to the theologians at the wake for our dead God, we return to open the last testament and assess the legacy, and we find ourselves bereft. We have inherited a plentiful amount of physical wealth—but almost nothing of those values, and the myths and symbols from which they come, which are the basis for responsible choice.

Friedrich Nietzsche, who in the Victorian age saw with amazing astuteness what was coming, was one of the first to announce that "God is dead." But he, in contradistinction to the proclaimers of the divine demise in our day, dared to confront the consequences. "What did we do when we unchained this earth from its sun? . . . Whither do we move now? Away from all suns? Do we not fall incessantly? Backward, sideward, forward, in all directions? Is there yet any up and down? Do we not err as through an infinite naught? Do we not feel the breath of empty space? Has it not become colder? Is not night and more night coming on all the while? . . . God is dead!"[6] With profound irony, Nietzsche puts this description of the wild disorientation of the self, and the paralysis of will which results, in the mouth of a madman. "The tremendous event is still on its way," the madman says at the end of this parable. It is now upon us; and is indeed a tremendous event—that man stands at the point where he can be present at the birth of a new world or can preside at the destruction of humanity itself.

Thus, the crisis in will does not arise from either the presence or absence of power in the individual's world. It comes from the contradiction between the two—the result of which is a paralysis of will.

THE CASE OF JOHN

Our clinical work gives some analogies to this crisis of will and throws light on our general problem. My colleague, Dr. Sylvano Arieti, in an important paper in which he points out that catatonia is a disorder of the will and not of the motor apparatus, goes on to indicate that the catatonic, in his pathological world, is caught in the same inner deadlock as we are in our world of reality. The catatonic's problem hinges on *values* and *will*, and his immobility is one expression of the contradiction he experiences.

Dr. Arieti describes a patient, John, Catholic, an intelligent professional in his thirties, who was referred to him because of his repeatedly increasing anxiety. This anxiety reminded John of the time ten years previously when he had developed a full catatonic episode. Wanting to prevent a recurrence of the event, he sought treatment. I shall give some excerpts from Arieti's case report, particularly with respect to the original catatonic episode.[7]

> John, one of four children, recollected attacks of anxiety going back to his early childhood. He remembered how much he needed to cling to his aunt who brought him up. The aunt had the habit of

undressing in his presence, causing him mixed feelings of excitement and guilt. Between nine and ten there was an attempted homosexual relation with his friend, and fleeting homosexual desires thereafter, and also the customary masturbation. . . . He had a special admiration for horses, because "They excreted such beautiful feces coming from such statuesque bodies."[8]

He did well in school, and after puberty became very interested in religion, considered becoming a monk especially in order to control his sexual impulses. This control was in a certain way opposite to that of one of his sisters who was leading a very promiscuous life. . . . After college he decided to make a complete attempt to remove sex from his life. He also decided to go for a rest and vacation at a farm for young men where he could cut trees. On this farm, however, he became anxious and depressed. He resented the other fellows increasingly, whom he felt were rough and profane. He felt that he was going to pieces. He remembered one night saying to himself, "I cannot stand it any more. Why am I in this way, so anxious for no reason? I have done no wrong in my whole life." But he would control himself by thinking what perhaps he was experiencing was in accordance with the will of God.

Obsessions and compulsions acquired more and more prominence. He found himself "doubting and doubting his doubts, and doubting the doubting of his doubts," and possessed by intense terror. One day in the terror he observed a discrepancy between what he wanted to perform and the action that he really carried out. For instance, when he was undressing and wanted to drop a shoe, he instead would drop a log. . . . He was mentally lucid and perceived what was happening, but he realized he had no control over his actions. He thought he could commit crimes, even kill somebody. He said to himself, "I don't want to be damned in this world as well as in the other. I am trying to be good and I can't. It is not fair. I may kill somebody when I want a piece of bread."

Then he felt as if some movement or action he would make could produce disaster not only to himself but to the whole camp. By not acting or moving he was protecting the whole group. He felt that he had become his brother's keeper. The fear became so intense as actually to inhibit any movement. Petrified, in his own words, he "saw himself solidifying, assuming statuesque positions." He was aware of one purpose—to kill himself—better to die than to commit crimes. He climbed a big tree and jumped down, but was taken to the hospital with minor contusions. In the hospital he would not move at all. He was like a statue of stone.[9] During his hospitalization John made 71 suicide attempts. Although he generally was in a state of catatonia he would occasionally make impulsive acts such as tearing the strait jacket to pieces and making a rope to hang himself.

When Dr. Arieti asked him why he had to repeat these suicidal attempts, he gave two reasons—the first to relieve the feeling of guilt and prevent himself from committing crimes. But the second reason was even stranger—to commit suicide was the only act which would go beyond the barrier of immobility. *Thus, to commit suicide was to live; the only act of life left to him.*

One day his doctor said to him, "You want to kill yourself. Isn't there anything at all in life that you want?" With great effort John mumbled, "Eat, to eat." The doctor took him to the patients' cafeteria and told him, "You may eat anything you want." John immediately grabbed a large quantity of food and ate in a ravenous manner.

Without going into the rest of the details of John's catatonia and his overcoming of it, let us note several things. First, the homosexual stimulation he was exposed to at the camp. Second, the refuge he sought in religious feeling. Third, the obsessive-compulsive mechanism and the fact that the anxiety which was first connected with any action that had to do with sexual feelings became extended to practically every action. Every action became loaded with a sense of responsibility, a moral issue. Every motion was not considered as a fact but as a value. Arieti notes that John's "feelings were reminiscent of the feelings of cosmic power or negative omnipotence experienced by other catatonics who believe that by acting they may cause the destruction of the universe."[10]

We see in John a radical conflict in will, tied up with the values he held. To me, the doctor's question, "Don't you want something?" is very significant, since it shows the importance of getting at the simple wish, the point where every act of will starts. Arieti points out that when one bears a tremendous responsibility as John did, his passivity is entirely understandable. It is not transference or conformism in the hypnotic sense. "The patient follows orders because these orders are willed by others, and therefore he does not have the responsibility for them." This is parallel, in extreme form, to the fact that in our confused age people go apathetic, comparable to John's stupor, and unconsciously yearn for someone to take responsibility for them.

Such a patient is in a "state where volition is connected with a pathologically intensified sense of value, so that torturing responsibility reaches the acme of intensity when a little movement of the patient is considered capable of destroying the world." "Alas!" Arieti continues, "this conception of the psychotic mind reminds us of its possible actuality today, when the pushing of a button may have such cosmic effects! Only the oceanic responsibility of the catatonic could include this up-to-now unconceived possibility."[11]

In relatively normal persons, in contrast to John, the beleaguered will takes refuge in half-measures that temporarily promise it some viability. Thus, at the time of a crisis of will, we observe the dilemma of the *protest*. When I asked certain faculty groups about the sentiment of students on their campuses concerning the Vietnam war, they responded that the division was not between those who were "pro" and "con" with respect to the war, but rather between the protesters on one side and those protesting against the protesters on the other. Now protesting is partially constructive, since it preserves some semblance of will by asserting it negatively—I know what I am *against* even if I cannot specifically know what I am *for*. Indeed, the capacity of the infant of two or three to take a negative stand against his parents is very important as the beginning of human will. *But if will remains protest, it stays dependent on that which it is protesting against.* Protest is half-developed will. Dependent, like the child on parents, it borrows its impetus from its enemy. This gradually empties the will of content; you always are the shadow of your adversary, waiting for him to move so that you can move yourself. Sooner or later, your will becomes hollow, and may then be forced back to the next line of defense.

This next defense is *projection of blame*. We find an illustration in every war of this unwitting confession of failure to integrate the daimonic. In the Vietnam war, for example, Secretary Rusk and the Administration blamed the Viet Cong for the escalation, and the Viet Cong—and those in this country opposed to the war—blamed Rusk and our own Administration. The self-righteous security that is achieved by means of this blaming of the other gives one a temporary satisfaction. But beyond the gross oversimplification of our historical situation which this exhibits, we pay a more serious price for such security. *We have tacitly given the power of decision over to our adversary.* Blaming the enemy implies that the enemy has the freedom to choose and act, not ourselves, and we can only *react to him*. This assumption, in turn, destroys our own security. For in the long run, we have, against our intention, given him all the cards. Will is thus further undermined. We see here an example of the self-contradictory effect of all psychological defensiveness: *it automatically hands the power over to the adversary*.

In these unsatisfactory measures, the activity of will becomes more and more tautological and repetitive, and finally tends toward apathy. And if apathy cannot be transmuted into an impetus to move to a higher state of consciousness in order to embrace the problem at hand, the person or group tends to surrender the capacity for willing itself. If apathy is to be avoided in such paralysis of will, the individual needs to ask sooner or later, Is there possibly something going on in myself that is a cause of, or contributes to, my paralysis?

WILL IN PSYCHOANALYSIS

How have psychology and psychoanalysis confronted the crisis in will? We earlier noted how Freud's destruction of Victorian "will power" was one expression of the undermining of will and decision in our whole age. And we also observed that analysts themselves are concerned about the predicament into which this confusion of will throws us. Pointing out that we have "gained determinism but lost determination," Wheelis goes on in the paper we quoted above to remind us, "The crucial importance of will lies in the fact that . . . [it] may nevertheless be the decisive factor in translating equilibrium into a process of change."[12]

Thoughtful persons in all branches of psychology as well as in other disciplines, such as philosophy and religion, have been asking pointed questions about what the process of psychoanalysis itself does to the patient's will. The conclusions of some are negative. "Psychoanalysis is a systematic training in indecision," charges Silvan Tomkins, professor at Princeton and the University of the City of New York, who himself had a number of years of analysis. "Psychoanalysis is in fact the disease of which its therapy purports to be the cure," a trenchant remark reputed to Karl Kraus, referred, similarly, to the fact that psychoanalysis plays into modern man's tendency to surrender his autonomy.

There have been indications for several years that the science and profession of psychoanalysis were moving into a state of crisis. One expression of this crisis—which is now present among us and cannot be evaded—is the turning against psychoanalysis on the part of outstanding members of the orthodox Freudian groups.[18] Their speeches sound very much like the "God-is-dead" plaint of some present-day theologians. And indeed, the god of psychoanalysis may actually be dead to the extent that, like the god of the theologians, it was wrongly conceived.

Central in the roots of this crisis lies the failure of psychoanalysis to solve the problem of will and decision.

For if the complete determinism in theory for which Freud argued were true in practice, no one could be cured in psychoanalysis. The opposite is likewise true: If we assumed a complete indeterminism, i.e., that we could make ourselves over in bland freedom by any New Year's whim or resolution, no one would need to bother to come for psychotherapy. Actually, we find that people's problems are stubborn, recalcitrant, and troublesome—but we find they *can* change. And so we need to look further for what changes them.

Academic psychologists tended also, no matter what the individual psychologist himself believed about his own ethical actions, to accept the position that as psychologists we were concerned only with what was determined and could be understood in a deterministic framework. This limitation of perception inevitably tended to put blinders on our perception; we made our man over into the image of what we let ourselves see. Psychologists tended to repress the problem of power, particularly irrational power. We took literally Aristotle's dictum that man is a rational animal by assuming that he is *only* that, and that irrationality is merely a temporary aberration to be overcome by right education of the individual or, if the pathology is somewhat more severe, by re-education of his maladjusted emotions. There was, of course, in Alfred Adler's psychology a concern with power, but that has generally been taken as merely a subhead to his beliefs in social inferiority and the struggle for security. Freud's assumptions about primitive cannibalism and the aggressive instinct have the element of power in them. But this also tends to be rationalized away in that it is used in referring only to severe pathology. The repression of power enabled psychology more readily to discard will and hold to a theoretical determinism, since the critical daimonic effects of determinism did not then come out into the open.[14]

But in psychoanalysis and psychotherapy, where therapists dealt with living, suffering people, the problem of the undermining of will and decision became increasingly critical. For the theory and process of psychoanalysis and most other forms of psychotherapy inevitably played into the passive tendencies of the patient. As Otto Rank and Wilhelm Reich in the 1920's began to point out, there were built-in tendencies in psychoanalysis itself that sapped its vitality and tended to emasculate not only the reality with which psychoanalysis deals but the power and inclination of the patient to change. In the early days of psychoanalysis, when revelations of the unconscious had an obvious "shock value," this problem did not come out into the open as much. And in any case with hysterical patients, who formed the bulk of those Freud worked with in his early formative years, there does exist a special dynamic in what Freud could call "repressed libido" pushing expression. But now, when most of our patients are "compulsives" of one form or another, and everybody knows about the Oedipus complex, and our patients talk about sex with an apparent freedom which would have shocked Freud's Victorian patients off the couch (and, indeed, talking about sex is the easiest way of avoiding really making any *decisions* about love and sexual relatedness), the predicament resulting from the undermining of will and decision can no longer be avoided. The "repetition compulsion," a problem that has always remained intractable and insoluble within the context of classical psychoanalysis, is in my judgment fundamentally related to this crisis of will.

Other forms of psychotherapy do not escape the dilemma of psychoanalysis, namely that the process of psychotherapy itself has built-in tendencies which invite the patient to relinquish his position as the deciding agent. The very name "patient" proposes it. Not only do the automatic, supportive elements in therapy have this tendency, but so does the temptation, to which patient and therapist easily succumb, to search for everything else as responsible for one's problems rather than one's self. To be sure, psychotherapists of all stripes and schools realize that sooner or later the patient must make some decisions, learn to take some responsibility for himself; but the theory and the technique of most psychotherapy tends to be built on exactly the opposite premise.

ILLUSION AND WILL

The denial of will and decision has been restated by psychologists and psychoanalysts in various ways. The late Freudian, Robert Knight, holds, for example, that the freedom to make choices experienced by a human being ". . . has nothing whatever to do with free will as a principle governing human behavior but is a subjective experience which is itself casually determined."[15] In this article, Knight consistently puts quotation marks around the word "freedom" to show, presumably, that it is an illusion. Choice and responsibility are illusions caused by prior states but, in turn, causal of future acts.

But—and here we arrive at the radical inconsistency—as *therapists,* the analysts could not help recognizing that the patient's act of choosing was of central importance. Freud, as a psychotherapist, took a view radically and amazingly different from his own theory. He writes in *The Ego and the Id* that ". . . analysis does not set out to make pathological reactions impossible, but to give the patient's ego *freedom* to choose one way or the other." (Italics Freud's.)[16]

Wheelis goes on to show the practical dilemma in which the therapist is caught in his actual therapy:

> Toward the end of analysis the therapist may find himself wishing that the patient were capable of more "push," more "determination," a greater willingness to "make the best of it." Often this wish eventuates in remarks to the patient: "People must help themselves"; "Nothing worth while is achieved without effort"; "You have to try." Such interventions are seldom included in case reports, for it is assumed that they possess neither the dignity nor effectiveness of interpretation. Often an analyst feels uncomfortable about such appeals to volition, as though he were using something he didn't believe in, and as though this would have been unnecessary had only he analyzed more skillfully.[17]

Psychoanalysts then found themselves in the curious, anomalous position of believing that the patient must have an illusion of freedom in order to change, and they therefore must cultivate this illusion, or at least do obeisance to it. The paradox, for example, that Knight's statement of the problem poses is well described by two reviewers. "As psychotherapy progresses the experience of freedom increases, so that successfully analyzed people report experiencing more freedom in the conduct of their lives than they did prior to psychotherapy. If this freedom is illusory, the purpose of therapy, or at least the result of successful therapy, is to restore an illusion even though most therapists believe that successful therapy increases the accuracy with which the patient perceives himself and his world."[18] Some analysts, indeed, admit openly that they are engaged in the cultivation of an illusion, and undertake to rationalize this in their theory.[19]

Consider what this means. We are told that an *illusion* is most significant in effecting personality change; that truth is not fundamentally (or is only theoretically) relevant to actions, but *illusion* is. Thus, we are to strive not for truth but for an illusion. We are to believe in definitions of the world by which we cannot live. Or, if we do try strictly to live by them, we shall, as Wheelis rightly suggests, slide back into a passive impotence that leads to apathy and depression.

I do not need to labor the point that this resolution of the dilemma is untenable. Even we analysts could not live by such an illusion—for how is it possible (without considerable pathology) to commit one's self if one knows in advance he is committing himself to an illusion? Furthermore, if patients need to believe in illusions, the possibilities of illusion are, unlike truth, infinite—who is to decide *which* illusion the given patient is to live by? Are we to take the illusion which "works"? If so, then our concept of truth has been wrong; for if the illusion genuinely works, it cannot be entirely illusion. Indeed, the statement that the illusion is most decisive for change is essentially an antirational (and thus, anti-scientific) one, for it implies that at the level of behavior the truth or falsehood of a concept is irrelevant. This cannot be accepted; if it seems to be true, there must be some truth in what we call "illusion" and some illusion in what we call truth.

Another solution has been proposed from a different angle. Recognizing that freedom and will have to be given some place in the psychoanalytic structure of personality, the later "ego" analysts such as Hartmann, Rapaport, and others, have developed the concept of the "autonomy of the ego." The ego, then, is assigned the

function of freedom and choice. But the ego is, by definition, a *part* of the personality; and how can a *part* be
free? Rappaport has written his paper on the "Autonomy of
Ego," Jung once wrote a chapter on "The Autonomy of
the Unconscious," and we could, following Walter B.
Cannon, write a paper on "The Autonomy of the Body."
Each of these would have a partial truth. But would not
each also be importantly wrong? Neither the ego nor the
body nor the unconscious can be "autonomous," but can
only exist as parts of a totality. And it is in this totality
that will and freedom must have their base. I am convinced that the compartmentalization of the personality
into ego, superego, and id is an important part of the
reason why the problem of will has remained insoluble
within the orthodox psychoanalytic tradition.

We know in our practice of psychoanalysis that *lack of
freedom* is shown in all aspects of the patient's organism.
It is shown in his body (muscular inhibitions) and in
what is called unconscious experience (repression) and
in his social relationships (he is unaware of others to the
extent he is unaware of himself). We also know experientially that as this person gains freedom in psychotherapy, he becomes less inhibited in bodily movements, freer
in his dreams, and more spontaneous in his unthought-
out, involuntary relations with other people. This means
that autonomy and freedom cannot be the domain of a
special part of the organism, but must be a quality of the
total self—the thinking-feeling-choosing-acting organism.
I shall show below, when discussing the concept of intentionality, that will and decision are inseparably linked
with id as well as ego and superego, if we are to use
Freudian terms. Something of profound significance is
going on—in spontaneity, feeling, symbolic meanings—
in each decision one makes *prior* to anything which might
be termed an "ego function." Bettelheim is entirely correct, in my judgment, when he emphasizes that a strong
ego is not the cause of decisions but the result.[20]

Does not the concept of "autonomy of the ego" have
the same difficulties as the old one of "free will," in posit-
ing some special part or organ of the personality as the
seat of choice? If we strip the concept of its sophisticated
clothes, it becomes something akin to Descartes's theory
that the pineal gland, the organ at the base of the brain

between body and head, was the place where the soul was located. To be sure, ego psychoanalysis has the positive aspect of reflecting the pressing concerns of contemporary man with his problems of autonomy, self-direction, and choice. But it is also caught in the contradictions with which these problems inescapably confront us.

Psychoanalysis and psychology, in all their representations, reveal, with the inconsistency and contradiction which lie therein, the dilemma of will and decision that Western man today experiences. It is a sign of Freud's usual honesty that he frankly states that he is trying to give the patient "freedom to choose" even though he knows this is directly contradictory to his theory. He did not quail before contradiction nor leap to too easy a solution. But as the culture has evolved since Freud, it has become less and less possible to survive in this contradiction.

In this book, I propose a solution to this problem. I do it on the basis of my belief that we have omitted a dimension of human experience which is important, indeed critical, to human will. An illustration of the dilemma is given in a passage by Hudson Hoagland:

> Let us assume that I am an omnipotent physiologist with a complete knowledge of the physiology, chemistry, and molecular activities of your brain at any given moment. With this knowledge I can then predict precisely what you will do as a result of the operation of your brain's mechanisms, since your behavior, including your conscious and verbal behavior, is completely correlated with your neural functioning. But this only applies if I do not tell you my prediction. Suppose that I tell you what you will do as a result of my complete knowledge of your brain. In doing this I shall have changed the physiology of your brain by furnishing it with this information. This makes it possible for you then to behave in a way quite different from my prediction. If I were to try to allow beforehand for the effects of telling you my prediction, I would be doomed to an endless regression—logically . . . chasing my own tail in an effort to allow for the effects of allowing for the ef-

fects of allowing for the effects, indefinitely.[20]

Human awareness and consciousness—that is, knowing —introduce unpredictable elements into our man. And man is the creature who obstreperously insists on knowing. The change of consciousness which this involves is both "outside" and "inside," consisting of forces operating on the individual from the world and the attitude of the person who is *attending* to these forces. We can note that one's awareness in Hoagland's example would involve such things as becoming aware of forgotten and buried events in childhood and other aspects of the "depth" experiences which emerge in therapy.

This is—to predict our later discussion—the problem of *intentionality* in contrast to mere *intention*. Intentionality, in human experience, is what underlies will and decision. It is not only prior to will and decision but makes them possible. Why it has been neglected in Western history is clear enough. Ever since Descartes separated understanding from will, science has proceeded on the basis of this dichotomy, and we tried to assume that "facts" about human beings could be separated from their "freedom," cognition could be separated from conation. Particularly since Freud, this is no longer possible—even though Freud, without full justice to his own discoveries, clung to the old dichotomy in scientific theory. Intentionality does not rule out deterministic influence, but places the whole problem of determinism and freedom on a deeper plane.

EIGHT

WISH AND WILL

> Between the conception
> And the creation
> Between the emotion
> And the response
> Falls the Shadow
>   Life is very long
>   —T. S. ELIOT

We cannot rest with the contradictions we have seen in psychology and psychotherapy. Nor can we leave will and decision to chance. We cannot work on the assumption that ultimately the patient "somehow happens" to make a choice or slides into a decision by ennui, default, or mutual fatigue with the therapist, or acts from sensing that the therapist (now the benevolent parent) will approve of him if he does take such and such steps. I propose that we need to put decision and will back into the center of the picture—"The very stone which the builders rejected is the head of the corner." Not in the sense of free will against determinism, nor in the sense of denying what Freud describes as unconscious experience. These deterministic, "unconscious" factors certainly operate, and those of us who do therapy cannot escape having this impressed upon us many times in an hour.[1]

The issue, rather, is not against the infinite number of deterministic forces operating on every person. We shall keep our perspective clear if we agree at the outset that there are certain values in determinism. One is that a belief in determinism, as in Calvinism or Marxism or behaviorism, allies you with a powerful movement. The fact that one is most free to act energetically and with abandon—as is the Marxist—by virtue of being allied to a determinism is one of the paradoxes of our problem.

Another value is that the determinism releases you from most of the innumerable petty and not-so-petty issues that you must settle every day; these are all settled beforehand. A third value is that a belief in determinism overcomes your own self-consciousness: sure of yourself, you can charge ahead. For determinism in this sense is an enlarging of human experience by placing the issues on a deeper level. But if we are true to our experience, we must find our freedom on the same deeper level.

This paradox precludes our ever talking of "complete determinism," which is a logical contradiction. For if it were true, there would be no need to demonstrate it. If someone does set out to demonstrate, as often used to occur in my college days, that he is completely determined, I would agree with his reasons and then add to his list a number of ways in which he is determined by unconscious dynamics which he may not be aware of and, indeed, is determined (possibly for the reasons of his own emotional insecurity) to make this very argument for absolute determinism. I could go on to make the logical rebuttal that if his present argument is simply a result of his being completely determined, he is making the argument without consideration of whether it is true or false, and, therefore, that he and we have no criteria for deciding that it is true. This logical self-contradiction of complete determinism is, I believe, irrefutable. But I would probably choose—remaining existential—rather to point out to my questioner that in the very raising of these questions, and by taking the energy to pursue them, he is exercising some significant element of freedom.

In therapy, for a better example, no matter how much the patient is the victim of forces of which he is unaware, he is orienting himself in some particular way to the data in the very revealing and exploring of these deterministic forces in his life, and is thus engaged in some choice no matter how seemingly insignificant; he is experiencing some freedom, no matter how subtle. This does not at all mean that we "push" the patient into decisions. Indeed, I am convinced that it is only by the clarification of the patient's own powers of will and decision that the therapist can avoid inadvertently and subtly pushing the patient in one direction or another. My argument is that self-consciousness itself—the person's

potential awareness that the vast, complex, protean flow
of experience is *his* experience, a fact that often takes
him by surprise—unavoidably brings in the element of
decision at every point.

I have had the conviction for a number of years, a
conviction which has only been deepened by my experience as a psychoanalyst, that something more complex
and significant is going on in human experience in the
realm of will and decision than we have yet taken into
our studies. And I am convinced that we have omitted
this realm to the impoverishment of both our science of
psychology and our understanding of our relations with
ourselves and others.

Our task in these chapters is to explore these problems.
We shall first take up the interrelation between will and
wish, and then the deeper meanings of wish. We shall
proceed to an analysis of *intentionality*. Finally, we shall
apply what we have learned to the practice of therapy.
The underlying questions all the way through will be,
Can we find through such explorations new insight into
the meaning of human volition and a new basis for solutions to the problems of will and decision?

THE DEMISE OF WILL POWER

To begin with, the terms "will power" and "free will" are
dubious, to say the least, and perhaps no longer even
helpful if they were available. "Will power" expressed
the arrogant efforts of Victorian man to manipulate his
surroundings and to rule nature with an iron hand, as
well as to manipulate himself, rule his own life in the
same way as one would an object. This kind of "will"
was set over against "wish" and used as a faculty by
which "wish" could be denied. Victorian man sought, as
Ernest Schachtel has put it, to deny that he had ever
been a child, to repress his irrational tendencies and so-
called infantile wishes as unacceptable to his image of
himself as a grown-up and responsible man. Will power,
then, was a way of avoiding awareness of bodily and
sexual urges and of hostile impulses which did not fit the
picture of the controlled, well-managed self.

I have not infrequently observed in patients that the

emphasis on "will power" is a reaction formation against their own repressed passive desires, a way of fighting off their wishes to be taken care of; and the likelihood is that this mechanism had much to do with the form that will took in Victorianism. Will was used to deny wish. Speaking in clinical terms, this process results in a greater and greater emotional void, a progressive emptying of inner contents. This impoverishes imagination and intellectual experience as well; it stultifies and suffocates longings and yearnings as well as wishes. No one needs to remind us of the great stores of resentment, inhibition, hostility, self-rejection, and related clinical symptoms which can develop as a result of this repressive kind of will power.

A woman in her late twenties—since we shall refer back to her, we shall give her a name, Helen—informed me at the beginning of her therapeutic treatment that her motto had always been, "where there's a will, there's a way." This motto seemed to fit her executive job, which required a lot of routine as well as serious decisions, and her respectable New England background in a typically upper middle-class family. She gave the impression at first of being a "strong-willed" person. The only trouble was that one of her most pronounced symptoms was compulsive, promiscuous sexual activity; she seemed incapable of saying no. Whatever the cause, this symptom —no doubt aided by the fact that she was a pretty girl— was directly contradictory to her "will power," as she could easily see. She would also "wolf" food, occasionally eating everything left on the plates by others at breakfast, paying the price of a stomach ache and later struggling to diet to keep her figure. Her job revealed similarly driven patterns—she would work for fourteen hours at a stretch but never seem any farther ahead. It soon came out, with a good deal of painful weeping, that, despite her superficial social success, she was a profoundly lonely and isolated person. She talked of longings for her mother expressed in the half-fantasy, half-memory of sitting with her in the sun when she was a little girl, and a recurrent dream of wanting to be encircled again by waves of the ocean. She dreamt that she went home and knocked on the door, but her mother, on opening the door, did not recognize her and closed the door in her face. The historical fact was that her mother had suffered a serious depression and had been hospitalized in mental institutions for a good deal of the several years after the girl's birth.

So what we see in our patient is a lonely, pathetic infant, overcome with longing for what she never had. It seemed clear that the great stress of "will power" was a frantic "reaction formation," a desperate endeavor to compensate for the symptoms of her unfulfilled infantile needs, a strategy of living on despite these painful early longings. It is not surprising—such is the irony and "balance" of the complex processes of human consciousness—that her symptoms were of the compulsive, driven type. This is precisely will gone awry; will turned self-destructive, directed against the person herself. Life is saying to her—if we may put it figuratively, in terms of her motto—where there are such longings and unfulfilled needs, will is exactly *not* the way.

We note, furthermore, that her problem was not mere *defiance* of her parents, as we normally see it in adolescent behavior. That would show the "will" still present and active, though negative, and a situation not too difficult to deal with. Our patient's problem was more serious—an emptiness, a vacuity, a longing to fill something which from infancy had always been empty. This kind of pattern can lead to critical problems of apathy if the "will" breaks down before the dependent longings have been brought to consciousness and to some degree integrated. The early trauma taught Helen as an infant that she must remove her wishes, for they carried a degree of despair which would have probably sent her into psychosis. "Will power" was the means by which she accomplished this. But the neurosis then takes revenge exactly in the area in which the problem originated.

FREUD'S ANTI-WILL SYSTEM

Psychoanalysis was brought into being by the failure of will. It is not surprising that Freud, observing in his Victorian culture how regularly will was used in the service of repression, should have developed psychoanalysis as an antiwill system. In Freud, as Professor Paul Ricoeur puts it, the phenomenon of will is crushed in the dialectic of instinct on one side and authority, in the form of the superego, on the other. Freud's observation that will is under three masters, id, superego, and external world, leaves will lost—or, if not actually lost, powerless under its masters. Needing very much to succeed in the world, Helen had an active conscience; but world, id, and super-ego—if one accepts this formulation—were hopelessly grinding her motto "where there's a will, there's a way" into pathetic mockery and extorting a painful price in her masochistic guilt.

Freud saw will as an implement in the service of re-pression, no longer a positive moving force. Seeking the force and the motive of human activity, he looked in-stead into the "vicissitudes of instincts," the "fate of the repressed libido," and so on. Object-choice, in the Freud-ian system, is not choice in a real sense, but a function of the transposition of the historical vicissitudes. Indeed, Freud sees "will" as the devil of the whole system, in that will has the negative function of setting resistance and repression into motion. Or, if the term "devil" begs the question, we can use a sophisticated name for it, which Wheelis supplies, namely "counterphobic" maneu-ver.[2] This marks the moment when the "unconscious became heir to the power of will."

What are the sources of this destruction of will in Freud's theory? One source is obvious: Freud's accurate clinical observation. A second source is cultural; Freud's theory was consistent with and an expression of the alien-ation it described. It must not be forgotten that Freud spoke out of and reflected an objectivistic, alienated, market-place culture. As I have indicated elsewhere, the very overemphasis on will power in Victorian times was part and parcel of the compartmentalization that fore-shadowed the culture's collapse, which indeed occurred in 1914. The overemphasis on will power was parallel to the increasingly rigid pattern of "will" of the compulsive neurotic before his whole system breaks down. The alien-ation of Victorian man from himself, under the rubric of *will*, is expressed in Freud's system under the rubric of the opposite pole, namely wish.

A third reason is that Freud needed to replace will be-cause of the requirements of his scientific model, his aim and desire being to make a deterministic science based on the image of nineteenth-century natural science. He thus needed a quantitative, cause-and-effect system: he speaks of his mechanisms as "hydraulics," and in his last book, libido is given the analogy of an "electro-magnetic" charge.

A fourth reason for Freud's seeking to destroy will was exactly why we are now interested in rediscovering it on a more profound basis: namely, to deepen human experience, to place these phenomena on a level which would reflect more adequately a dignity and respect for human life. For, contrary to its intention, Victorian "will power," by implying that every man was "master of his fate" and could decide the whole course of his life by a resolution on New Year's Eve or on a chance whim in a Sunday-morning church service, actually belittled life, robbed it of dignity, and cheapened human experience.

That some of these aspects of Freud, like the last two, are contradictory, should not daunt us; one of the marks of his greatness was that he could live with such contradictions. He might well have countered such a charge with the lines of Walt Whitman, "I contradict myself? Very well, I contradict myself."

THE WISH

In attacking the morbid psychological processes of "will power," Freud developed his far-reaching emphasis on the "wish." It is not "will" but "wish" that moves us. "Nothing but a wish can set the mental apparatus in motion," he says time and again. Since we are setting out to explore the implications of wish, it is helpful to point out that wish is also assumed to be the "force" in other, more or less deterministic, psychological systems as well. In the Hullian type of behaviorism, "wish" is present as the desire and need to reduce tension, an emphasis surprisingly akin to Freud's definition of pleasure as the reduction of tension. In general, our sciences of man assume the usual adaptational and evolutionary wishes, that people wish "to survive" and "live long."

The word "wish," let us hasten to say in view of the fact that in our post-Victorian day we still tend to impoverish the term by making it a concession to our immaturity or infantile "needs," may be seen in processes much more extensive than the residue of childhood. The correlates of "wish" can be found in all phenomena of nature down to the most minute pattern of atomic reaction; for example, in what Alfred North Whitehead and Paul Tillich call the negative-positive movements in all particles of nature. Tropism is one form, in its etymological sense of the innate tendency in biological organisms to "turn toward." If, however, we stop with "wish" as this more or less blind and involuntary movement of particle toward another or of one organism toward another, we are inexorably pushed to Freud's pessimistic conclusion of the "death instinct" taken literally, namely, the inevitable tendency of organisms to move back to the inorganic state. If wish is *only a force,* we are all involved in an abortive pilgrimage which consists of simply moving back to the state of the inorganic stone again.

But wish also has the element of *meaning.* Indeed, it is the particular confluence of force and meaning which constitutes the human wish. This "meaning" element is certainly present in Freud's concept of wish and is one of his central contributions, even though he speaks, contradictorily, as though wish were only blind force. He was able to use the wish with such fecundity—particularly in fantasies, free associations, and dreams—because he saw in it not simply a blind push but a tendency which carried meanings. Despite the fact that when he writes about wish fulfillment and satisfaction of libidinal needs, and talks as if the wish were only an economic quantity, a force by itself the context he assumed is the point of the meeting of meaning with force.

In the first few weeks of life, for example, the infant may be thought of as indiscriminately and blindly pushing its mouth toward the nipple; any nipple, human or rubber, will do.[3] But with the emergence and development of consciousness and the capacity to experience one's self as subject in a world of objects, new capacities arise. Chief among these is the use of symbols and the relating to life by way of symbolic meanings. From then on, the wish is more than merely a blind push; it carries a meaning as well. The nipple becomes breast—and how different the words are! The former is an anatomical description of the part of the body that gives us our rations for survival. The latter is a symbol which brings in a total experience—the warmth, the intimacy, even the beauty and possible love which go with feminine care.

I am aware of the difficulties this dimension of symbolic meaning introduces for a natural science of man. Nevertheless, we must take man, our object of study, as we find him—a creature who relates to his life by way of symbolic meanings which are his language. It is thus methodologically unsound and empirically inaccurate to reduce the wish to mere force. After the emergence of consciousness in man, *wishes are never merely needs, nor merely economic*. I am attracted sexually by one woman, not by another; it is never just a matter of sheer, stored-up quantities of libido, but rather my erotic "force" channeled and formed by the diverse meanings the first woman has for me. We should qualify our "never" in the previous sentence with two exceptions. One is artificial situations, like soldiers stationed in the arctic for twelve months, in which certain aspects of experience are simply and consciously bracketed. Another exception is in pathology, when a person is driven by indiscriminate sexual urges toward any male or female, like our patient Helen. But here we have a state precisely defined as pathological; and it is an important proof of my point that indiscriminate sexuality goes against a significant element in the human wish. I do not know what Louis XVI was bracketing when he said, "Any woman will do, just give her a bath and send her to a dentist." But I do know that when people who are not kings and not radically disturbed have sexual relations with someone fairly frivolously, let us say, in a chance meeting or in carnival, they find themselves afterwards investing the other person, possibly only in fantasy, with tenderness or virtue or special attributes that have some meaning for them. *Disgust* is also an expression of a humanly meaningful wish or, more specifically, a frustration of it. In instances of almost purely anonymous sexual relationship, as it occurs for example in some homosexual practices, the later reaction in which the person feels disgust also demonstrates the point we are making. My experience as a therapist suggests that the human being has to make the creature with whom he has sexual relations in some way personal, even if only in fantasy, or else suffer depersonalization himself.

This carries the corollary that discussions and approaches in therapy based on such concepts as "control of id impulses" and "integration of primary processes" all miss the point. Is there ever such a thing as a primary process as such? Only in very severe pathology or in our own abstracted theory. The former is the situation in which meaningful symbolic processes break down, as in our patients; the latter is when our own symbolism is used as therapists. What we have is not an organism constituted by primary processes and the control of them, but a human being whose experience involves wishes, drives, and needs experienced and known by him, and by us if we can understand him, in symbolic meanings. *It is the symbolic meanings that have gone awry in neurosis, and not the id impulse.*

The human wish, we are saying, is not merely a push from the past, not merely a call from primitive needs demanding satisfaction. It also has in it some selectivity. It is a forming of the future, a molding by a symbolic process which includes both memory and fantasy, of what we hope the future will be. The wish is the beginning of orienting ourselves to the future, an admission that we *want* the future to be such and such; it is a capacity to reach down deep into ourselves and preoccupy ourselves with a longing to change the future. Note that I say *beginning*, not the end; I am perfectly aware of "wish fulfillment," wishes as a substitute for will, and so on. I am saying that there is no will without a prior wish. The wish, like all symbolic processes, has a *progressive* element, a reaching ahead, as well as a *regressive* pole, a propulsion from behind. The wish thus carries its *meaning* as well as its *force*. Its motive power lies in the conjunction of this meaning and force. We can now understand why William Lynch should hold that "to wish is the most human act."[4]

ILLNESS AS THE INABILITY TO WISH

Further data are given for our enlarging of the significance of wish from another quarter. That is the fact of the illness, emptiness, and despair which is caused by a person's inability to wish. T. S. Eliot shows this on a broad cultural scale in *The Waste Land*. The unforgettably vivid incidents in this epoch-making poem sing out over and over again, with the cumulative power of a symphony. The main character, a lady of leisure satiated with sex and luxury, says to her lover:

> "What shall I do now? What shall I do?
> I shall rush out as I am, and walk the street
> With my hair down, so. What shall we do tomorrow?
> What shall we ever do?"
>   The hot water at ten.
> And if it rains, a closed car at four.
> And we shall play a game of chess,
> Pressing lidless eyes and waiting for a knock upon
>   the door.

>   (II:131—138)

We can identify in the poem some of the characteristics of the contemporary emotional and spiritual wasteland. One is the desperate lack of communication: when the lady asks her lover why he does not talk to her, and implores him to tell her what he's thinking, he answers only,

> I think we are in rats' alley
> Where the dead men lost their bones.
>   (II:115—116)

To cease wishing is to be dead, or at least to inhabit a land of the dead. Another characteristic is satiety: if wishes are thought of only as pushes toward gratification, the end consisting of the satisfying of the need, the poem is saying that *emptiness and vacuity and futility are greatest where all wishes are met*. For this means that one stops wishing.

But Eliot, writing poetically of the most unpoetic subjects, is more profound than that—and our psychology could well be also. He describes the underlying cause of this situation, in a word, as *sterility*. It is a literal sexual sterility in the particular myth he takes as the basis for his poem, the legend of a man called the Fisher King who ruled over a Waste Land. This very old legend has to do with fertility of land, spring following the "waste land" of winter; and later, the myth became worked into the King Arthur stories, the Holy Grail becoming the means of healing the Fisher King. "The land was barren and dry and was to remain so until a knight of purity should arrive to heal the Fisher King, who is wounded in the genital organs."[5] The essence of the sterility is futility, aimlessness, purposelessness, lack of zest in life; these are associated with the radical blocking off of consciousness. "It is the unawareness of the woman that is so terrible. . . ."[6] This, in turn, is interpreted by Eliot as due to a lack of faith, which in part comes from severing one's self from the great symbolic experiences in the tradition of our historical culture. He sets his contemporary boudoir in a milieu of references to Shakespeare, Milton, and Ovid, but the woman has no awareness at all of the beauty that surrounds her. He sets the sexual affair amid allusions to the great passionate lovers of the past like Dido and Aeneas and Antony and Cleopatra—but sex for this lady and her lover, far from being passionate, is no longer even a "futile panting palm to palm."

Eliot is saying, in effect, that without faith we cannot *want* anymore, we cannot *wish*. And this includes sexual wants: without faith we become impotent, genitally as well as otherwise. The religious context of the poem can be interpreted in the terms I am using in this chapter—that there is a dimension of meaning expressed in the symbolism of the wish, that this is what gives the wish its specifically human quality, and that without this meaning, even the emotional and sexual aspects of wanting become dried up. The poem was written in 1922, early in the age of optimism when we believed that peace and prosperity were just around the corner and that it was only a matter of a few years' progress until all our needs would be met; the "jazz age" of F. Scott Fitzgerald when the only pessimism was a romantic, nostalgic, self-pitying melancholy. Though this is the most discussed poem of our age, few people in that day, no matter how gripped by the poem they were, must have realized how predictive it was; and I would wonder if even Eliot knew how clinical psychotherapy would later substantiate his prediction of apathy and impotence.

Eliot, like a number of the existentialists, did not believe that an answer was yet possible in the culture in which he wrote the poem. The "time was not ripe," in Heidegger's terms; in Tillich's *Kairos* not yet present. He has the Knight going only as far as the Chapel Perilous:

> There is the empty chapel, only the wind's home,
> It has no windows, and the door swings,
> Dry bones can harm no one.
>
> (V:388—390)

He does not see any real hope of revival at that time and, at the conclusion of the poem, the Fisher King is still

> Fishing, with the arid plain behind me
> Shall I at least set my lands in order?
> London Bridge is falling down falling down
>   falling down.
>
> (V:424—426)

I find this turning of the Fisher King to *technical* pursuits very gripping, setting his "lands in order" as one does when anxiety blocks one's deeper intentionality. The technical preoccupation is especially striking when set in juxtaposition to that powerful line, "London Bridge is falling down. . . ." Though the time was obviously not ripe for an answer in 1922, it may be more ready for a resolution in our age.

There is in this poem, moreover, a kind of wishing that goes way below the question of the relieving of genitalia or the filling of the stomach. This is the imaginative yearning expressed in the "lidless eyes . . . waiting for a knock upon the door." On its simplest plane, biologically and psychologically, we see echoed here the myth of Sleeping Beauty, waiting for the kiss of the prince. Except that the princess, in her naïveté, sleeps; wheras our lady, in her despair, has lidless eyes which cannot be closed in rest. On a deeper level, there seems to me in this "waiting for a knock upon the door" a profound wishing that still takes place in despair, a waiting that may be pictured as a wish for a state beyond despair, as is implied in *Waiting for Godot*. But it also has within it the hope for the way out, however latent, the dynamic beginning of the wish for constructive possibilities that transcend the emptiness, futility, and apathy.

LACK OF CAPACITY TO WISH

In the past few years, a number of persons in psychiatry and related fields have been pondering and exploring the problems of wishing and willing. We may assume that this confluence of concern must be in answer to a strong need in our time for new light on these problems.

In his penetrating interpretations of literature in its relation to depth psychology, Father William Lynch develops the thesis that it is not wishing which causes illness but *lack of wishing*. He holds that the problem is to deepen people's capacity to wish, and that one side of our task in therapy is to create the ability to wish. He defines wish as a "positive picturing in imagination."[7] It is a transitive verb—to wish involves an *act*. There is an autonomous element in the wish which Lynch relates to an act of imagination; "every genuine wish is a creative act."[8] I find support for this in therapy: it is indeed a positive step when the patient can feel and state strongly, "I *wish* such and such." This, in effect, moves the conflict from a submerged, unarticulated plane in which he takes no responsibility but expects God and parents to read his wishes by telepathy, to an overt, healthy conflict over what he wants. On the basis of the theological myth of creation, Lynch says, "God exults when man comes through with a wish of his own."[9]

Lynch then goes on to point out something that is generally overlooked, namely that *the wish in interpersonal relationship requires mutuality*. This is a truth shown in its breach in many myths, and brings the person to his doom. Peer Gynt in Ibsen's play runs around the world wishing and acting on his wishes; the only trouble is that his wishes have nothing to do with the other person he meets but are entirely egocentric, "encased in a cask of self, sealed up with a bung of self." In *The Sleeping Beauty*, by the same token, the young princes who assault the briars in order to rescue and awaken the slumbering girl "before the time is ripe," in the words of the fairy tale, are exemplars of behavior which tries to force the other in love and sex before the other is ready; they exhibit a wishing without mutuality. The young princes are devoted to their own desires and needs without relation to the Thou. If wish and will can be seen and experienced in this light of autonomous, imaginative acts of interpersonal mutuality, there is profound truth in St. Augustine's dictum, "Love and do what you *will*."

But Father Lynch, and certainly St. Augustine, were not naïve about human nature (just as Freud was not). They knew full well that this wishing is stated in ideal terms. They knew that the trouble is precisely that man does wish and will against his neighbor, that imagination is not only the source of our capacity to form the creative mutual wish but it is also bounded by the individual's own limits, convictions, and experience; and, thus, there is always in our wishing an element of doing violence to the other as well as to ourselves, no matter how well analyzed we may be or how much the recipient of grace or how many times we have experienced satori. Lynch calls this the *"willful"* element, willful here being the insistence of one's own wish against the reality of the situation. Willfulness, he holds, is the kind of will motivated by defiance, in which the wish is more *against* something than *for* its object. The defiant, willful act, says Lynch, is correlated with fantasy rather than with imagination, and is the spirit which negates reality, whether it be a person or an aspect of impersonal nature, rather than sees it, forms it, respects it, or takes joy in it.

The autonomous, spontaneous element in wishing and willing is also present in the significant new studies of will by the psychiatrist Leslie Farber.[10] Dr. Farber demarcates two realms of "will," the first consisting of an experience of the self in its totality, a relatively spontaneous movement in a certain direction. In this kind of willing, the body moves as a whole, and the experience is characterized by a relaxation and by an imaginative, open quality. This is an experience of freedom which is anterior to all talk about political or psychological freedom; it is a freedom, I would add, presupposed by the determinist and anterior to all the discussions of determinism. In contrast, the will of the second realm, as Dr. Farber sees it, is that in which some obtrusive element enters, some necessity for a decision of an either/or character, a decision with an element of an *against* something along with a *for* something. If one uses the Freudian terminology, the "will of the Super-Ego" would be included in this realm. Farber makes these contrasts, using will in this second sense: we can will to read but not to understand, we can will knowledge but not wisdom, we can will scrupulosity but not morality. This is illustrated in creative work. Farber's second realm of will is the conscious, effortful, critical application to the creative endeavor, in preparing a speech for meeting or revising one's manuscript, for example. But when actually giving the speech, or when hopefully creative "inspiration" takes over in our writing, we are engrossed with a degree of forgetfulness of self. In this experience, wishing and willing become one. One characteristic of the creative experience is that it makes for a temporary union by transcending the conflict.

Farber emphasizes that the temptation is for the second realm to take over the first; we lose our spontaneity, our free flow of activity, and will becomes effortful, controlled—i.e., Victorian will power. Our error, then, in the words of Yeats, is that "will tries to take over the work of imagination." As I understand it, what Farber is describing as will of the first category is very close to what Lynch calls "wish." And they are both, Lynch in "wish" and Farber in his realm of "spontaneous will," giving very good descriptions of something to which we shall devote our next chapter, *intentionality*.

I shall offer here some provisional definitions. *Will is the capacity to organize one's self* so that movement in a certain direction or toward a certain goal may take place. *Wish is the imaginative playing with the possibility* of some act or state occurring.

But before we move on to more intricate questions, we must do two things. One is to block in a rough dialectic of the interrelation of will and wish. This is intended to show some of the phenomenological aspects that must be taken into consideration. "Will" and "wish" may be seen as operating in polarity. "Will" requires self-consciousness; "wish" does not. "Will" implies some possibility of either/or choice; "wish" does not. "Wish" gives the warmth, the content, the imagination, the child's play, the freshness, and the richness to "will." "Will" gives the self-direction, the maturity, to "wish." "Will" protects "wish," permits it to continue without running risks which are too great. But without "wish," "will" loses its life-blood, its viability, and tends to expire in self-contradiction. If you have only "will" and no "wish," you have the dried-up, Victorian, neopuritan man. If you have only "wish" and no "will," you have the driven, unfree, infantile person who, as an adult-remaining-an-infant, may become the robot man.

WILLIAM JAMES AND WILL

The other task that must be done before exploring intentionality is to consider William James, that psychologist-philosopher American-man-of-genius, who struggled all his life with the problem of will. His experience will launch us on our way.

One of my esteemed colleagues, writing of James's "severe depression" and the fact that "for a number of years he was on the verge of suicide," asks us "not to judge him harshly" for those aspects of maladjustment.[11] I take a different view. I believe that understanding the depressions James suffered and the way he dealt with them increases our appreciation and admiration for him. True, all his life he was plagued by vacillation and an inability to make up his mind. In his last years, when he was struggling to give up his lecturing at Harvard, he would write in his diary one day, "Resign," the next day, "Don't resign," and the third day, "Resign" again. James's difficulty in making up his mind was connected with his inner richness and the myriad of possibilities for him in every decision.

But it was precisely James's depressions—in which he would often write of his yearning for "a reason for wishing to live four hours longer"—which forced him to be so concerned with will, and precisely in the *struggle against these depressions that he learned so much about human will*. He believed—and, as a therapist, I believe that his judgment here is clinically sound—that it was his own discovery of the capacity to will which enabled him to live a tremendously fruitful life up to his death at sixty-eight, despite his depressions and his continual affliction with insomnia, eye troubles, back disorders, and so on. In our own "age of the disordered will," as it has been termed, we turn to William James with eagerness to find whatever help he can give us with our own problem of will.

He begins his famous chapter on will, published in 1890,[12] by summarily dismissing *wish* as what we do when we desire something which is not possible for achievement, and contrasts it with *will*, which exists when the end is within our power. If with the desire there is a sense that attainment is not possible, we simply *wish*. I believe that this definition is one of the places where James's Victorianism shows through; wishes are treated as unreal and childlike. Obviously, no wish is possible when we first wish it. It *becomes* possible only as we wish it in many different ways, and through considering it from this side and that, possibly over a great period of time, we generate the power and take the risk to *make* it happen.

But then James launches into what turns out to be one of the most thrilling treatises on will in literature, which I can only touch on. There is, first, the "primary" type, which is distinguished by the fact that it does not require a whole series of decisions. We decide to change our shirt or begin to write on a paper, and once we start, a whole series of movements is set going by itself; it is ideomotor. This "primary will" requires absence of conflict. James is here trying to preserve spontaneity. He is taking his stand against Victorian will power, the exercise of the separate faculty called "will power" which must have failed him dismally in his own life and led him into the paralysis which expressed itself in his depressions. Now we know in our day a lot more about this so-called "absence of conflict," thanks chiefly to psychoanalysis, and that infinitely more is going on in states which seem without conflict.

He then touches on the "healthy will" which he defines as action following vision. The vision requires a clear concept and consists of motives in their right ratio to each other—which is a fairly rationalistic picture.[13] Discussing unhealthy will, he rightly focuses on the *obstructed will*. One illustration of this that he cites is the state that exists when our eyes lose focus and we are unable to "rally our attention." "We sit blankly staring and do nothing." The objects of consciousness fail to touch the quick or break the skin. Great fatigue or exhaustion marks this condition; "and an apathy resembling that then brought about is recognized in asylums under the name of *abulia* as a symptom of mental disease."[14] It is interesting that he relates this apathy only to mental disease. I, for one, believe this is the chronic, endemic, psychic state of our society in our day—"The neurotic personality of *our* time."

The question then boils down to, Why doesn't something *interest* me, reach out to me, grasp me? And James then comes to the central problem of will, namely *attention*. I don't know whether he realized what a stroke of genius this was. When we analyze will with all the tools modern psychoanalysis brings us, we shall find ourselves pushed back to the level of *attention* or *intention* as the seat of will. The effort which goes into the exercise of the will is really effort of attention; the strain in willing is the effort to keep the consciousness clear, i.e., the strain of keeping the attention focussed. The "once-born" type of well-adjusted person doesn't need much effort, James comments, but heroes and neurotics need a lot. This leads him to a surprising, though very keen, statement of an identity between *belief, attention,* and *will:*

> Will and Belief, in short, meaning a certain relation between objects and the Self, are two names for one and the same *psychological* phenomenon.[15]
> The most compendious possible formula perhaps would be that *our belief and attention* are the same fact.[16]

He then beguiles us with one of his completely human and earthy illustrations. I cite it in detail because I wish to come back to it in discussing the unfinished aspects of James' concept of will:

> We know what it is to get out of bed on a freezing morning in a room without a fire, and how the very vital principle within us protests against the ordeal. [The scene is New England before the advent of central heating.] Probably most persons have lain on certain mornings for an hour at a time unable to brace themselves to the resolve. We think how late we shall be, how the duties of the day will suffer;

we say, "I *must* get up, this is ignominious," and so
on. But still the warm couch feels too delicious, and
the cold outside too cruel, and resolution faints
away and postpones itself again and again just as it
seemed on the verge of the decisive act. Now how
do we ever get up under such circumstances? If I
may generalize from my own experience, we more
often than not get up without any struggle or decision at all. We suddenly find that we *have* got
up. A fortunate lapse of consciousness occurs; we
forget both the warmth and the cold; *we fall into
some revery connected with the day's life,* in the
course of which the idea flashes across us, "Hollo! I
must lie here no longer"—an idea which at that lucky
instant awakens no contradictory or paralyzing suggestions, and consequently produces immediately
its appropriate motor effects. It was our acute consciousness of both the warmth and the cold during
the period of struggle which paralyzed our activity. . . .[17]

He concludes that the moment the inhibition ceases, the
original idea exerts its effect, and up we get. He adds,
with typical Jamesian confidence, that "This case seems
to me to contain in miniature form the data for an entire
psychology of volition."

Let us now take, for our special examination, James's
own example. We note that just when he gets to the heart
of the problem of will in this illustration there comes a
remarkable statement. He writes, "We suddenly find that
we *have* got up." That is to say, he jumps over the whole
problem. No "decision at all occurs," but only a "fortunate lapse of consciousness."

But, I ask, what went on in that "fortunate lapse of
consciousness"? True, the paralyzing bind of his ambivalence was released. But that is a negative statement and
doesn't tell us why anything else happened. Surely we
cannot call this just a "lucky instant," as James does, or
a "happenstance!" If our basis for will rests on the mere
"luck" or "happenstance," our house is built upon the
sands indeed, and we have no basis for will at all.

Now I do not mean to imply that so far James, in this
example, has not said something. He has, and it is very

important: the whole incident shows *the bankruptcy of Victorian will power,* will consisting of a "faculty" which is based upon our capacity to force our bodies to act against their desire. Victorian will power turned everything into a rationalistic, moralistic issue—e.g., the attraction of the warmth of the bed, the giving in to of which is ignominious, as opposed to the so-called "superego" pressure to be "upright," that is, up and working. Freud described at length and self-deceit and rationalization involved in Victorian will power and, I believe, dethroned it once and for all. The example shows James's own struggle against the paralyzing effects of Victorianism, in which the goal becomes twisted into a self-centered demonstration of one's own character and the real moral issue gets entirely lost in the shuffle.

So we return to our crucial question. What went on in that "fortunate lapse of consciousness"? James only tells us that "we fall into some revery connected with the day's life." Ah, here lies our secret! Psychotherapy has brought us a good deal of data about that "revery" which James did not have—and I do not believe that we "fall" into it at all.

For purposes of clarity, I shall state here my own argument concerning the "unfinished business" in James's concept of will. *I propose that a whole dimension of experience is left out by James, as it is also omitted by us in contemporary psychology.* The answer does not lie in James's conscious analysis or in Freud's analysis of the unconscious, but in a dimension which cuts across and includes both conscious and unconscious, and both cognition and conation.

To this dimension, which has been known historically as *intentionality,* we now turn.

NINE

INTENTIONALITY

> Learning is not the *accumulation* of scraps of knowl-
> edge. It is a *growth*, where every act of knowledge
> develops the learner, thus making him capable of
> constituting ever more and more complex objectivities
> —and the object growth in complexity parallels the
> subjective growth in capacity.
>
> —HUSSERL, AS INTERPRETED BY
> QUENTIN LAUER

As we have been exploring the deeper significance of
wish, we have noticed that a curious theme has been constantly emerging. Something more is going on in a wish
than meets the eye. This theme is implied when Lynch
speaks of the "autonomous" element in wishing, or when
he and Farber both speak of the relation of the wish to
imagination and spontaneity. And the theme is present
especially when we consider the *meaning* of the wish, that
aspect of the wish in human beings that goes beyond
mere force and is expressed in language, art, and other
symbols. The same theme was also present as the big
"X" which James leaped over in his illustration of getting
out of bed on a cold morning.

This theme, running through our discussion like an
obligato, is *intentionality*. By intentionality, I mean the
structure which gives meaning to experience. It is not to
be identified with intentions, but is the dimension which
underlies them; it is man's capacity to have intentions.
It is our imaginative participation in the coming day's
possibilities in James's example out of which comes the
awareness of our capacity to form, to mold, to change
ourselves and the day in relation to each other. James's
reverie as he lay in bed is a beautiful, albeit denied, expression of it. Intentionality is at the heart of conscious-

ness. I believe that it is also the key to the problem of
wish and will.

First, what does the term mean? We shall define it in
two stages; the preliminary stage is the fact that our intentions are decisive with respect to how we perceive the
world. This afternoon, for instance, I go up to see a
house in the mountains. Suppose, first, that I am looking
for a place which some friends can rent for the summer months. When I approach the house, I shall question whether it is sound and well-built, gets enough sun,
and other things having the meaning of "shelter" to me.
Or suppose that I am a real-estate speculator: then what
will strike me will be how easily the house can be fixed
up, whether it will bring a price attractively higher than
what I shall have to pay for it, and other things meaning "profit." Or let us say that it is the house of friends I
am visiting: then I shall look at it with eyes which see it
as "hospitality,"—its open patio and easy chairs which
will make out afternoon talk more pleasant. Or, if this is
a cocktail party at the house of friends who have snubbed
me at a party at my house, I find myself seeing things
that indicate that anyone would prefer my cottage to
theirs, and other aspects of the invidious envy and "social
status" for which we human beings are notorious. Or,
finally, if this afternoon I am outfitted with my water-
color materials and bent on doing a sketch, I shall see
how the house clings to the side of the mountain, the pattern of the lines of the roof leading up to the peaks above
and sweeping away into the valley below, and, indeed,
now I even prefer the house ramshackle and run down
for the greater artistic possibilities this gives me.

In each one of these five instances, it is the same house
that provides the stimulus, and I am the same man responding to it. But in each case, the house and experience have an entirely different meaning.

But this is only one side of intentionality. The other
side is that it also *does* come from the object. Intentionality is the bridge between these. It is the structure of
meaning which makes it possible for us, subjects that we
are, to see and understand the outside world, objective as
it is. In intentionality, the dichotomy between subject and
object is partially overcome.

THE ROOTS OF INTENTIONALITY

The concept seems to me so important, and has been so neglected in contemporary psychology, that I ask the reader to go with me into an exploration of its meaning. Its roots are to be found in ancient thought: Aristotle said, "What is given to the eyes [in our terms, what is perceived] is the *intention* of the soul" Cicero speaks of "the soul as the *tension* of the body."[1] But the specific concept of intentionality itself was introduced into western thought by Arabic philosophers in early medieval times, and became central for the thought of the Middle Ages. It then meant how we know reality, that is, it was an epistemology. Two kinds of intentionality were made distinct: *intensio primo*, referring to knowing particular things—that is, objects which actually exist; and *intensio secundo*, the relations of these objects to general concepts —that is, knowing by conceptualization.

All of this presupposes that we could not know a thing unless we already, in some way, participated in it. For St. Thomas Aquinas, intentionality is what the intellect grasps about the thing understood. He states, in language unfortunately not made easier for us by the translator, "The intellect through a species of being informed in the act of intelligence, forms itself some intention of the understood thing."[2] We note the words "being informed" in the passive voice, followed later by *form* in the active voice. I take this to mean that in the process of knowing, we are *in-formed* by the thing understood, and in the same act, our intellect simultaneously *gives form* to the thing we understand. What is important here is the word "in-form," or "forming in." To tell someone something, to in-form him, is to *form* him—a process that can sometimes become very powerful in psychotherapy by the therapist's saying just one sentence, or one word, at the right moment. How different this is from the indoctrination many of us got in graduate school, that information is simply dry data, external to us, which we manipulate!

Intentionality thus begins as an *epistemology,* a way of knowing reality. It carries the meaning of reality as we know it.

Our theme is carried a giant step forward by Immanuel Kant's "second Copernican revolution" in modern thought. Kant held that the mind is not simply passive clay on which sensations write, or something which merely absorbs and classifies facts. What really happens is that objects themselves conform to our ways of understanding.[3] A good example of this is mathematics. These are constructs in our minds; but nature conforms, "answers," to them. As Bertrand Russell was to say about physics a century and a half after Kant, "Physics is mathematical not because we know so much about the physical world, but because we know so little; it is only its mathematical properties that we can discover."[4] Kant's revolution lay in making the human mind an active, forming participant in what it knows. Understanding, itself, is then constitutive of its world.

In the last half of the nineteenth century, the concept of intentionality was reintroduced by Franz Brentano, whose forceful lectures at the University of Vienna both Freud and Husserl attended. Brentano believed that consciousness is defined by the fact that it *intends* something, points toward something outside itself—specifically, that *it intends the object*. Thus, intentionality gives meaningful contents to consciousness.

Though Freud, so far as I know, never mentions Brentano in his writings, it is clear that he was more than just an anonymous auditor at Brentano's lectures. There is evidence, I am told, of Freud's active participation in the class, and also that Brentano at one time gave him a recommendation. It would seem to me that the intentionality implicit in Freud's views is one of the not-too-rare cases of the influence of the ideas of one man on another in such a germane way that they become part and parcel of the second man's thought and may seem to have always been his. Intentionality is built into the warp and woof of Freud's approach to free association, dreams, and fantasies. The reason Freud does not mention the concept explicitly may be the same reason it has been left out of other aspects of our academic and scientific psychology; Freud wanted to establish a natural-science form of psychology for his psychoanalysis, and explicit intentionality—the "missing link" between mind and body—makes such a task infinitely more difficult, if not impossible. Take, for example, Freud's endeavor to make an "economic" theory out of libido, with the significant variable being the changes in the economic quantities of excitation. One can assume a certain force, let us say, of sheer sexual desire, with glandular and neuromuscular correlates in the whole body as well as specific excitation in the sexual organs. But it turns out that a person's libido is no fixed quantity at all, but rises and falls with the associations he or she has of the loved one and the father, mother, past lovers, *et al.*, and that these symbolic meanings—which are qualitative—have more significance and force as a variable than the quantity of libido. Freud, indeed, was the one who, above all, taught us of these very meanings which destroy his own or any other sheer quantitative interpretation.

Edmund Husserl, the disciple of Brentano who was to become the father of modern phenomenology, extended the concept to the whole of our knowledge. Consciousness, he pointed out, never exists in a subjective vacuum but is always consciousness *of* something. Consciousness not only cannot be separated from its objective world, but, indeed constitutes its world. The upshot is that "meaning is an intention of the mind," in Husserl's words.[5] The act and experience of consciousness itself is a continuous molding and remolding of our world, self related to objects and objects to self in inseparable ways, self participating in the world as well as observing it, neither pole of self or world being conceivable without the other. This, of course, does not mean that we cannot bracket for the moment the subjective or objective side of the experience. When I measure my house to see how much paint it will take to repaint it, or when I get a report on some endocrinological tests on my child, I bracket for the moment how I feel about it: I want only to understand as clearly as I can these measurements. But *then* my responsibility is to put these objective facts back into the context in which they have meaning for me—my project to paint my house, or my caring for the health of my child. I believe that one of our serious errors in psychology is to bracket out part of experience and never put it back together again.

Heidegger then took the next step by removing Husserl's concept "out of the thin air" of Platonic idealism and extending it to the total feeling, valuing, acting human being. He did this by his concept of care (*Sorge*). Care is constitutive of our world in a sense analogous to Kant's understanding. Man is the being, Heidegger says over and over again, who is concerned about Being. And when man fails to be, we could add from our therapeutic observations of states of conformism and depersonalization, he loses his being, that is, loses his potentialities. There is a close, inner relationship between caring and intentionality, suggested already by the fact that the root word "tend"—to take care of—is the center of the term intentionality.

A word itself embodies a cumulative, creative wisdom in that it is the product of centuries of molding, forming, and re-forming on the part of an infinite number of people who are trying to communicate something important to themselves and to the fellow members of their culture. Let us see what help we can find in understanding "intentionality" and its related terms "intend" and "intention" by tracking down their etymological sources.

All of these terms come from Latin stem *intendere*, which consists of *in* plus *tendere, tensum,* the latter, interestingly enough, meaning "to stretch," and from which we get our word "tension." This tells us immediately that intention is a "stretching" toward something.

Now a fact which may be surprising to many readers, as it was to me, is that the first meaning given for "intend" in *Webster's*[6] does not have to do with "purpose" or "design," as when we say, "I intend to do something," but is rather, *"to mean, signify."* Only secondly does Webster give the definition "to have in mind a purpose or a design." Most people in our voluntaristic Victorian tradition have tended to skip over the primary and central meaning and to use the concept only in its derivative meaning of conscious design and purpose. And since our psychology soon became able to prove that such conscious designs and purposes were mostly illusions and that we are not at all creatures of these nice, freely-chosen, voluntary plans, we were constrained to throw out the whole kit of "intents" with the caboodle of "intentions." We had known already that the road to hell is paved with good intentions, and we now saw that these intentions,

good or bad, were figments of our own self-conceit anyway. But if you change "self-conceit" to "self-concern"
and realize that there is no knowledge or act at all without this self-concern—that everything has its concern or
intent in it, and that we know our world by virtue of
these intents—if you make these shifts from the pejorative to the positive form of the same words, how different
the implication is!

The more significant aspect of intention is its relation
to *meaning.* We use this in one form in the legal phrase
asking, What is the *intent* of the law? when referring to
its meaning. "Intent" is "the turning of the mind toward
an object," *Webster's* tells us in the first definition,
"*hence,* a design, purpose."[7] The design and purpose come
after the "hence." That is to say, the voluntaristic aspects
of the experience lie in the fact that already the mind is
turned toward an object which has a certain import and
meaning for us.

All the way through this etymology is, of course, that
little word "tend." It refers to movement toward something—*tend* toward, *tend*ency. To me, it seems to be the
core of our whole quest; its presence there in the center
is a perpetual reminder that our meanings are never purely "intellectual" or our acts purely results of pushes from
the past; but in both we are moving *toward* something.
And *mirabile dictu,* the word also means, as we briefly
saw, "to take care of"—we tend our sheep and cattle, and
we tend to ourselves.

Thus, when Husserl says, "Meaning is an intention of
the mind," he includes both the *meaning* and the *act,* the
movement toward something. He points out this dual
meaning in the German language: the word *meinung*
which signifies either opinion or meaning, has the same
stem as the German verb *meinen,* "to intend." In pondering the English language at this point, I was surprised—
being brought up to think that the objective fact was the
epitome of everything and occupied the place next to
God if not indeed His Throne itself—to find that we also
have that dual import. When I say, "I mean the paper is
white," you take my sentence as giving you merely a
statement of fact; it is a unilateral equivalence, "A" is
"B." But when I say, "I mean to turn the corner, but the

car skids," you take my "mean" as my intention, a statement of my commitment and conviction. Only later will
we see if I can make it come true.

The conclusion, therefore, to which our argument points
is that every *meaning has within it a commitment.* And
this does *not* refer to the use of my muscles *after* I
get an idea in order to accomplish the idea. And most
of all, it does *not* refer to what a behaviorist might say
on reading these paragraphs, "Just as we've always said
—the consciousness is only in the act anyway, and we
might as well study only the muscular action, the behavior, to start with." No, our analysis leads to exactly
the opposite conclusion, that a sheer movement of the
muscles, as the larynx in talking, is exactly what you
don't have. You have, rather, a human being *intending*
something. And you cannot understand the overt behavior
except as you see it in relation to, and as an expression
of, its intention. Meaning has no meaning apart from
intention. Each act of consciousness *tends toward* something, is a turning of the person toward something, and
has within it, no matter how latent, some push toward a
direction for action.

Cognition, or knowing, and conation, or willing, then
go together. We could not have one without the other.
This is why commitment is so important. If I do not
will something, I could never *know* it; and if I do not
know something, I would never have any content for my
willing. In this sense, it can be said directly that man
makes his own meaning. Note that I do not say that he
only makes his meaning, or that it is not dialectically related at every instant to reality; I say that if he is not
engaged in making his meaning, he will never know reality.

My task, so far, has been to define the concept of intentionality. I have emphasized that it contains both our
knowing and our forming reality, and that these are inseparable from each other. From the point of view of
intentionality, James's reverie as he lies in bed is entirely
sensible, and his sudden act of getting up is not at all a
will-o'-the-wisp "lucky instant" or "fortunate happening,"
but an understandable and reliable expression of his *"connection with the day's events."* It is his "imaginative participation" in the day and the events of the day, which is

reaching out to him, grasping him, that accomplishes the getting up.

EXAMPLES FROM PSYCHOANALYSIS

I wish now to give some examples from psychoanalysis of the problem of intentionality. Take the fascinating instances of a patient who cannot perceive some obvious thing not because anything is wrong with his eyes or his neurological functioning or anything of that sort, but because *the intentionality in which he is trapped makes it impossible for him to see it.*

A patient of mine presented data the very first session that his mother tried to abort him before he was born, that she then gave him over to an old-maid aunt to raise the first two years of his life, after which she left him in an orphan's home promising to visit him every Sunday, but rarely putting in an appearance. Now if I were to say to him—being naïve enough to think it would do some good—"Your mother hated you," he would hear the words but they might well have no meaning whatever for him. Sometimes a vivid and impressive thing happens—such a patient cannot even *hear* the word, such as "hate," even though the therapist repeats it. Suppose my patient is a psychologist or psychiatrist. He might then remark, "I realize all of this seems to say my mother didn't want me, didn't love me, but those are simply foreign words to me." He is not prevaricating or playing a game of hide-and-seek with me. It is simply a fact: *the patient cannot permit himself to perceive the trauma until he is ready to take a stand toward it.*

This experience is surely not foreign to anyone: we sense that we shall be fired from our job, that someone we love will die imminently. But what goes on is a curious inner conversation with ourselves, "I know I *will* be able to see this later on, but I cannot see it now." This is simply a way of saying, "I know it is true, but I cannot yet permit myself to see it." The world can be too overwhelming if we are not able to take a stand toward a traumatic happening but also are unable to escape seeing it. Schizophrenia is one reaction to such a dilemma. Sometimes the therapist makes the mistake of setting out to drum into the patient's head an obvious truth which the patient has not been able to admit—for example, telling a woman that she does not love her baby. What often happens then is that the patient, if she does not quit therapy, develops some other, probably worse, block between herself and reality.

Intentionality presupposes such an intimate relationship with the world that we would not be able to go on existing except if we could block the world out at times. This should not be called simply by the condemnatory term "resistance." I do not doubt the reality of resistance, as Freud and others elucidated it, but I am emphasizing here a broader, structural phenomenon. That is, "every intention is an attention, and attention is I-can," as Merleau-Ponty puts it.[8] We are, therefore, unable to give attention to something until we are able in some way to experience an "I-can" with regard to it.

The same principle is evident, also in exceedingly interesting ways, in memory. Patients often need one or two years of analysis before they can remember some obvious event in their childhood. When they suddenly do recall the event, has their memory gotten better? Of course not. But what *has* happened is a change in the patient's relation to his world, generally by way of his increased capacity to trust the therapist and, accordingly, himself, or there is a reduction of his neurotic anxiety for other reasons. His relation to intentionality—in contrast to his mere conscious intention, which was assumedly there to begin with—has changed. *Memory is a function of intentionality.* Memory is like perception in this regard; the patient cannot remember something until he is ready to take some stand toward it. "Recovery of childhood memories," Franz Alexander puts it, "is not the cause but the result of analysis."[9]

All of this hinges on the inseparability of knowing and willing, of cognition and conation, which we see nowhere more clearly than in psychotherapy. Patients come for therapy because they are aware that they cannot act in their lives because they don't *know*—aren't aware of drives from their "unconscious," don't know their own mechanisms, have never become conscious of the childhood genesis of these mechanisms, and so on. But if this is the only approach, the patient will lie there on the couch for eight or nine years, never acting because he doesn't yet know enough; and psychoanalysis, in the words of Silvan Tomkins, becomes "systematic training in indecision."

But it is also an error for therapy to reach in the opposite direction, as several schools have done of late, and insist that the function of the therapist is to clarify "reality" for the patient and get him to act accordingly. This makes the therapist the psychic policeman of the society, whose job is to help the patient conform to the mores of our particular historical period—about which it can only be said that, if they are still viable at all, they are of exceedingly dubious merit. Our only way to avoid both errors is to move the problem to the deeper plane of intentionality.

My thesis here is that the function of psychoanalysis should be to push "intention" toward the deeper, wider, organic dimension of intentionality. Has it not been always the function of psychoanalysis to demonstrate that there never is a purely conscious intention, that we—whether we literally are murderers or not—are always pushed by the "irrational," daimonic, dynamic forces of the "dark" side of life that Schopenhauer and Nietzsche, as well as Freud, talked about? Freud dethroned deliberation as the motive for actions. Whatever we do, infinitely more than our "rational" reasons and justification is involved. Psychoanalysis gives the data that makes the necessary distinction, as well as the necessary connection, between intention and intentionality.

We must now pause to distinguish intentionality from "purpose" or "voluntarism." Intentionality is a form of epistemology, which neither purpose nor voluntarism are. Intentionality involves *response,* which neither purpose nor voluntarism do. Not solipsistic, intentionality is an assertive response of the person to the structure of his world. Intentionality gives the basis which makes purpose and voluntarism possible.

A patient's *voluntary* intention, so far as he is aware of it, may be to get to his hour with me on time, to tell me this or that important thing that has happened to him, to relax and be completely honest. But his unconscious intentions, in contrast, may well be to please me by playing the role of the "good patient," or to impress me with

how brilliant his free associations are, or to force my un-
conditioned attention by describing what catastrophic
things he may do to himself and others. Intention is a
psychological state; I can set myself voluntarily to do
this or that. Intentionality is what underlies both conscious and unconscious intentions. It refers to a state of
being and involves, to a greater or lesser degree, the *totality* of the person's orientation to the world at that
time. And what is most interesting is the times in psychotherapy when strong voluntary intention—correlated with
"will power"—blocks the way to the person's intentionality, and is just what keeps the patient from communicating with the deeper dimensions of his experience. Our
William James, struggling there in bed with his Victorian
will power and remaining paralyzed for as long as he
struggled, is an engaging example. And as long as he
struggled in that way, we could be sure that he would
remain paralyzed.

Intentionality, as I am using the term, goes below levels
of immediate awareness, and includes spontaneous, bodily elements and other dimensions which are usually
called "unconscious." This has positive as well as negative implications. For example, my *intention* at this moment is to put these ideas, which seem important to me,
into readable form and to finish this chapter in the not-
too-distant future. But unless I am participating in an *intentionality* which is more than that—i.e., unless I am
committed to writing as good and true a book as I can
—I shall accomplish only a pedestrian job. I shall produce nothing of genuine significance or originality. For
in my pressure to get the chapter done, I will be blocking off new ideas which might well up in me, new insights
and forms emerging from the preconscious and unconscious dimensions of experience. Intention goes with conscious purpose. But the gift of psychoanalysis is the
depth dimension, a contribution which vastly enlarges intention, and indeed pushes it from a conscious purpose
to the more total, organic, feeling and wishing man, the
man who is the product of his past as well as moving
toward the future. Psychoanalysis will not let intention
rest as simple intention, but pushes it to the deeper,
wider, organic plane of intentionality.

We have said that intentionality gives the underlying structure for wishing and willing. Speaking psychoanalytically, intentionality gives the structure within which repression and the blocking off of conscious intentions takes place. Freud made it undeniably clear, in his use of "free association," that associations which seem merely random are not at all random. In free association, the thoughts and memories and fantasies take their form, their pattern, their meaningful theme (which the patient, or any one of us engaging in free association not on the couch but in normal thinking and creativity, may not at all catch at the moment) from the fact that they are *his* fantasies, *his* associations, coming out of *his* way of perceiving the world and *his* commitments and problems. It is only afterwards that the person himself can see and absorb the meaning that has been in these apparently random, disconnected things he is saying. *Free association is a technique of going beyond mere conscious intention and giving one's self over to the realm of intentionality.* It is in the basic, more inclusive realm of intentionality that these deeper meanings lie; but it is also here where we find the patient's reasons for his repression in the first place. I believe that the long-run impact of Freud and psychoanalysis will be to deepen and enlarge our understanding of intentionality.

PERCEPTION AND INTENTIONALITY

On the desk before which I sit lies a sheet of paper. If I have in mind to make some notes on the paper for my manuscript, I see the sheet in terms of its whiteness; has it already been scribbled upon? If my intention is to fold it into a toy plane for my grandson, I see the paper in its sturdiness. Or if my intent is to draw a picture on it, I see the rough, coarse-grained texture of the paper inviting my pencil and promising to make my lines more interesting. It is the same piece of paper in each case, and I am the same man responding to it. But I see three entirely different pieces of paper. It makes no sense, of course, to call this "distortion": it is simply an example of the infinite variety of meanings a given event, a given pattern of stimulus and response, can have.

An intention is a turning of one's attention toward something. In this sense, perception is directed by intentionality. This can be illustrated by the fact that consciousness consists of a figure-ground constellation. If I look at the tree, the mountain is a background; if I look at the mountain, the reverse is the case: the mountain then becomes the figure and the rest the foreground. The selective, either/or character of perception is one aspect of intentionality: I cannot look at one thing at this instant without refusing to look at another. To say "yes" means for that moment I must say "no" to something else. This is one example of how conflict is of the essence of consciousness. The conflict, which is part and parcel of intentionality, is the beginning of volition, and the beginning of volition is present in the structure of consciousness itself.

But we must now hasten to say that this selecting process—I look here rather than there—is not at all simply a using of neck and eye muscles to turn the head and line of vision in my picking out the object to which I attend. A more intricate and much more interesting process is occurring. It is the inner process of *conceiving* the object so that I can *perceive* it. Such is the amazingly intimate interrelation of my subjective experience with what goes on in the objective world: I cannot *per*ceive something until I can *con*ceive it. Professor Donald Snygg has reminded us of that memorable event when the people in a primitive society were unable to see Captain Cook's ship when it sailed into their harbor because they had no word, no symbol, for such a ship.[10] What they did perceive I do not know—possibly a cloud or animal; but at least it was something they did have a symbol for. Language, or the symbolizing process, is our way of *con*ceiving that we may *per*ceive.

The word "conceive" is used in our society to mean to become pregnant, and the analogy is not inappropriate. For the act of perceiving also requires the capacity to bring to birth something in one's self; if one cannot, or for some reason is not yet ready, to bring to birth in himself some position, some *stance* toward what he is seeing, he cannot perceive it. From our examples in psychoanalysis, it is clear that the patient cannot get insights, perceive truths about himself and his life, until he is ready to take some stand toward the truth, until he is able to *con*ceive them.

The stem of both perceive and conceive is the Latin *capere*, which means to take, to seize. Even the word "apprehend" has the same active rather than passive quality, coming as it does from *prehendere,* to seize with the hand. (How far removed this is—the wisdom inhering in the evolution of these words—from the passive picture most of us had learned about perception, namely, of a stimulus occurring and making an imprint upon the retina!) The sexual as well as the pregnancy analogy is not out of place: both perception and conception are an active forming of the world that goes on in the intercourse between the living being, man, and the world to which he is related. The new idea is born, the new view of Cézanne's trees is created, the new technical invention is made. Consciousness *creates* in the sense that it conceives its knowledge; but this is a continuous, reciprocal, attracting and counter-attracting, responsive relationship between subject and object, not unlike sexual intercourse. It is not the mere relation between master and slave. If we take the time-honored metaphor of the sculptor and his clay, we must see that the clay also *forms* the sculptor; the clay conditions what he does, limits and even changes his intentions, and, thus, also forms *his* potentialities and consciousness.

If intentionality is a significant process in perception, as I believe it is, more is the misfortune that the dimension has been left out of consideration in psychological studies. Instead of leaving it specifically *out* of the picture—which I think in itself has contaminated our work —we ought to figure intentionality directly *in*. This means taking account of the experimenter's bias. Robert Rosenthal has already demonstrated how the expectations, the "intentions" of the experimenter, do influence the results.[11] We should also figure in the intentionality of the human subjects in any experiment. What underlies the intentions of your colleagues in participating in your experiment? What is the intentionality of the subjects in the classroom to whom you are giving the Thematic Apperception Test? It has been amazing, indeed, that we have seemed to believe that these things would not make any difference.

In any case, may I emphasize that time and again, when reading psychological studies, I have the conviction that the psychologist is studying something different from what he thinks he is studying. He will not actually know what he is getting unless he can clarify on the level of intentionality the situation of the participating persons.

This takes us to the threshold of the relation of the body to intentionality. But before we cross that threshold, however, we must clear up a common misunderstanding. Intentionality is not to be confused with introspection. It is not a looking into or at ourselves to find such and such. It is not a looking that transforms me into an object. It does not have to do with "spection," as Paul Ricoeur points out, or splitting me into a "spectator" and "actor." The common tendency to connect intentionality with introspection is another comment on how difficult it is in our day to get over the habit, after Descartes' original dichotomy, of making everything into object or subject. Intentionality is shown in the act itself. By my act I reveal myself, rather than by looking *at* myself. The imputation that is correlated with intentionality is not a speculative matter, but an act which, because it always involves responding, is responsible.

THE BODY AND INTENTIONALITY

Victorian man used his will to push down and suppress what he called "lower" bodily desires. But one surely cannot be a man of decision without taking bodily desires into consideration. Our discussion of wish in the previous chapter indicates that bodily wishes must be brought into integration with will, or else the one will block the other. The body consists of the muscular, neurological, and glandular correlates of intentionality, such as increased adrenalin secretion when we are enraged and want to strike something, increased speed of heart beat when we are anxious and want to run, engorgement of the sexual organs when we are sexually excited and want to have intercourse. In therapy, when a patient in a given hour is blocked off from his wishes and intentionality in general, a good place to start is for the therapist simply to help the patient become aware of his bodily feelings and his bodily state at that moment.

William James was very much concerned with the body. We can see this in his staunch insistence on the importance of sensations and in his view of emotions as the perception of inner bodily changes. There is a parallel in the preoccupation of that other Victorian, Freud, with sex and instinct. In each of these men, we see the Victorian's endeavor to come to terms with *a body from which their culture had alienated them.* Each dealt with the body as a tool, an instrument, unaware that this is an expression of the very alienation he sought to overcome.

When I was ill with tuberculosis two and a half decades ago, I found that my inherited "will power" was strangely ineffective. In those days, the only cure was bed rest and carefully graduated exercise. We could not will ourselves to get well, and the "strong-willed," dominating type of person sick with TB generally got worse. But I found that listening to my body was of critical importance in my cure. When I could be sensitive to my body, "hear" that I was fatigued and needed to rest more, or sense that my body was strong enough for me to increase my exercise, I got better. And when I found awareness of my body blocked off (a state similar to what patients have in analysis when they say they are not "with it"), I got worse. This may seem like a poetic and "mystical" viewpoint for someone seriously ill to be indulged in, but actually it was a hard-rock, empirical issue of whether I would live or die. As far as I could judge, this was true for the other patients as well. This bodily awareness sometimes comes spontaneously, but by no means necessarily so. "Will is a listening," Pfanders states,[12] which brings to mind particularly the "listening" to the body. In our society, it often requires considerable effort to listen to the body—an effort of sustained "openness" to whatever cues may come from one's body. In recent years, the work of the body re-educationalists, the teachers of exercise and of Yoga, have brought out the significant interrelation between the capacity to listen to the body and psychological well-being. The presence of volition is betrayed in the phrases we use, such as I "accept" fatigue, I "agree" to rest, I "consent" to follow my physician's (or teacher's) recommendation, I "adopt" a regimen. There is, therefore, a willing which is not merely against bodily desires but *with* the body, a willing from within; it is a willing of *participation* rather than *opposition*.

"Will moves through desire," said Aristotle. The fact that I am an individual. Since I am a body, separate with all the glandular changes that go therewith—the fact that they are *embodied* desires—means that I cannot escape taking some stand in regard to them. That is to say, if I have a *wish*, I cannot avoid willing about it, even if only to deny that I have the wish. Pure detachment works only if we can disengage our bodies. Hence, the outright denial of awareness of wishes generally involves doing violence to one's body.

My body is an expression par excellence of the fact that I am an individual. Since I am a body, separate from others as an individual entity, I cannot escape putting myself on the line in some way or other—or refusing to put myself on the line, which is the same issue. One may try to conform to someone else psychologically, be an imprint of the other in *ideas;* but Siamese twins *bodily* are very rare. The patient who cannot experience himself as bodily separate from another, say his mother, is generally representative of a serious pathological illness, often of the schizophrenic kind. The fact that my body is an entity in space, has this motility and this particular relation to space which my movements give it, makes it a living symbol of the fact that I cannot escape in some way or other "taking a *stand*." Will, as Paul Ricoeur emphasizes, is *embodied* will. Thus, so many words having to do with will refer to our physical place —"taking a position," accepting a "viewpoint," choosing an "orientation." Or we say that someone is "upright," "straight," or the opposite, "prone," "cringing," "ducking," all referring to will and decision as shown through the position of the body. Peer Gynt in Ibsen's play could never become an individual self so long as he followed the spirit of the Boyg and went "around," walked "crooked"; he achieved some selfhood only when he walked "straight through," as Ibsen expresses the stance of the man of single-minded will.

Even more interesting is the body as a *language* of intentionality. It not only expresses intentionality; it *communicates* it. When a patient comes in the door of my consulting room, intentionality is expressed in his way of walking, his gestures; does he lean toward me or away? Does he talk with a half-closed mouth; and what does his voice say when I stop listening to the words and listen only to the tone? Not only in the therapeutic hour but in real life as well our communication has, much more than we are aware of it, the subtle character of the dance, the meaning communicated by virtue of the forms we continuously create by our bodily movements.

In their research at Wisconsin with schizophrenics, Carl Rogers and his associates give some vivid pictures of intentionality and the body with patients who could not or would not communicate, at least for some months, except through the language of the body. Eugene Genlin tells, for example, of coming to the ward to do therapy with a hostile patient who would never speak.[13] At first, the patient immediately ran away at Dr. Genlin's coming. Then, the patient remained longer before running, and finally stood there for the hour while Genlin stood beside him. In his fugitive flutter of his eyes at moments of fear, in the tremor of his mouth hovering on the verge of crying or smiling, in all these expressions, there is a language which can be more significant, and is surely more eloquent, than most spoken words. Obviously, it communicates much more than the bright intellectualized talking of the sophisticated patient who chatters for months in order to avoid awareness of his own underlying feelings.

WILL AND INTENTIONALITY

In one of his sonnets, Shakespeare writes of his going to bed at night weary with the day's travel. He continues,

> But then begins a journey in my head
> To work my mind, when body's work's expir'd;

> For then my thoughts—from far where I abide—
> *Intend* a zealous pilgrimage to thee,
> And keep my drooping eyelids open wide . . .[14]

In this use of the word *intend,* Shakespeare has the act already present in the intention. In our day, we would say "intend *to make* a zealous pilgrimage to thee"; we see the act as separate, as something which must be brought in explicitly, something added *after* you've put your mind to it, made a decision. Shakespeare wrote when English, as is always the case with languages in their classical periods, had a special vitality and power which was characterized by the inseparability of intent and act. Our later language reflects the dichotomy between mind and body: we assume that the intent and act are separate as a matter of course; we have to state the "making" by itself. The emphasis in this chapter has been that Shakespeare's usage represents not only the more poetic but the more accurate version psychologically. It is what we experience prior to the artificial abstraction. The separation of intention and act is an artificial posture and does not accurately describe human experience. The act is in the intention, and the intention in the act.

Professor Paul Ricoeur offers the following example.[15] I am taking a trip. The trip is not just an objective matter—i.e., as seeing myself already there. It is also *to be done,* a project to be done *by me.* It is a possibility for realization by me as much as lies in my power. Ricoeur points out that in this projecting of a trip, we are dealing with future structures, but it is not accurate to say disparagingly that this is "just" subjective. It is not less objective because it has to do with the future, with non-resolved structures. It is an unjustified reduction on the part of Wittgenstein and the positivists—and the behaviorists are to be included at this point—to make the world only out of objective facts. "I can" is part of the world. This point is particularly important in therapy, for patients come to us because they cannot say "I can," but only "I can't." In order to understand the "I can't," we must also see the "I can" behind it, of which it is the negation.

It cannot have escaped the reader's attention, as it has not mine, that all through this chapter the word "will," in connection with intentionality, is also the same word we use for the future tense in English. Will and intentionality are intimately bound up with the future. Both meanings—simple future, something will happen; and personal resolve, I will make it happen—are present in varying degrees in each statement of intentionality. "I will come to New York in September" may have very little of resolve and be almost entirely a simple statement of the future. But "I will get married" or "I will write a poem" are much less a comment on the future and mostly a statement of a resolve. The future does not consist of simply a state of time which is going to occur, but contains the element, "I will make it so." Power is potentiality, and potentiality points toward the future: it is something to be realized. The future is the tense in which we promise ourselves, we give a promissory note, we put ourselves on the line. Nietzsche's statement, "Man is the only animal who can make promises," is related to our capacity to posit ourselves in the future. We are reminded here also of William James's fiat, "Let it be so." The hopelessness of many patients, which may be expressed in depression, despair, feelings of "I can't," and related helplessness, can be usefully seen, from one point of view, as the inability to see or construct a future.[16]

It is in intentionality and will that the human being experiences his identity. "I" is the "I" of "I can." Descartes was wrong in his famous sentence, "I think, therefore, I am," for identity does not come out of thinking as such, and certainly not out of intellectualization. Descartes's formulation leaves out, as we have previously indicated, exactly the variable that is most significant; it jumps from thought to identity, when what actually occurs is the intermediate variable of "I can." Kierkegaard mocked Hegel's similarly oversimplified and intellectualistic solution that "potentiality goes over into actuality" when he proclaimed that potentiality does go into actuality, *but the intermediate variable is anxiety*. We could rephrase it, "potentiality is experienced as *mine*—my power, my question—and, therefore, whether it goes over into actuality depends to some extent on me—where I throw my weight, how much I hesitate," and so on. What happens in human experience is "I conceive—I can—I will—I am." The "I can" and "I will" are the essential

experiences of identity. This saves us from the untenable
position in therapy of assuming that the patient develops
a sense of identity and *then* acts. On the contrary, he
experiences the identity *in* the action, or at least in the
possibility for it.

I have elsewhere pointed out that anxiety and potentiality are two sides of the same experience.[17] When
potentiality for sexual intercourse emerges at adoles-
cence, the young person not only feels zest and self-worth
at his new powers, but also normal anxiety, since these
powers will now involve him in a complex pattern of
relationships, some potentially very important, in which
he will have to act. Normal, constructive anxiety goes
with becoming aware of and assuming one's potentialities.
Intentionality is the constructive use of normal anxiety.
If I can have some expectations and possibility of acting on my powers, I move ahead. But if the anxiety becomes overwhelming, then the possibilities for action are
blotted out. Thus Paul Tillich points out that pronounced
neurotic anxiety destroys intentionality, "destroys our relationship to meaningful contents of knowledge or will."
This is the anxiety of "nothingness." Without intentionality we are indeed "nothing."

Tillich goes on, interestingly enough, to relate intentionality to vitality, and then to courage:

> Man's vitality is as great as his intentionality: they
> are interdependent. This makes man the most vital
> of all beings. He can transcend any given situation
> in any direction and this possibility drives him to
> create beyond himself. Vitality is the power of cre-
> ating beyond oneself without losing oneself. The
> more power of creating beyond itself a being has
> the more vitality it has. The world of technical cre-
> ations is the most conspicuous expression of man's
> vitality and its infinite superiority over animal vi-
> tality. Only man has complete vitality because he
> alone has complete intentionality. . . . If the correla-
> tion between vitality and intentionality is rightly un-
> derstood one can accept the biological interpretation
> of courage within the limits of its validity.[18]

Overwhelming anxiety destroys the capacity to per-

ceive and conceive one's world, to reach out toward it
to form and re-form it. In this sense, it destroys intentionality. We cannot hope, plan, promise, or create in severe anxiety; we shrink back into a stockade of limited
consciousness hoping only to preserve ourselves until the
danger is past. Intentionality and vitality are correlated
by the fact that man's vitality shows itself not simply as
a biological force, but as a reaching out, a forming
and re-forming of the world in various creative activities.
The degree of one's intentionality can thus be seen as
the degree of one's courage. Tillich describes the Greek
concept of *arête*, meaning a combination of strength
and value, and the Roman *virtus*, having a similar union
of masculine strength and moral nobility. "Vitality and
intentionality are united in this ideal of human perfection,
which is equally removed from barbarism and from moralism."[19]

Taking a final lead from the origin of the word itself,
we can go further and relate intentionality to "intensity"
of experience, or to the degree of "intentness" in life.
There have been a number of attempts to identify what
we mean by vitality in the psychological sphere: such
words as "aliveness" and so on are used, but without
anyone's having much conviction that he has said anything. Does not intentionally give us a criterion for de-
fining psychological vitality? The degree of intentionality
can define the aliveness of the person, the potential degree of commitment, and his capacity, if we are speaking of a patient, for remaining at the therapeutic task.

TEN

INTENTIONALITY
IN THERAPY

> Neither in the theoretical nor in the practical sphere
> do we care for, or go to help to, those who have no
> head for risks, or sense for living on the perilous edge.
> —WILLIAM JAMES

In turning now to therapy, we have a twofold purpose. First, to arrive at some suggestions on how intentionality and will may be used in clinical work with people in psychological difficulty. Second, to see what light the practical examples cast upon the question which is still most important, namely, What are intentionality and will? Psychotherapy should give us a spring of data, the richness and depth of which are unique, on how wish, will, and intentionality are experienced by living, feeling, suffering people.

In our discussion of intentionality, I may have given —against my intention!—the impression that there was an ideal way of willing, a willing by participation, which puts one in harmony with one's body and world. That is one realm of wishing and willing. But what of the *conflict* of will? Surely this conflilt remains and requires us to push on to another realm. As William James touchingly puts it, the simple, once-born person may have little of it, but the hero and the neurotic have plenty—as he had reason to know. Neurosis can roughly be defined as a conflict between two ways of *not fulfilling* one's self. To borrow James's example, neither staying in bed because it's warm, nor getting up to demonstrate your own noble character adds a mite to your stature. If James had been my patient and began an hour with a story of such a conflict about getting out of bed, I would have agreed immediately—silently or outspokenly—with his *wish:* it *is* nice to lie in a warm bed on a cold morning. Furthermore (and perhaps more to the point), it brings the added satisfaction of demonstrating one's autonomy by protesting against that rigid society which orders you to be up and working. And perhaps staying in bed expresses both horns of James's dilemma toward his father—that extraordinary man who loved much but required much. Only by admitting and affirming the *immediate* wish can we get to the deeper level of what he *genuinely* wishes—that is, to the events of the day.

Therapy, in clarifying the intentionality of the patient, shifts the fight to the real battlefield. It helps the patient and ourselves to fight the conflict on grounds in which a genuine fulfillment is possible; it shifts the struggle to one between authentic fulfillment and nonfulfillment. The reverie which William James fell into concerning the possibilities of the day, which I have insisted is not a chance "fall," shows that on the level of intentionality, he was indeed a man who obviously had a profoundly vital interest in living and a dedication to what he could do.

My task as a therapist is to be conscious, as best I can, of what the intentionality of the patient is in a particular session. And if the session is not simply one in a fairly consistent progression but represents some crisis, as many hours do, my task is to draw out this intentionality so that the patient cannot escape becoming aware of it too. And that, very often, is no easy task.

CASE OF PRESTON

The session from which I will now give some verbatim quotations was one which took place in the seventh month of analysis.[1] The patient, a writer, one of whose symptoms was a fairly steady and sometimes exceedingly severe "writer's block," was a sophisticated and gifted man of forty. He had had five years of previous analysis before coming to me.

The previous analysis had helped him to some extent; he was now able to hold down a job, having before lived off his wife's inherited income. But he still had severe anxiety, depression, and sexual problems. (For reasons I won't go into, the previous analyst felt that these could

not be cured.) In any case, when he wrote to me a
month after breaking off with the previous therapist in a
state of painful, almost incapacitating tension and despair, I agreed to see him. My motives for deciding to
work with him were partly because of the challenge of-
fered by this kind of person of inner resources and stature who hasn't gotten help, at least in a basic sense,
from his previous analysis. Therapy ought to be able to
help persons of this kind, and if it doesn't, we should
know why. The fact that he was a very sophisticated
person who knew almost everything about the field is
partly why I was more active and challenging during this
hour than I would be with some other patients.

If I may state at the outset a conclusion related to our
discussion here: I now believe that one reason psychoanalysis doesn't "take," doesn't get to the basis of the
problems of persons like Preston in a certain number of
cases, is that the intentionality of the patient is not
reached. He, therefore, never fully commits himself, is
never fully *in* the analysis, never has a full encounter.

Five months before the session I now report took place,
he had arrived at an hour in great perturbation over his
struggle, which had gone on for several weeks, to finish
writing an important article. In that session, I felt that
he desperately wanted help, and—varying my technique,
as I often do—I had plunged directly and specifically
into the practical problem of his block, asking what went
on as he sat down at the typewriter and so on. After
that hour, he had gone back to his studio and had written
what he judged was the best article he had ever done, a
verdict later borne out objectively. I mention this prior
incident because it probably had something to do with
his conscious *intentions* in contrast to his *intentionality*
in the hour I am now presenting.

When he came in this hour, he threw himself on the
couch and sighed audibly.

PRESTON. I'm stuck in my writing worse than I've ever
   been. Stupidest thing—a simple piece I'm trying to do.
   This play is modest, minor. I can't do a thing . . .
   Worst block in I don't know how long, as long as I've
   been writing . . . I have a stack of paper like that.
   [*Gestures*] It's a clear test of my psychical condition

. . . nothing in the work . . . it's not magic I expect . . . Just seems to be a spectacular illustration of my perversity . . . Something's gotta happen . . . it means I got to go back to the office this afternoon—didn't want to. I have other things to do—it's got to be done by tomorrow night . . . deadline. It's hard—don't understand why it should be so particularly burdensome. [*Pause*] I don't know whether to just continue to talk about it or leave it alone, go on to other things.

THERAPIST. I prefer to let you decide, let you go on as you wish.

PRESTON. [*Sighs deeply*] I'm so used to myself as a stage manager around here . . . I might just be doing this to avoid talking about something else, I mean. I can't control my behavior in all this. I started out this A.M. in good shape, good spirits to write this piece . . . and whammo! Now, of course, the pressure is building up like mad . . . I can't think of what to do . . . well . . . I don't know whether . . . to talk about it . . . It's nothing . . . you know . . . it's just a minor piece.

This was said in a lackadaisical, disinterested voice, his mouth barely open as he talked. After sighing considerably he went on:

Last night I had some dreams, don't remember them but I remember I almost had them . . . if I had remembered, something would have broken through . . . I would have been in touch with myself . . . a thin wall . . . why I can't break through it . . . I was thinking before I came in . . . there's so much weight of habit behind me, behind my sickness, you know, that every time I seem to get anywhere, see something, or something changes—it's like a pinprick in those self-seal tires, you know . . . Something has to be done . . . My anxiety is building up . . . I was tense all day . . . I try to neutralize it . . . I have masochistic fantasies . . . While trying to write, every five minutes I'd get up, go to the toilet, get a drink . . . I have a pile this high of pages . . . [*Gestures*] . . . somehow it would write itself . . . I never could start out well . . . eventually it changes . . . I have no interest in it . . . I don't think about it . . . I'm

the worst I ever was. It's a habit . . . I have no interest in it.

During the first fifteen minutes of this hour, I was almost entirely silent, trying to hear, naïvely and simply,
what he was doing in these communications. What does
he want? What is he after this morning? Is he asking for
help, as was the case in the similar hour five months
ago? When I heard his lackadaisical tone, I did not
think so. We cannot conclude that he wishes help with
the problem of writing in the face of all these remarks,
"I'm not interested in it," and "Somehow it would write
itself." Nevertheless, he is very upset; this is obvious
and genuine. Does he want some magical intervention
to do it for him? There is certainly an element of this
in Preston's style of life: the first dream he had reported
in the analysis, which had come in the second week, was
of his being in a hospital and being given a truth serum.
At first it didn't work; then he felt dizzy, and he and
the attendant believed it was working; but he then, at
the end of the dream, was afraid that "what would come
out would not be what they wanted to hear." I believed
there was an element of this present today, and that he
needed to make himself "dizzy" in a masochistic way to
"receive the magic." But I did not think this was the
main thing going on. Besides, there is that arresting
sentence in the early dream—that he was afraid what
would come out would not be what they wanted to hear.
This is a striking way of saying that the magic is not
the issue, but "what would come out"—his concealed attitude and feelings toward the "they" (including centrally me, the giver of the serum in the dream). This is his
intentionality, as we have been using the term here. And
the fact that this came up in a dream, and, therefore,
under less conscious distortion, made me take it with
special concern.

As I was trying to hear what was going on today, I
then recalled his manner of walking in and throwing
himself on the couch at the beginning of the hour. I had
picked up the feeling, without my being consciously
aware of it at that time, that he seemed to be angry.
This was now supported by his way of talking, his mouth
mostly closed, emitting words between clenched teeth.

My hypothesis, accordingly, was that what was going on was anger, or more specifically, rage at me.

Should I interpret to him what I sensed? If I had, he probably would have nodded his head, agreed, and nothing would have happened, except that he would retreat a little more solidly behind his stockade, possibly showing some half-covert irritation. Or he would say that I was simply wrong, and again we'd be at the same point. If the intentionality is anger or is in other ways negative, rational discussion is ruled out by definition. We cannot draw out intentionality by a verbal interpretation as such. Preston makes the point more than clear for us by that marvelous symbol, "I'm a self-seal tire." Whatever prick he is given will affect him no more than it would such a tire, and he will be sealed right up again.

I must, rather, make him *experience* his anger with me, get him to live out with me what he is doing. It is arrogant for me, as therapist, to think that the patient goes through all these writhings and sufferings just for my benefit: but I happen to be the other person in the room with him at the moment, the personal embodiment of his interpersonal world. Thus I am the one the intentionality is directed toward, played out with, regardless of all the genetic transference elements in it. I am with him here both as a real person in my own right and as a representative of the world of persons in relation to whom he can experience and live out his conflicts in his *intra* and *inter*personal world.

After the first quarter of an hour, the following exchanges then took place between us.

THERAPIST. What you've been doing since the beginning of the hour is to tell me it will write itself . . . you have nothing to do with it . . . you dump it in my lap . . . you ask me even whether to talk about it . . . you're outside it . . . nothing you can do about it.

PRESTON. [*Pause*] It's something I can't control . . . A major part of my life has no center . . . my own center doesn't function. Sure I put it outside, nothing I can say . . . [*Getting more heated when I don't pick this up*] I can't change it.

I felt this reference to "no center in his life," which

could well have come out of some of my own writing
which he had read, was bait to hook me into a discussion with him. I responded merely, "Yup."

PRESTON. I can't . . . It's not willful—or strategic. How,
how! . . . I sat at my typewriter and I worked . . .
I tried and I tried . . . God damn it. What in hell am
I supposed to do? . . . The piece is not anything hard
. . . I worked—the material didn't frighten me . . .
it wasn't dull—nothing much . . . Knew what I had to
say . . . knew my language . . . I knew what my
judgments were . . . I sat at the typewriter, nothing
came, nothing, nothing, nothing! I had a pile this high
of paper—all variations over and over of the same
words. . . . *Now!* [*Shouts*] What in hell am I supposed to do?

THERAPIST. You're asking me, aren't you?

PRESTON. Sure!

THERAPIST. You're asking me—that in itself puts it outside you. [*Pause*]

PRESTON. Awright, right now . . . I feel very, very irritated . . . Oh, boy! . . . I don't feel like saying anything . . . I feel trapped right now . . . I feel like
killing somebody . . .

THERAPIST. You're furious.

PRESTON. I know I am.

THERAPIST. Furious at me.

PRESTON. Yeah, that's true.

THERAPIST. You said a few minutes ago the reason you
can't do it is you have no will. But the reason you
have no will is you put yourself always outside it.
You have nothing to do with it, it'll write itself. If
there's no man at the typewriter, who's going to write
it?

PRESTON. I have no will to put myself inside it. Consciously I do, but will is all unconscious anyway. Night
before last, I *consciously* wanted to screw this girl.
[*He refers here to an incident when he was impotent
two nights before.*]

THERAPIST. What you told me in the session yesterday
was exactly that you *didn't* want to screw her.

PRESTON. Well, I mean I thought I wanted to . . . Or

I *ought* to want to—Oh, God, I don't know! [*On the theory that the best defense is a good offense, he shifts his tactics.*] Since last fall, I haven't changed one bit. I'm just as bad as I ever was—as bad as when I came to you.

What I want to do by bringing out that he is "dumping it in my lap" will be obvious to the reader: I am making him confront his fiction that "it will write itself," he "has nothing to do with it." I am spotlighting his *intentions* in order to make him experience the conflict between those and his *intentionality.* He came this morning assumedly with the intention of getting help with the problem of his writing block. But we saw at the very beginning of the hour the clear contradiction between his lackadaisical attitude and tone of voice and the fact that he is really suffering and up against a serious problem. These two themes are contradictory on the level of intention; but they must have some unity and be both encompassed in whatever is his intentionality. This whole part of the hour can be seen as this conflict between intention and intentionality coming into the open and inescapably experienced with whatever affect goes along with it (in this case, rage). When I say, "If there's no man at the typewriter, who's going to write it?" the obvious answer from him would be, "You, May, will write it for me" (cause it magically to be written). But when this is drawn into the open, it is so patently absurd that he doesn't say it. When the conflict does come out clearly, Preston then utters that fascinating statement about will. If I had discussed this with him, what would have turned out would be useless intellectualization and we'd miss the point: but if we take it in the context, we find him beautifully stating the contradiction between what he thought he wanted consciously (intention) and his "underlying will" (intentionality). Intelligent persons like Preston, in the heat of affect in psychoanalysis, often utter quite amazing insights without any realization of the import of what they are saying. I think his sentence, "Will is all unconscious anyway" is such a statement.

If the reader accuses me of "trapping" the man, I would answer, Yes, that's exactly what I am trying to do

—or, more accurately, trapping the conflict, and thus forcing it into the open. If my hypothesis is wrong—that is, if I misread what was going on and it was not anger at me—these sentences would simply fall like seeds on stone: he would not react. Or he would simply tell me that I'm wrong and perhaps then point out what was going on; or he might react with greater despair and hopelessness. If the therapist is wrong about the intentionality, the upshot is that the therapeutic exchanges simply don't work.

When this patient experiences the full impact of the conflict in consciousness, he turns in an accusing rage on me—I haven't helped him at all; he's just as bad as when he came to me. This rage is certainly to be expected: we see it in prototype in Oedipus' rage at Tiresias, when Tiresias was the voice by which Oedipus' conflict came into full consciousness.

The tapescript goes on from that last interchange:

THERAPIST. Well, one thing is clear today, you're angry at me. Let it come.

PRESTON. That's not it. Well, maybe it is . . . God damn it anyway. What the hell! I'm through, I'm finished. I'm washed out. I can't do it. I'm just hanging on to this job by a thread. I'll lose this job. I won't be able to pay you. I'll tell them, "I couldn't do your piece, I'm neurotic." They'll be happy with that. So off I go, back to the intellectual salt mines.

THERAPIST. Well, that'll give you a great deal of revenge on me, won't it? You'll go to hell . . . be a bum . . . can't do a thing . . . can't pay me.

PRESTON. Well I didn't mean it that way. It's not true, anything I say is not true, that's why it's so damn frustrating . . .

THERAPIST. One thing that is true today, you're angry at me. You've been angry since you came in at the beginning of the hour. What makes you not write, makes you tense, is your anger.

PRESTON. *Why* am I angry? *What* am I angry at? *What* does it mean, I'm angry? *What's* the sense in being angry? . . . I'll not talk.

THERAPIST. It has nothing to do with all these why's and what's. The hell with that. You'll not talk, that's an excellent way to tie my hands. It's your way of being angry, to tie my hands.

PRESTON. So I tell you. Big deal! So what then?

THERAPIST. What do you want me to do?

PRESTON. I don't know. My feeling of anger, when I think about it, it goes.

After this rage experienced in the encounter with me, my statement, "What do you want me to do?" is, I think, very important. It is one of those questions—"What do you wish from me today?" or the slightly more shocking one, "Why did you come today?"—which I often ask, and not infrequently when the patient directs a hostile question at me. It is a direct way of bringing out his intentionality. If I had tried to do this before he fully experienced his rage, he would have sloughed it off with a platitude: isn't it obvious that he wants me to help him with his writing block? But now that the question cannot be avoided, *the first real despair of the hour* emerges.

PRESTON. I can't help it because I start thinking . . . I can't . . .

At this point of despair, I make a summary interpretation.

THERAPIST. You tell me you can't do anything about writing. You tell me you're angry, but can't tell me anything about that because you're thinking. Well, one thing you *can* do is tell me your feelings. Yesterday, you spent most of the hour telling me you have to remain sick. When you told me what happened in your writing, what you say is exactly that you did not try —you got up to get a drink every five minutes or God knows what. What I hear today is not "I can't" but over and over again the shout, "I won't." I don't mean you can change this by an act of will—for God's sake; if it were so easy why are we here? But behind your "can't" is an angry, stubborn battle. A battle going on with me today. Also going on with your father. What you told me a few minutes ago is exactly what would have infuriated your father most of all. You'd lose your job, have no money, go to hell, be a bum.

His tone of voice. which of course isn't conveyed in the type, is entirely different in the next response from the lackadaisical, do-my-bidding-god-damn-you tone of the first part of the hour. He speaks now with an open mouth and with earnestness, wanting to communicate.

PRESTON. I told you I was the same as when I came here. No, I'm a lot changed. It looks like I'm the same. Why? Because the conflict is a lot more dangerous. The edge is sharper . . . I see it now and I didn't then. What's come out is, I must have you seeing me as sick. Exactly when I got angry is when you refused to believe I couldn't change . . . Oh . . . oh . . . so sick, sick [*In tone of mocking himself*]. You didn't say a word . . . You had to take me as sick. It was as though you were saying, "It's all bullshit." . . . You were believing I could do it. I wanted you to believe I couldn't. I don't want to do it. No satisfaction in doing well. Satisfaction comes from being sick. I'm a martyr!

THERAPIST. Exactly.

PRESTON. I'm a martyr, I'm noble, sensitive, I can't do it. That's a tragedy. What I was saying yesterday, I must be impotent—that's the martyr to girls—impotent . . . Now I'm in a situation where it doesn't work. Why I need to be sick. Why I need to show I can't live. I'll die if I'm a success. I'll die if I am healthy. They can't turn me out, can't abandon me. "How could you do this to a sick person?" If I am self-sufficient, well, you'd turn me out. "Get out of my room, get out of this house!" I'd be abandoned . . . I didn't belong in the world.

THERAPIST. At least it's clear, you abandon yourself—you treat yourself as if you don't belong in the world. That's just what you did in your writing today. If you came here and said, "I worked hard, I did it," what's special to that? But if you say, "I can't do a damn thing," that's the *real* tragedy.

PRESTON. That's why I am so enraged when you don't accept "I can't." I was angry. I'm not angry now. I was. I was so angry I couldn't talk. I kept my mouth closed like this. What could be clearer?

THERAPIST. Yes, you were enraged at exactly the point where I wouldn't go along with "I can't."

This illustrates what was said in the previous chapter, that the therapist takes the patient in terms of the "I can" behind his "I can't." I don't imply, of course, that our verbalizing to the patient the "I can" side is going to help, or even that we necessarily should verbalize it; it may take a long time before the "I can" is a practical possibility and can be realized by him. My point is that the patient can discuss and talk about the "I can't" from now till doomsday without the talk being viable at all, or having power to change him or even to give him emotional relief, unless the "I can" is part of the polarity. It is the "I can" that makes talking about the "I can't" dynamic, makes it hurt, and draws upon some motivation to change. Otherwise "I can't" is resignation, and may have, at first, a kind of bittersweet, nostalgic, and romantically cynical satisfaction, but soon becomes merely empty and mocking.

When the patient is genuinely helpless and despairing, I would not challenge him in this way, for obvious reasons—the chief one being that he would not need it. What is important here is that the "I can't write" is used by Preston as a strategy to crack the whip over my head. It is a cover for the real "I can't," which is not "I can't write," but "I can't afford to get well, or I'll be turned out, abandoned, unloved," as he later puts it. It *is* a serious threat to patients when you believe in their "I can," even though you don't do this at all exhortatively or moralistically, but simply as a realistic belief stemming from knowledge (and some healthy faith) that people do change and grow. The reason it is a threat is not simply that it makes him responsible; it is the more subtle and profound threat that he has no world to which he can orient himself. My not fitting into the world he has continuously built for himself all his life severely shakes his self-world relationship.

Later in the hour he goes on, most of this part of the session crying:

PRESTON. I was trying desperately to say, "I'm sick." And

why? What I forgot to say earlier . . . I first thought
of it when you mentioned my father. Why I should
have left this out! I said that what I was writing had
nothing to do with the block today. It certainly does.
The play was about a father, mother, and son, the son
just back from the war. The son was going out to ruin
after two days' at home, just as I did when I came
back from war. The father was standing, tense. The
son said to the mother, "I'm going out; father never
said he loved me" . . . Then the son thought, maybe
I didn't tell him. Then he said, "Pop, I do love you."
Father is tense, then he breaks down and they embrace.
I pretend I don't want it . . . I want my father to
say, "I love you, you can do it." [*Pause*] I want my
father to put his arm around me and say "I love you.
You're all right. You can work, you really can . . .
You have the right to live." I don't have my father's
sanction. Something more. Mother gave in to me . . .
made over me . . . and there was tension. But father,
no . . . Father only said, "Stay away from girls." Father never let me go out. I want my father to say,
"You can. You can!" He said, "You can't . . . you
won't live."

In the remainder of the session, he brings out the feelings he has had about people loving him only because of
his fame, and his contradictory fear that if he becomes
more famous, he will not be loved. His own inner conflict—the *intra*psychic aspect which comes out when the
interpersonal encounter is engaged—is well expressed in
the following sentence taken from this last part: "I function like a mirror—two persons, one in one direction,
one in the other."

How shall we summarize what is occurring here? There
is first the *conscious intention* of the patient. It was, so
far as he was aware of it, "I find myself blocked in my
task of writing; I feel like hell over being blocked." He
was not aware that the feeling-like-hell is anger and resentment over the fact that he should be up against such
a problem to begin with, but would feel it as a generalized upset with the resulting intent, "I shall make an emer-
gency appeal to get Dr. May to do something about
this."

Then, as I see it, we arrive at his intentionality, his way of relating to me as a whole, which was present when he came in, though on a level of unawareness. It consisted of anger and resentment against me, an aggressive cracking of the whip, which he unwittingly reveals to us in that nice symbol, "I'm a theater director here." It took the form of a struggle to get me to take over, to put the writing on my shoulders, and so on. I liken this to the demands of a small child in bed; the Prince commanding the adults to serve him and being enraged, meanwhile, that his promise (which assumedly he got from his mother) is not fulfilled. The rage which comes out is, on one side, rage that *he* should be in such a block, a humiliating insult added to injury since the Prince should be able to wave his wand, the pen, and turn out great writing. He could not have verbalized what I have just described if I had asked him at the beginning of the hour; yet I would hesitate to call it "unconscious." It was being lived out, present in the language of his bodily movements, spoken symbolically in his way of relating to me. It is the bridge connecting varying levels of awareness and consciousness.

But then something comes out which can properly be called unconscious—the repressed element in his saying that the play he saw the night before had nothing to do with his upset. When I refuse to go along with "I can't," the repressed memory comes out. In my judgment, only after the encounter with me could one break through this repression. He was then able to remember that the play he saw did have a good deal to do with his conflict, and no doubt much to do with why he had the severe block *this* particular morning. ("If I write well and succeed, father won't love me.")

In the last third of the hour, the problems of intrapsychic conflicts appear. His anger has under it a yearning to be loved, the fear of being thrown out and abandoned; the only way one can be loved, especially by women, is by being sick, in need, a failure. These have a great deal to do with genetic factors, his childhood experiences, and so on, which are the proper area of psychoanalysis and which I do not neglect but are not our area of inquiry here. But these realms cannot be reached without the exploration of wish and will—that is to say, without the intentionality first coming into the open.

Some readers may be asking in the course of our discussion of intentionality, What is the difference between this and "acting out" in therapy? And they might press the point with the question, Does not the emphasis on the act as an inseparable part of the intent amount to a recommendation of "acting out"?

"Acting out" is a transmuting of an impulse (or intent) into overt behavior in order to avoid insight. To see the full implications of a desire or intention, to get insight about its meaning, typically upsets one's self-world relationship more and is, therefore, more anxiety-creating and painful than to act out the desire physically, even if one gets rebuffed or hurt in the latter process. At least, if one can keep the whole problem on the level of muscular behavior, one doesn't have to face the more difficult threat to his self-esteem. This is why "acting out" is rightly associated with infantile, psychopathic and sociopathic character types. Acting out occurs not on the level of consciousness, but on the level of "awareness" which, as I shall indicate in the next section, is the capacity that the human being shares with animals, the more primitive developmental level prior to consciousness. In adult patients, acting out is generally an endeavor to discharge the desire or intention without having to transmute it into consciousness. It is not easy to live with intentionality without acting it out; to live in a polarity of intent and act means to live with one's anxiety. Hence, if patients cannot escape into the act, they try to avoid the tension by doing the opposite, by denying the whole intention itself.

The sophisticated patient uses the method—and this seems to me to be the usual method nowadays—of intellectualizing the intention and thereby denying its affect, emasculating and draining off the whole experience. Nowadays, when the patient experiences a hatred for and a desire to kill his father, he generally knows that he does not have to get a gun and do it. But if he then detaches himself from the whole thing by reminding himself, "Everybody gets such thoughts in psychoanalysis; it's simply part of the Oedipus complex," talking about it forever will do no good and will only solidify his defenses against working through whatever real problem he has with his father. What such a patient is doing is precisely taking the *intentionality* out of the experience. He emasculates it so that he really doesn't intend anything, doesn't move toward anything, and discusses a detached idea. Detachment and psychopathic acting out are the two opposite ways to escape confronting the impact of one's intentionality, the former being the method of the intellectualizing, compulsive-obsessional type, and the latter being the method of the infantile, psychopathic type.

What we want the patient to do is to genuinely experience the implications and meaning of his intention; and "to experience" includes the act but defined *in the structure of consciousness* and not physically. When we emphasize that the intention has its act within the structure of consciousness, two things are implied: one, that the act must be felt, experienced, and accepted as part of *me* along with its social implications; and two, that I am thereby freed from the need to act it out physically. Whether or not I do act it out behaviorally in the world is a problem on a different plane. If I have faced my intentionality, I can hope to make the decision in the outside world.

Psychoanalysis ought to be the place par excellence of experiencing intentions and their implied actions and meaning—the "playground of intentionality," to borrow Freud's phrase about transference—without the patient's having to transform this into overt behavior. To be sure, therapists are taking some risk that harmful acting out may occur since whenever the patient genuinely experiences something, there is risk. But when the patient gets emotionally upset at becoming conscious of his desire to kill his father, the affect can and ought to be used in the service of *changing his relationship to his father*. Such hatred and desire to kill, when present in adult life, generally turn out, in my experience, to be expressions of dependency on the father. The normal, constructive outcome is that through insight into the meaning of the experience as well as abreacting the affect, he will "kill" his own excessive tie to his father and thereby gain greater emotional independence. This illustration, no doubt, sounds oversimplified, but I hope it shows the distinction between experiencing the intention and its implications in consciousness, and psychopathic acting out. Both the psychopathic and the detached types are struggling to escape confronting the meaning of their intentionality. The whole import of what we have been trying to do in these chapters on intentionality is to restore and make central this meaning of the act. Thus, the concern with intentionality can be the genuine undermining of acting out in psychoanalysis.

Another point needs to be made here. Intentionality is based upon a meaning-matrix which patient and therapist share. Every person, sane or insane, lives in a meaning-matrix which he, to some extent, makes—i.e., it is individual—but he makes it within the shared situation of human history and language. This is why language is so important: it is the milieu within which we find and form our meaning-matrix, a milieu which we share with our fellow human beings. "Language is every man's spiritual root," says Binswanger. By the same token, we state that history is every man's cultural body. The meaning-matrix comes before any discussion, scientific or other, since it is what makes discussion—as in psychotherapy—possible. We can never understand the meaning-matrix of a patient, or anyone for that matter, by standing purely objectively outside it. I must be able to participate in my patient's meanings but preserve my own meaning-matrix at the same time, and thus unavoidably, and rightfully, interpret for him what he is doing—and often doing to me. The same thing holds true in all other human relationships as well: friendship and love require that we participate in the meaning-matrix of the other but without surrendering our own. This is the way human consciousness understands, grows, changes, becomes clarified and meaningful.

STAGES IN THERAPY

The process of therapy with individual patients involves bringing together the three dimensions of wish, will, and decision. As the patient moves from one dimension to the next in his integration, the previous dimension is incorporated and remains present in the one that follows. Intentionality is present on all three dimensions.

We discussed wish, will, and decision earlier in this book. It is now significant that we return to them after our discussion of intentionality. For intentionality is essential for the complete understanding of wish, will, and decision. We shall now show more fully the meaning of our problem by describing practical therapy on all three levels.

The first dimension, *wish*, occurs on the level of *awareness*, the dimension which the human organism shares with animals. The experiencing of infantile wishes, bodily needs and desires, sexuality and hunger, and the whole gamut of infinite and inexhaustible wishes which occur in any individual is a central part of practically all of psychotherapy from that of Rogers on one hand to the most classical Freudian on the other. For the human being, experiencing these wishes may involve dramatic and sometimes traumatic anxiety and upheaval as the repressions which led to the blocking off of the awareness in the first place are brought out into the open. On the significance and necessity of unmasking repression—dynamic aspects which are beyond the scope of our present discussion—various kinds of therapy differ radically; but I cannot conceive of any form of *psychotherapy* which does not accord the process of awareness a central place. The conditioning therapies, of Wolpe and Skinner for example, do not aim to bring out these aspects of awareness. I would not call them psychotherapy, however, but rather what their name implies, *behavior* therapy—reconditioning, re-education, retraining of habit patterns.

The experiencing of wishes may come out in the simplest forms—the desire to fondle or be fondled, the wishes associated originally with nursing and closeness to mother and family members in early experience. In adult experience, wishes may vary from sexual intimacy to the touch of the hand of a friend or the simple pleasure of wind and water against one's skin; and it goes all the way up to the sophisticated but naïve experiences which may come in a dazzling instant when one is standing near a clump of blooming forsythia and is suddenly struck by how brilliantly blue the sky looks when seen beyond the sea of yellow flowers. This immediate awareness of the world continues throughout life at a hopefully accelerating pace, and is infinitely more varied and rich

than one would gather from most psychological discussions.

This growing awareness of one's body, wishes, and desires—processes which are obviously related to the experiencing of identity—normally also bring heightened
appreciation of one's self as a being and a heightened
reverence for being itself. It is at this point that the
eastern philosophies, like Zen Buddhism, have much to
teach us.

Let us glance again at the case of Helen, the patient
we described in our chapter on wish and will, who used
"where-there's-a-will-there's-a-way" as a reaction-forma-
tion against her powerful yearning to be encircled in her
mother's arms. We noted that this yearning seemed to
originate in her first two years of infancy when her depressed mother had been taken away to a mental hospital. At the beginning of therapy, Helen was not aware
that she had these wishes for her mother's love and tenderness and for being enclosed in fondling arms (though
she got it promiscuously from the various men she slept
with). She was aware only of generalized depression,
sadness, and grief under the hurried, driven surface of
her life. Her emerging awareness and acceptance of these
infancy wishes, her experiencing them in the therapeutic
hours, brought out some overt anger, a good deal of resentment, helplessness, and feeling ashamed of her "weakness," accentuated passivity for a time, alternating with
rage, and so on, down the line. I mention these things to
show that bringing to awareness these important, long-
denied wishes is not at all easy, not at all a childish
game of wishing. It is typically traumatic and can be
highly upsetting. Hence, we find the regression that often
occurs in psychoanalysis. Nor do we bring into consciousness these wishes merely for the sake of "letting off
steam," or "getting the affect out"—though I think the
genuine experiencing of the affects is essential, along with
the inevitably attending sadness, grief, and mourning for
the lost past. But the fact, more significant than the sheer
affect-release, is that the wishes point to a meaning. Hel-
en began to discover the relation between her frustrated
love for her mother and what she wanted to get from
the endless line of boy friends; her use of sex and intimacy as oral gratification; and her defiant, competitive

needs. ("If mother and father won't give me love, I'll show them how I can get it!") And this, in accordance with the usual development of rage and resentment in a neurosis, will be a way which, among other things, will make the parents very angry.

There is, however, a further stage that is not infrequent in our culture: a more *structuralized* form of the above, in which the patient has developed the goal of "not wanting," a kind of cynical or despairing aim of not wishing for anything. In my experience, this goes with obsessional, compulsive personality types. The person lives by the formula "It is better not to want," "To want exposes me," "To wish makes me vulnerable," "If I never wish, I'll never be weak." Our culture plays up to this in a curious, backhanded way. On one hand, the society seems to promise that all our wishes will be granted—avalanches of advertising guarantee to make one a blonde or redhead overnight and have one out of her stenographer's chair and on a jet bound for Nassau by the weekend. The Horatio Alger myth has long since been destroyed, but not the myth that all things will be given to us. But there also seems to be in our culture a curious cautiousness—"You'll get these abundant gratifications only if you don't *feel* too much, don't let on you want too much." The result is that, instead of conquering the world like Alger, we should wait passively until the genie of technology—which we don't push or influence, only *await*—brings us our appointed gratifications. All of this is a part of the rewards which go with belief in the vast myth of the machine in the twentieth century.

However one may interpret this culturally, the upshot is the same: people carry within them a great number of wishes to which they react passively and which they hide. Stoicism, in our day, is not strength to overcome wishes, but to hide them. To a patient who, let us say, is interminably rationalizing and justifying this and that, balancing one thing against another as though life were a tremendous market place where all the business is done on paper and tickertape and there are never any *goods,* I sometimes have the inclination in psychotherapy to shout out, "Don't you ever *want* anything?" But I don't cry out, for it is not difficult to see that on some level the patient does want a good deal; the trouble is he has formulated and reformulated it, until it is the "rattling of dry bones," as Eliot puts it. Tendencies have become endemic in our culture for our denial of wishes to be rationalized and accepted with the belief that this denial of the wish will result in its being fulfilled. And whether the reader would disagree with me on this or that detail, our psychological problem is the same: it is necessary for us to help the patient achieve some emotional viability and honesty by bringing out his wishes and his capacity to wish. This is not the end of therapy but it is an essential starting point.

We note that the *body* is particularly important in wishing. A number of times the word has come up as we discussed this dimension—wishing for fondling of the body, awareness chiefly as a bodily enterprise, and so on. The body is important in this stage of therapy as a language. Wishes, and the intentionality underlying wishing, are expressed in subtle gesture, ways of talking and walking, leaning toward or away from the therapist—all of which comprise a language that, because it is unconscious, is more accurate and honest than what the patient consciously articulates. This is the general reason the body needs to be accepted, aye exulted in, lusted in, loved, and respected. Conflicts will emerge as the "bodily armor" is undermined, in Wilhelm Reich's phrase; they will always be there as part of bodily expression. But conflicts can be met constructively, while nothing at all will occur positively if the body remains walled off.

FROM WISH TO WILL

The second dimension is the transmuting of awareness into self-consciousness. This is correlated with the distinctive form of awareness in human beings—consciousness. The term *consciousness,* coming etymologically from *con* and *scire,* means "knowing with." Strictly speaking, self-consciousness, in the normal sense in which we are using the term here, is a redundancy; consciousness itself includes my awareness of my role in it. On this level, the patient experiences I-am-the-one-who-has-these-wishes. This is the dimension of accepting one's self as having a world. If I experience the fact that my wishes are not simply blind pushes toward someone or something, that *I* am the one who stands in this world where touch, nourishment, sexual pleasure, and relatedness may be possible between me and other persons, I can begin to see how I may do something about these wishes. This gives me the possibility of *in-sight*, or "inward sight," of seeing the world and other people in relation to myself. Thus, the previous bind of repressing wishes because I cannot stand the lack of their gratification on one hand, or being compulsively pushed to their blind gratification on the other, is replaced by the fact that I myself am involved in these relationships of pleasure, love, beauty, trust. I then have the possibility of changing my own behavior to make them more possible.

The generic term for self-conscious intentions is for our use, will. This term reflects the active flavor and self-assertiveness of such intentional acts.

On this dimension, *will* enters the picture not as a denial of wish but as an incorporation of wish on a higher level of consciousness. The experiencing of the blue of the sky behind forsythia blossoms on the simple level of awareness and wish may bring delight and the desire to continue or renew the experience; but the realization that I am the person who lives in a world in which flowers are yellow and the sky so brilliant, and that I can even increase my pleasure by sharing this experience with a friend, has profound implications for life, love, death, and the other ultimate problems of human existence. As Tennyson remarks when he looks at the flower in the crannied wall, ". . . I could understand what God and man is." This is the dimension on which human creativity emerges. The human being does not stop with the naïve delight, but he paints a picture, or he writes a poem, which he hopes will communicate something of his experience to his fellowmen.

WISH AND WILL TO DECISION

The third dimension in the process of therapy is that of *decision* and *responsibility*. I use these two terms together, with some redundancy, to distinguish them both from will. Responsibility involves being responsive to, *respond-*

ing. Just as consciousness is the distinctively human form
of awareness, so decision and responsibility are the distinctive forms of consciousness in the human being who
is moving toward self-realization, integration, maturity.
Again, this dimension is not achieved by denying wishes
and self-assertive will but incorporates and keeps present
the previous two dimensions. *Decision,* in our sense, creates out of the two previous dimensions a pattern of acting and living which is empowered and enriched by
wishes, asserted by will, and is responsive to and responsible for the significant other-persons who are important
to one's self in the realizing of the long-term goals. If
the point were not self-evident, it could be demonstrated
along the lines of Sullivan's interpersonal theory of psychiatry, Buber's philosophy, and other viewpoints. They
all point out that wish, will, and decision occur within
a nexus of relationships upon which the individual depends not only for his fulfillment but for his very existence. This sounds like an ethical statement and *is.* For
ethics have their psychological base in the capacities of
the human being to transcend the concrete situation of
the immediate self-oriented desire and to live in the dimensions of past and future, and in terms of the welfare
of the persons and groups upon whom his own fulfillment
intimately depends.

Professor Ernest Keen formulates this, my third dimension of decision, as follows:

> Emerging out of my self consciousness is my
> experience of myself as a "valuing self" and a "be-
> coming self." The terms here have to be less precise
> perhaps because this experience is more highly indi-
> viduated. This "emerging" involves an integration or
> synthesis of my bodily awareness and my self con-
> sciousness, or, one might say, of my wish and my
> will. Reserving an additional level for the wholistic
> functioning of a person's Being in intercourse with
> the world reflects not only the dialectical nature of
> "decision" but also the important insight that intend-
> ing with one's whole being is more than the sum of
> the parts of wishing and willing. A "decision" is nei-
> ther a wish nor an act of will, nor an additive com-
> bination of the two. Wishing for something against

my will is like being tempted to steal the candy bar; willing something against my wish is like denying that I like candy; deciding something is like putting myself on record (to myself) that I shall (or shall not) endeavor to get it. Hence making a decision is a commitment. It always involves the risk of failure, and it is an act that my whole Being is involved in.[2]

HUMAN FREEDOM

Our final question is the relation of man's will to his freedom. William James was entirely correct in pointing out that this is an ethical, not a psychological, question. But the question, as James also saw, cannot be avoided. Some answer is always presupposed in everyone's life and work, and it is only the mark of honesty to make this clear.

The impact of Freud and the new psychology has been to vastly increase the sphere of determinism or necessity. We see as never before how much we are creatures of conditioning and how much we are driven and molded by our unconscious processes. If our freedom is only to choose in the areas which are left over, the negative space that remains when determinism has taken over the rest, we are lost indeed. Freedom and choice shrink and become only the crumbs from the table thrown to us temporarily until new determinisms are discovered. Man's will and freedom then become childish absurdities.

But this is a naïve and primitive view of will and freedom and must be discarded. One thing which is clear since Freud is that the "first freedom," the naïve freedom of the Garden of Eden before the "fall" into consciousness or the infant before the struggle to achieve and enlarge consciousness, is a false freedom. The present struggle with the machine is the same question all over again. If our freedom is what is left over, what the machine *can't* do, the whole issue is lost to start with: we are doomed when, in some future day, a machine can be invented to do it. Freedom can never be dependent upon a suspension of necessity, by God or science or anything else. Freedom can never be an *abnegation of law,* as though our "will" operated only in a temporary margin of relief from determinism. But the planning, the forming, the imagination, the choosing of values, the *intentionality* are the qualities of human freedom.

Freedom and will consist not in the abnegation of determinism but in our *relationship* to it. "Freedom," wrote Spinoza, "is the recognition of necessity."[3] Man is distinguished by his capacity to know that he is determined, and to choose his relationship to what determines him. He can and must, unless he abdicates his consciousness, choose how he will relate to necessity, such as death, old age, limitations of intelligence, and the conditioning inescapable in his own background. Will he accept this necessity, deny it, fight it, affirm it, consent to it? All these words have an element of volition in them. And it should, by now, be clear that man does not simply "stand outside" in his subjectivity, like a critic at the theater, and look at necessity and decide what he thinks of it. His intentionality is already one element in the necessity in which he finds himself. Freedom lies not in our triumphing over objective nature, or in the little space that is left to us in our subjective nature, but in the fact that we are the men who experience both. *In our intentionality, the two are brought together, and in our experiencing both, we already change both.* Intentionality not only makes it possible for us to take a stand vis-à-vis necessity, but requires us to take this stand. This is illustrated ad infinitum in psychotherapy, when the patient argues rigid determinism, generally when he is discouraged or wishes to escape the meaning of his intentions. And the more he is "determined to be a determinist"—the more he argues (which already is intentionality) that he has nothing whatever to do with the fate that is bearing down upon him—the more he is making himself in fact determined.

Nietzsche spoke often of "loving fate." He meant that man can face fate directly, can know it, dare it, fondle it, challenge it, quarrel with it—and love it. And though it is arrogance to say we are the "masters of our fate," we are saved from the need to be the victims of it. We are indeed *co-creators of our fate.*

Psychoanalysis requires that we should not rest with

intentions, or conscious rationalizations, but must push on to intentionality. Our consciousness can never again be the simple one, based on the belief that because we think something consciously, it is necessarily true. Consciousness is an immediate experience, but its meaning must be mediated by language, science, poetry, religion, and all the other aspects of the bridges of man's symbolism.

We share with William James the perplexity of living in a transitional age, he at the beginning and we, it is hoped, near the end of it. One thing he was clear about: even though a man can never know for certain and even though there are no absolute answers and never will be, man has to act anyway. After the five years in his late twenties and early thirties, when he was paralyzed with his own depression and scarcely able to will the simplest thing, he decided one day that he could make an act of will to believe in freedom. He *willed* freedom, made it his fiat. "The first act of freedom," he writes, "is to choose it." He was convinced afterwards, that this act of will was what enabled him to deal with and transcend his depression. It is at least clear in his biography that at that point, the highly constructive life which continued right up to his death at sixty-eight began for him.

This *fiat* became an integral part of the Jamesian view of will. Among the many sensations greeting us, the many stimuli affecting us, we have the power to throw our weight on this possibility rather than that. We say in effect, "Let *this* be the reality for me." The fiat "Be it so!" is James's leap; it is his statement of commitment.

He knew that in an act of will a man was doing something more than what met the eye; he was creating, forming something which had never existed before. There is risk in such a decision, such a fiat, but it remains our one contribution to the world which is original and underived. I have been critical of James's theory of will in that he omits intentionality, the heart of the problem. But in the *human act* of will, in which every man starts at the beginning and can only say with Socrates in his decision to drink the hemlock, "I do not know, but I believe" and take the leap, James is still great indeed. Since his words ring with the sincerity and power of one who has hammered them out on the anvil of his own suffering and ecstasy, we can do no better than to quote him:

> The huge world that girdles us about puts all sorts
> of questions to us, and tests us in all sorts of ways.
> Some of the tests we meet by actions that are easy,
> and some of the questions we answer in articulately
> formulated words. But the deepest question that is
> ever asked admits of no reply but the dumb turning
> of the will and tightening of our heartstrings as we
> say, *"Yes, I will even have it so!"* . . .
>
> The world thus finds in the heroic man its worthy
> match and mate; and the effort which he is able to
> put forth to hold himself erect and keep his heart
> unshaken is the direct measure of his worth and func-
> tion in the game of human life. He can *stand* this
> Universe. . . . He can still find a zest in it, not by
> "ostrich-like forgetfulness" but by pure inward will-
> ingness to face the world [despite all the] deter-
> rent objects there. . . .
>
> *"Will you or won't you have it so?"* . . . we are
> asked it every hour of the day, and about the largest
> as well as the smallest, the most theoretical as well
> as the most practical things. We answer by *consents
> or non-consents* and not by words. What wonder that
> those dumb responses should seem our deepest organs
> of communication with the nature of things! . . .
> What wonder if the amount which we accord of it
> be the one strictly underived and original contribu-
> tion which we make to the world![4]

PART III

Love and Will

ELEVEN

THE RELATION OF
LOVE AND WILL

> Sexual passion is the cause of war and the end of
> peace, the basis of what is serious, and the aim of the
> jest, the inexhaustible source of wit, the key to all al-
> lusions, and the meaning of all mysterious hints . . .
> just because the profoundest seriousness lies at its
> foundation. . . . But all this agrees with the fact
> that the sexual passion is the kernel of the will to live,
> and consequently the concentration of all desire;
> *therefore in the text I have called the genital organs
> the focus of will.* —SCHOPENHAUER

It is a curious thing that Schopenhauer, old misanthrope
as he is often called by the thin-skinned, should have, in
this section referred to above, called sexual passion the
"kernel of the will to live" and the "genital organs the
focus of will." He here expresses a truth of the relationship of love and will, indeed the interdependence of them
in a way which runs contrary to modern man's conven-
tional understanding. Power—which we can for the moment identify with will—and love, even sexual love, are
considered to be antithetical. I believe that Schopenhauer
was right, that they are not opposites but closely related.

Our discussion of the daimonic has shown that self-affirmation and self-assertion, obvious aspects of will, are
essential to love. We discuss them together in this book
because they are interrelated in ways which are crucial
to the personal lives of all of us, as well as specifically to
psychotherapy.

Both love and will are conjunctive forms of experience. That is, both describe a person reaching out, moving toward the other, seeking to affect him or her or it
—and opening himself so that he may be affected by the
other. Both love and will are ways of molding, forming,

relating to the world and trying to elicit a response from it through the persons whose interest or love we covet. Love and will are interpersonal experiences which bring to bear power to influence others significantly and to be influenced by them.

LOVE AND WILL BLOCKING EACH OTHER

The interrelation of love and will is shown, furthermore, by the fact that each loses its efficacy when it is not kept in right relation to the other; each can block the other. Will can block love. This can be seen particularly in the "will power" of the inner-directed type of man, as he appears in Riesman's studies.[1] This was the man who was often the powerful captain of industry and finance in the early decades of this century and was our link to the great emphasis that was placed on individual will power which characterized the end of the Victorian Age.[2] This was the period in which a man could talk of his "unconquerable soul" and could proclaim, "I am the captain of my fate." But if my soul is really unconquerable, I shall never fully love; for it is the nature of love to conquer all fortresses. And if I must cling to being the master of my fate, I shall never be able to let myself go in passion; for passionate love always has tragic possibilities. Eros, we have seen in an earlier chapter, "breaks the limbs' strength," and "overpowers the intelligence in all its shrewd planning."

An example of will blocking love can be seen in the father of a young student-patient of mine, who was the treasurer of a large corporation. He telephoned me to talk about "maximizing the effectiveness of his son's treatment" exactly as though we were at his company board meetings. When the son became sick with a minor illness in college the father immediately flew to the scene to take charge; the same father became furious when his son held hands and kissed his girl friend on the front lawn of their resort home. At dinner, the father told how he had entered into negotiation to buy the company of a friend of the son's but, having become irritated over the slowness of the negotiations, had called up the would-be partners and told them to "forget the whole thing."

He showed no awareness that he was sending another company into bankruptcy with the snap of his fingers. This father was a public-spirited citizen, the chairman of several committees for civic betterment; and he could not understand why, when he had been treasurer of an international corporation, his subordinates secretly referred to him as the "hardest S.O.B. in Europe." The strong "will power" which the father thought solved all his problems, actually served at the same time to block his sensitivity, to cut off his capacity to *hear* other persons, even, or perhaps *especially*, his own son. It is not surprising that this exceedingly gifted son failed in his college work for several years, went through a beatnik period, and ultimately had a tortuous time permitting himself to succeed in his own profession.

Typical of the inner-directed genre, the father of my patient could always take care *of* others without caring *for* them, could give them his money but not his heart, could *direct* them but could not *listen* to them. This kind of "will power" was a transfer into interpersonal relationships of the same kind of power that had become so effective in manipulating railroad cars, stock transactions, coal mines, and other aspects of the industrial world. The man of will power, manipulating himself, did not permit himself to see why he could not manipulate others in the same way. This identifying of *will with personal manipulation* is the error that sets will in opposition to love.

It is a sound hypothesis, based on a good deal of evidence in psychotherapeutic work, that the unconscious guilt which parents like this carry because they manipulate their children leads them to be overprotective and overpermissive toward the same. These are the children who are given motor cars but not moral values, who pick up sensuality but are not taught sensitivity in life. The parents seem vaguely aware that the values on which their will power was based are no longer efficacious. But they can neither find new values nor give up the manipulative will. And the fathers often seem to act on the assumption that their will therefore has to do for the whole family.

This overemphasis on will, which blocks love, leads sooner or later to a reaction to the opposite error, *love which blocks will*. This is typically seen in the generation made up of the children of parents like the father we described above. The love proposed in our day by the hippie movement seems to be the clearest illustration of this error. "Hippie love is indiscriminate," is a common principle within the movement. Hippie love emphasizes immediacy, sponstaneity, and the emotional honesty of the temporary moment. These aspects of hippie love are not only entirely understandable reactions against the manipulative will of the previous generation, but are values in their own right. The immediacy, spontaneity, and honesty of the relationship experienced in the vital *now* are sound and telling criticisms of contemporary bourgeois love and sex. The hippies' revolt helps destroy the manipulative will power which undermines human personality.

But love also requires enduringness. Love grows in depth by virtue of the lovers experiencing encounters with each other, conflict and growth, all over a period of time. These cannot be omitted from any lasting and viable experience of love. They involve choice and will under whatever names you use. Generalized love, to be sure, is adequate for generalized, group situations; but I am not honored by being loved simply because I belong to the genus "man." The love which is separated from will, or the love which obviates will, is characterized by a passivity which does not incorporate and grow with its own passion; such love tends, therefore, toward dissociation. It ends in something which is not fully personal because it does not fully discriminate. Such distinctions involve willing and choosing, and to choose someone means not to choose someone else. This is overlooked among the hippies; the *immediacy* of love in the hippie development seems to end in a love that is fugitive and ephemeral.

Now spontaneity is a tremendous relief after the assembly-line, sex-on-Saturday-night artificiality of bourgeois love against which the hippies are rebelling. But what of fidelity and the lasting qualities of love? Erotic passion not only requires the capacity to give one's self over to, to let one's self be stimulated by, the power of the immediate experience. But it also requires that one take this event into one's own center, to mold and form one's self and the relationship on the new plane of consciousness which emerges out of the experience. This requires the element of will. Victorian will power lacked the sensitivity and flexibility which goes with love; in the hippie movement in contrast, there is love without the staying power which goes with will. Here we see another important illustration of the fact that love and will are inseparable from each other.

A final indication that the problems of love and will belong together is the similarity in their "solutions." Neither can be adequately dealt with in our day simply by new techniques, patching up the old values, restating old habits in more palatable form, or any other such device. We cannot content ourselves by painting the old building a new color; it is the foundations which are destroyed, and the "resolutions," by whatever name we may call them, require new ones.

What is necessary for "resolutions" is a new consciousness in which the depth and meaning of personal relationships will occupy a central place. Such an embracing consciousness is always required in an age of radical transition. Lacking external guides, we shift our morality inward; there is a new demand upon the individual of personal responsibility. We are required to discover on a deeper level what it means to be human.

IMPOTENCE AS AN EXAMPLE

The problem of sexual potency is especially interesting because it represents the *confluence of will and love.* Impotence is an expression of the fact that the person is trying to make his body do something—perform the sex act—which "it" doesn't want to do. Or, to put it slightly differently, the patient is trying to will his body to love when *he* does not love. We can't will potency; we can't will to love. But we can will to open ourselves, participate in the experience, allow the possibility to become a reality. Impotence is the failure not of intention, but of intentionality. For just as the language of sex is tumescence and erection of the penis in the man and excitement and readiness for intercourse in the woman, so the language of eros is fantasy, imagination, and the heightened sensitivity of the whole organism. And if the deeper but more subtle language of the second falls on deaf ears,

the more direct, insistent, and obvious language of the
body takes over to communicate the message by means
of sexual impotence.

The incident given in the previous chapter, that of
Preston's impotence, may be cited here in greater detail
to give us a picture of the dynamics of impotence as well
as the contrast between eros and sex. During that hour, I
asked Preston what fantasy was going on in his mind
that evening as he was undressing and on the brink of
going to bed with the girl. Understandably, it was difficult
for him to recall it since these images and the feelings
associated with them had to be repressed in the service
of trying to force himself ahead in the act. But, when he
did remember it, the fantasy he related was this: the
woman's vagina was a bear trap; she would take in his
penis, get him to impregnate her, have a baby, and thus
catch him for good. As he went on in telling the fantasy,
it became evident that he had experienced the situation
not only as his getting trapped by the woman and—as
contradictory as it sounds—as being seduced rather than
doing the seducing, but also as an expression of his own
countersadism toward her in that he went ahead in the
act, getting her more excited only to disappoint her. The
impotence, therefore, turns out to be an accurate expression of the denied symbolic meanings occurring in Preston's subconscious fantasies. Such fantasies are not at all
the result of whim, but are the accurate and necessary
expressions of his anxiety, his need to submit to the woman, and his revenge on her.

Fantasy is one expression of imagination. Both fantasy and imagination are capacities by which personal
meaning is given an act. Imagination is the home of intentionality and fantasy one of its languages. I use fantasy here not as meaning something unreal to which we
escape, but in its original meaning of *phantastikous*,
"able to represent," "to make visible." Fantasy is the language of the total self, communicating, offering itself,
trying on for size. It is the language of "I wish/I will"
—the projection in imagination of the self into the situation. And if one cannot do this, *he* will not be present in
the situation, sexual or other, whether his *body* is there
or not. Fantasy assimilates reality and then pushes reality
to a new depth.

IMAGINATION AND TIME

The positive side of the use of fantasy can be seen in other hours of Preston's. We take one example in which he speaks:

PRESTON. I thought about what we'd been talking about, how I ward off all experience, live behind protective walls. Then I made an act of will, saying, "So long as you protect yourself, you will be unhappy. Why can't you let go?" So I did. Then I began to feel Beverly attractive, and sexual relations seemed very enjoyable. But I had no erection yet. I was worried. Then I thought, Do you have to have intercourse every time? No. Then my erection came.

The good sexual relationship they then had was not, of course, the total answer to his problem. The deeper sources of his conflict were shown by what came up in the second half of that therapeutic hour after he said, "I can't afford to deserve Beverly's love." Then, talking about his mother and sister, he cried, "I can't give in to them. I have to get even with them. They'll go to their death. I won't give in." Obviously, this reveals a neurotic problem which has to be resolved. But the first part, the constructive "act of will," must go along with the second. Just as the second, unconscious aspects cannot be ignored, so the first, what he calls the act of will, likewise cannot be ignored. The two poles of the problem move dialectically, each helping the other.

We cannot will love, but we can will to open ourselves to the chance, we can *conceive of the possibility*—which, as patients testify, sets the wheels in motion. This flushes out what keeps us from conceiving of it, the source of the unconscious and repressed difficulties. We can then let our imaginations play on it, dwell on it, turn it over in our minds, focus on it, "invite" the possibility of love in fantasy.

This brings us to the problem of *time*. In cases of impotence we recognize an all too familiar pattern: the impression of being compulsively hurried: "We undressed *immediately*," the patient says, or, "We went to bed *im-*

mediately and I was impotent." In order to make ourselves do something about which we are in significant conflict, we act compulsively, trying to jump into it in order to outwit, or at least to get ahead of, the pursuing, repressed "hounds" of consciousness. "If it were done when 'tis done," as Macbeth classically states in his crucial moment, "then 'twere well it were done quickly" (I, 7). We must hurry in order not to let ourselves know consciously what, on another level, we know that we know. The fact that many people tend not to give themselves *time* to know each other in love affairs is a general symptom of the malaise of our day. We are the age, says John Galbraith referring to the motels along the highways, of "short order sex."

When I said above that we "*fly* to sex in order to avoid eros," the word "fly" can be taken in several senses. Fly means to go in haste: we experience a compulsion, little aware that it is our own anxiety which pushes us. Fly also can be taken as flight from—it would be well if it were done quickly before our fantasies catch up, before the voice of the conflict gets so strident that it takes away our erection and desire to have intercourse with the woman. The haste to engage in sex often serves to short circuit eros.

We arrive now at the fundamental relationship between *eros, time, and imagination.* Eros takes time: time for the significance of the event to sink in, time for the imagination to work, and if not "time to think," at least time to experience and to anticipate. This is why someone in love wants to be alone, wandering here and there by himself, not concentrating or trying to work; he is giving eros time to do its work. This significance of time is one of the characteristics which distinguishes eros from sex. Eros may seem to take effect simultaneously with the first glimpse of the other person (love at first sight is by no means necessarily neurotic or to be relegated to the immature). The suddenly beloved elicits a composite image from our experiences in our past or in our dreams of our future; we spontaneously experience him or her in relation to our personal "style of life" which we form and carry with us all our lives and which becomes clearer the more fully we know ourselves. But it takes time for the integrating process to take place, time for eros to be interwoven with the multitude of memories, hopes, fears, aims, ad infinitum which form the pattern we recognize as ourselves.

UNION OF LOVE AND WILL

Man's task is to unite love and will. They are not united by automatic biological growth but must be part of our conscious development.

In society, will tends to be set against love. For this there is an important genetic history. We have a memory, a "reminiscence" in Plato's sense, of a time when there was a union of ourselves with our mothers in the early experience of nursing at mother's breast. Then we were also at union with the universe, were wedded to it and had the experience of "union with being." This union yielded a satisfaction, calm happiness, self-acceptance, and elation. This is what is relived in meditation of the Zen or Hindu variety and in some drug experiences; it is a union with the universe which is shown in mysticism and produces a mild ecstasy, a blissful feeling that I am completely accepted by the universe. This is the backdrop of human existence implied in every myth of the Garden of Eden, every story of paradise, every "Golden Age"—a perfection which is deeply embedded in man's collective memory. Our needs are met without self-conscious effort on our part, as, biologically, in the early condition of nursing at the mother's breast. This is the "first freedom," the first "yes."[3]

But this first freedom always breaks down. And it does so because of the development of human consciousness. We experience our difference from and conflict with our environment and the fact that we are subjects in a world of objects—and even mother can then become an object. This is the separation between self and world, the split between existence and essence. Mythologically, it is the time when each child re-enacts the "fall" of Adam. This first freedom is inadequate because one cannot remain in it if we are to develop as a human being. And though we experience our separation from it as guilt (in Anaximander's sense of separation from the boundless), we must nevertheless go through with it.[4] But it remains the source of all perfection, the backdrop of all utopias, the perpetual feelings that there ought to be a paradise someplace, and the efforts—forever creative but forever doomed to disappointment—that make us try to recreate a perfect state like the early one in our mother's arms. We cannot—not because of something God does, or some chance accident, or some happenstance that might have been different. We cannot because of the simple development of human consciousness. But nevertheless, we still always seek, as when we write a good paragraph or do a good work of art. We "fall" anew, but we remain ready to arise and pit ourselves anew against our fate.

This is why human will, in its specific form, always begins in a "no." We must stand against the environment, be able to give a negative; this inheres in consciousness. Arieti points out that all will has its source in the capacity to say "no"—a "no" not against the parents (although it shows itself in coming out against them, representatives of the personal authoritative universe as they are). The "no" is a protest against a world we never made, and it is also an assertion of one's self in the endeavor to remold and reform the world. Willing, in this sense, always begins *against* something—which generally can be seen as specifically against the first union with mother. Small wonder that this is done with guilt and anxiety, as in the Garden of Eden, or with conflict, as in normal development. But the child has to go through with it, for it is the unfolding of his own consciousness which prods him. And small wonder that, though he affirms it on one level, on another he regrets it. This is one aspect of the acceptance of the daimonic. During a re-experiencing of this period, one patient dreamt of a "tiger" which he was wont to interpret as his mother. But the therapist, with a wisdom which comes from having a view of the whole, continuously remarked "The tiger is in *you*." He was by this means able to give up fighting it and assimilate it, take it in as part of his own strength, and, as a result, become more affirmative as a person.

Will begins in opposition, begins in a "no" since the "yes" is already there. The danger is that this stage of development will be interpreted negatively by the parents, as shown in their excessive anger or interpretation of the child's original "no" as personally against them;

and thus they may be seen by the child as opposing his development and autonomy. And he may, getting recriminations against choices, be tempted (and, to some extent, even give in to this temptation) to give it up, go back to the "bliss" (which is now a bliss only in quotation marks). This is the hankering, nostalgic and self-defeating, which we see in adult neurotics, to go back to the first union again. But the past cannot be resurrected or ever made real again.

This is why the reuniting of will and love is such an important task and achievement for man. Will must come in to destroy the bliss, to make possible a new level of experience with other persons and the world; to make possible autonomy, freedom in the mature sense, and consequent responsibility. Will comes in to lay the groundwork which makes a relatively mature love possible. No longer seeking to re-establish a state of infancy, the human being, like Orestes, now freely takes responsibility for his choices. Will destroys the first freedom, the original union, not in order to fight the universe forever—even though some of us do stop at that stage. With the first bliss of *physical* union broken, man's task is now the *psychological* one of achieving new relationships which will be characterized by the choice of which woman to love, which groups to devote himself to, and by the conscious building of those affections.

Hence, I speak of the relating of love and will not as a state given us automatically, but as a task; and to the extent it is gained, it is an achievement. It points toward maturity, integration, wholeness. None of these is ever achieved without relation to its opposite; human progress is never one dimensional. But they become touchstones and criteria of our response to life's possibilities.

TWELVE

THE MEANING OF CARE

Only the truly kind man knows how to love and
how to hate. —CONFUCIUS

There is a strange phenomenon about the Vietnam war.
It lies in the fact that the photographs from this war—
the movies for TV, the stills for the newspapers and
magazines—are different from those of any other war.
No more the pictures of victory, no more the planting of
the flag atop a mound as at Iwo Jima, no more the
triumphant marches through the streets. Amid the announcements in this war of the dead and wounded each
day, the counting of bodies because there is nothing else
to count, there comes something else: not a planned effect, or one consciously decided by someone's brain. It
comes from the photographers—those journeymen who
represent the unconscious of all of us, whose *stand* on
the war is irrelevant, who get one picture rather than another due to a stance of the body or a use of muscles,
whose sole concern is human interest. From these photographers come pictures of wounded caring for each other, of soldiers taking care of the injured, of a marine with
his arm around a wounded comrade, the wounded one
crying out in pain and bewilderment. What comes back
in the photos is, on this elemental level, *care.*

In a Vietnamese village, as reported in a recent TV
program, gas bombs had been thrown into holes and
huts to drive out of hiding any remaining Viet Cong.
Only women and children came out of the holes. One
child, about two, routed out with his mother, sat on her
lap looking up at a large Negro marine. The side of the
child's face was dirty with the smoke and soot from the
smoke bomb; he had been crying. He looked up with an
expression of bewilderment, now beyond crying, not

knowing what to make of such a world. But the camera shifted immediately to the black American marine looking down at the child, commanding and somewhat hideous in his battle uniform. He had exactly the same expression: bewilderment, his eyes wide as he stared down at the child, his mouth slightly ajar; but his stare did not move, remaining fixed on that child. What should he make of a world in which he does this? While the announcer of the program rattled on about how the gas is harmful for only ten minutes and then leaves no deleterious effects, the cameraman kept his camera focused on the face of the marine. Was the marine recalling that he too had once been a child in some Southern state, driven from caves and huts where he had been playing, recognizing that he too was of a race held to be "inferior"? That he too was once a child in a world at which he could only look out and up, a world causing pain for reasons no child can begin to fathom? Does he see himself in this child, see his bewilderment as a black child?

I do not think he ponders these things consciously: I think he only sees there another human being with a common base of humanity on which they pause for a moment in the swamps of Vietnam. His look is care. And the cameraman happens to see him—happens almost always now to see them so—and keeps his camera trained on his face; a subconscious reaching-out only for human interest, rendering to us an unconscious expression of the guilt of us all. And while the broadcaster gives in a bland voice the interminable lists of figures of wounded-dead-dead-wounded, the cameraman, anonymous at this moment and forever, representing only an outreach of our own blind and unconscious muscles, our own bodies, keeps his camera pointed at the face of the large black man staring down at the crying child, nameless in the whole sad quicksand of modern war.

This is a simple illustration of care. It is a state composed of the recognition of another, a fellow human being like one's self; of identification of one's self with the pain or joy of the other; of guilt, pity, and the awareness that we all stand on the base of a common humanity from which we all stem.

CARE IN LOVE AND WILL

Care is a state in which something does *matter;* care is the opposite of apathy. Care is the necessary source of eros, the source of human tenderness. Fortunate, indeed, is it that care is born in the same act as the infant. Biologically, if the child were not cared for by its mother, it would scarcely live out the first day. Psychologically, we know, from the researches of Spitz, that the child withdraws to his bed corner, withers away, never developing but remaining in a stupor, if as an infant he does not receive mothering care.

For the Greeks, Eros could not live without passion. Having agreed with that, we can now say Eros cannot live without care. Eros, the daimon, begins *physiologically,* seizing us and whirling us up into its vortex. It requires the necessary addition of care, which becomes the *psychological* side of Eros. Care is given power by nature's sense of pain; if we do not care for ourselves, we are hurt, burned, injured. This is the source of identification: we can feel in our own bodies the pain of the child or the hurt of the adult. But our responsibility is to cease letting care be solely a matter of nerve endings. I do not deny the biological pheonomena, but care must become a conscious psychological fact. *Life* comes from physical survival; but the *good life* comes from what we care about.

For Heidegger, care (*Sorge*) is the source of will. This is why he practically never speaks about will or willing, except when he is refuting other philosophers' positions. For will is not an independent "faculty," or a department of the self, and we always get into trouble when we try to make it a special faculty.[1] It is a function of the whole person. "When fully conceived, the care-structure includes the phenomenon of Selfhood," writes Heidegger.[2] When we do not care, we lose our being; and care is the way back to being. If I care about being, I will shepherd it with some attention paid to its welfare, whereas if I do not care, my being disintegrates. Heidegger "thinks of care as the basic constitutive phenomenon of human existence."[3] It is thus *ontological* in that it constitutes man as man. Will and wish cannot be the basis for care, but rather vice versa: they are founded on care[4] We could not will or wish if we did not care to begin with; and if we do authentically care, we cannot help wishing or willing. Willing is caring made free, says Heidegger[5] —and, I would add, made active. The constancy of the self is guaranteed by care.

Temporality is what makes care possible. The gods on Mount Olympus do not care—we here have our explanation for this fact which every one has patently seen and wondered about. The fact that we are *finite* makes care possible. Care also, in Heidegger's concept, is the source of conscience. "Conscience is the call of Care," and "manifests itself as Care."[6]

Heidegger quotes an ancient parable of care, which Goethe also used at the end of *Faust:*

> "Once when 'Care' was crossing a river, she saw some clay; she thoughtfully took up a piece and began to shape it. While she was meditating on what she had made, Jupiter came by. 'Care' asked him to give it spirit, and this he gladly granted. But when she wanted her name to be bestowed upon it, he forbade this, and demanded that it be given his name instead. While 'Care' and Jupiter were disputing, Earth arose and desired that her own name be conferred on the creature, since she had furnished it with part of her body. They asked Saturn to be their arbiter, and he made the following decision, which seemed a just one: 'Since you, Jupiter, have given its spirit, you shall receive that spirit at its death; and since you, Earth, have given its body, you shall receive its body. But since "Care" first shaped this creature, she shall possess it as long as it lives. And because there is now a dispute among you as to its name, let it be called *"homo,"* for it is made out of *humus* (earth).' "[7]

This fascinating parable illustrates the important point brought out by the arbiter Saturn, Time, that though Man is named *Homo* after the earth, he is still constituted in his human attitudes by Care. She is given charge of him in the parable during his temporal sojourn in this world. This also shows the realization of the three aspects of time: past, future, and present. Earth gets man in the past, Zeus in the future; but since "Care first shaped this creature, she shall possess it as long as it lives," i.e., in the present.

This excursion into ontology makes it clearer why care and will are so closely related, indeed are two aspects of the same experience. It also gives us a distinction between wishing and willing: wishing is like "a mere hankering, as though will stirred in its sleep," as Macquarrie writes, "but did not get beyond the dreaming of action."[8] Will is the full-blown, matured form of wish, and is rooted with ontological necessity in care. In an individual's conscious act, will and care go together, are in that sense identical.

This gives us, indeed *requires* of us, a clear distinction between care and sentimentality. Sentimentality is thinking *about sentiment* rather than genuinely *experiencing* the object of it. Tolstoy tells of the Russian ladies who cry at the theater but are oblivious to their own coachman sitting outside in the freezing cold. Sentimentality glories in the fact that I *have* this emotion; it begins subjectively and ends there. But care is always caring *about* something. We are caught up in our experience of the objective thing or event we care about. In care one must, by involvement with the objective fact, do something about the situation; one must make some decisions. This is where care brings love and will together.

Paul Tillich's term, *concern*—used normally with the adjective "ultimate"—I also take to be a synonym for what we are now discussing. But I prefer for our purposes here the simpler and more direct term, care. I could also use the term *compassion*, which may connote to many readers a more sophisticated form of care. But compassion, a "feeling with" someone, is already an emotion, a passion which may come and go. I choose the term care because it is ontological and refers to a state of being.

Care is important because it is what is missing in our day. What young people are fighting, in revolts on college campuses and in the sweep of protests about the country, is the seeping, creeping conviction that nothing matters; the prevailing feeling that one can't do anything. The threat is apathy, uninvolvement, the grasping for external stimulants. Care is a necessary antidote for this.

As open as the methods of the student revolts are to criticism, they still boil down to a struggle to preserve the "right below rights." The struggle is for the existence of the human being in a world in which everything seems increasingly mechanical, computerized, and ends in Vietnam. The rubric "Do not staple, mutilate, or fold" is, though unknown to the student, an acting out of Heidegger's statement that man is ontologically constituted by care. It is the refusal to accept emptiness though it face one on every side; the dogged insistence on human dignity, though it be violated on every side; and the stubborn assertion of the self to give content to our activities, routine as these activities may be.

Love and will, in the old romantic and ethical sense, are dubious concepts and, indeed, may be both unavailable and unusable in that framework. We cannot support them by the appeal to romance in this day when romance is on the way out, or by the appeal to "ought." Neither of these carry cogency any longer. But there remains the old, bed-rock question, Does something, or some person, *matter* to me? And if not, can I find something or someone that *does* matter?

Care is a particular type of intentionality shown especially in psychotherapy. It means to wish someone well; and if the therapist doesn't experience this within himself, or doesn't have the belief that what happens to the patient matters, woe unto the therapy. The common, original meaning of "intentionality" and "care" lies in the little term "tend," which is both the root of intentionality and the meaning of care. Tend means a tendency, an inclination, a throwing of one's weight on a given side, a movement; and also to mind, to attend, to await, to show solicitude for. In this sense, it is the source of both love and will.

THE MYTHOS OF CARE

I shall now refer to an episode in history very much like our own period, which may help us to understand the myth of care. After the Golden Age of classical Greece, when the myths and symbols gave the citizen an armor against inner conflict and self-doubts, we come down to the third and second centuries B.C. We find ourselves in a world with a radically different psychological mood from the time of Aeschylus and Socrates. On every side we find anxiety, inner doubts, and psychological conflict rampant in the literature. And this world is not unlike our own. As one student of that Hellenistic Age puts it:

> If you woke up one morning to discover that some miracle had transported you to Athens in the early years of the third century B.C., you would find yourself in a social and spiritual atmosphere not altogether unfamiliar. The political ideals of the city-state—liberty, democracy, national self-sufficiency—had lost their appeal in a world dominated by large-scale despotisms and shaken by economic crises and social unrest. The old gods retained their temples and their sacrifices, but had ceased to inspire a living faith. The master minds of the preceding century, Plato and Aristotle, seemed to have no message for the rising generation—no medicine for the prevailing mood of disillusionment, scepticism, and fatalism.[9]

Now and in the period immediately following, the writers are indeed aware of *angst*. Plutarch paints a graphic picture of an anxious man with the telltale symptoms of dread such as palm-sweating and insomnia.[10] Epictetus has one chapter entitled "concerning Anxiety," in which he gives his diagnosis of the state of anxiety and the rules for conquering it. "This man is disordered in the will to get and the will to avoid, he is not in the right way, he is feverish, for nothing else changes the complexion and causes a man to tremble and his teeth to chatter."[1] Lucretius bemoans the fact that anxiety is everywhere—dread of death, dread of the plague, dread of punishments which will occur after death, dread of superhuman spirits. In the midst of his poem *The Nature of the Universe*, he looks up into the heavens, "studded with flashing stars," and "then in hearts already racked by other woes a new anxiety begins to waken and rear up its head. We fall to wondering whether we may not be subject to some unfathomable divine-power, which speeds the shining stars along their various tracks."[12]

This source of anxiety which Lucretius mentions reminds us again of the anxiety nowadays concerning flying saucers, night lights that people fear may be visitations from other planets, gremlins, and so on. Some perceptive psychotherapists, like C. G. Jung, are convinced that modern man's change in relation to space produces much more hidden anxiety in the middle of the twentieth century than is generally admitted.[13]

There is more similarity between our modern age and this anxiety-ridden Hellenistic period than just these projections and hallucinations. Lucretius looked back at this third century and wrote a description which, apart from its poetic style, could be taken out of a contemporary newspaper as a portrait of the Great Society:

> Epicurus saw that, practically speaking, all that was wanted to meet men's vital needs was already at their disposal, and . . . their livelihood was assured. He saw some men in full enjoyment of riches and reputation, dignity and authority, and happy in the fair fame of their children. Yet, for all that, he found aching hearts in every home, racked incessantly by pangs the mind was powerless to assuage and forced to vent themselves in recalcitrant repining.[14]

Lucretius followed this up with an interesting effort at diagnosis. He concluded "that the source of this illness was the container itself." That is, man himself, or man's mind, was at fault. Epicurus believed, and Lucretius followed him with the devotion of a full believer, that if the natural world is explained to people in a completely rational way, they will be freed from their anxiety.

I propose, rather, that the source of this illness was that man had lost his world. The great change that had occurred was the loss of communication with this world, with others, and with himself. That is to say, the myths and symbols had broken down. And the human being, as Epictetus was later to phrase it, "does not know where *in the world* he is."[15]

A number of schools flourished during this Hellenistic period, which included not only the Stoics and Epicureans, but Cynics, Cyreniacs, and Hedonists, together with the traditional Platonists and Aristotelians. What is significant about these diverse schools is that they are no longer endeavors to discover moral reality like the Socratic school, or to construct systems of truth like Platonic and Aristotelian schools. They are rather methods of teaching people how to live in a world filled with psychological and spiritual conflicts. *The teachings of these schools now take on the character of overt psychotherapy, good or bad as it may be.*

Several of the schools saw people's problem centrally as how to control their passions, how to remain above the conflicts of life. The Stoics and Epicureans developed the doctrine of *ataraxia,* an attitude of "unshakability" toward life, a passionless calm attained, especially in the case of the Stoics, by an effort of strong will, and by a refusal to let one's self be touched by the ordinary emotions of grief, hardship, and loss of life. You should assert your mastery over outward events, or, if you could not do that, at least you should be unaffected by them. Great individual strength—*vide* the Roman legionnaire and governor—was often produced by the beliefs and practices of Stoicism.

But it was a strength gained at the price of suppression of all emotions, negative and positive alike. As attempts to give a kind of psychotherapy, the Epicurean and Stoic schools were much the same. "Both schools would have liked to banish the passions from human life," writes Dodds; "the ideal of both was . . . freedom from disturbing emotions, and this was to be achieved in the one case by holding the right opinions about man and God, and in the other by holding no opinions at all."[16]

The Epicureans sought to achieve tranquillity of mind and body by rationally balancing their pleasures, with special value placed on intellectual pleasures. This *seemed* to open the door to a life of gratification and to welcome in the joys of the senses. Epicurus "set bounds to desire and fear," Lucretius tells us, for "he made it clear that, more often than not, it was quite needlessly that mankind stirred up stormy waves of disquietude within their breasts."[17] But whatever the intentions of this control by setting bounds to fear were (which, interestingly enough, meant also setting bounds to desire), this method, in actual practice, led to an emasculation of the person's dynamic urges. One writer of the period even refers to the Epicureans as eunuchs.

The Hedonist tradition emphasized finding pleasure in sensual satisfaction. But these Hedonists were to discover, as Hedonists of other periods including our own were to learn, that sensual satisfaction sought for its own sake turns out to be strangely unsatisfying. One teacher in this school, Hegesias, despairing of ever attaining happiness, became the philosopher of pessimism; and his lectures in Alexandria had to be prohibited by Ptolemy because they resulted in so many suicides. This is the beginning of the time when the teacher or philosopher "conceives his lecture-room as a dispensary for sick-souls."[18]

Now the most impressive of all these endeavors to help man meet his anxiety is Lucretius'. Sensitive to human sufferings and poet that he was, he could not simply steel his feelings to the psychological and spiritual desolation around him. However much he might have yearned for *ataraxia,* his poet's nature did not permit him the detachment and capacity for repression necessary to achieve it. "The fears and anxieties that dog the human breast," he wrote, "do not shrink from the clash of arms or the fierce rain of missiles. They stalk unabashed among princes and potentates. They are not awe-struck by the gleam of gold or the bright sheen of purple robes"[19]

He knows that some of this anxiety is due to the meaninglessness of people's lives. "Men feel plainly enough within their minds a heavy burden, whose weight depresses them. If only they perceived with equal clearness the causes of this depression, the origin of this lump of evil within their breasts, they would not lead such a life as we now see all too commonly—no one knowing what he really wants and everyone forever trying to get away from where he is, as though mere locomotion could throw off the load."[20] Perceptive psychologist as well as poet, Lucretius adds concerning this bored rushing around, "In so doing the individual is really running away from himself." He continues:

> Often the owner of some stately mansion, bored stiff by staying at home, takes his departure, only to return as speedily when he feels himself no better off

out of doors. Off he goes to his country seat, driving his carriage and pair hot-foot, as though in haste to save a house on fire. No sooner has he crossed its doorstep than he starts yawning or retires moodily to sleep and courts oblivion, or else rushes back to re-visit the city.[21]

Lucretius throws himself with religious devotion into explaining the faith he had inherited from his master, Epicurus. He believed the deterministic understanding of the natural universe would cure us of our fears and anx-ieties.

As children in blank darkness tremble and start at everything, so we in broad daylight are oppressed at times by fears as baseless as those horrors which chil-dren imagine coming upon them in the dark. This dread and darkness of the mind cannot be dispelled by the sunbeams, the shining shafts of day, but only by an understanding of the outward form and inner workings of nature.[22]

Lucretius believed that if he could do away with the gods and the myths and help men to be enlightened, empirical, and rationalistic, he would have taken the nec-essary step to free people from their anxiety. Epicurus, seeing about him all the images of gods on coins and in statues, had made the error of many an empiricist, naïve as the error may seem to be, of believing that the gods were actually *objects*. He had cut the Gordian knot by exiling the gods way off to the interspaces between the worlds, safe from contact with the human species (little suspecting we would by now be getting ready to travel to those very spaces!). "For it is essential to the very na-ture of deity that it should enjoy immortal existence in utter tranquillity, aloof and detached from our affairs. It is free from all pain and peril, strong in its own re-sources, exempt from any need of us, indifferent to our merits and immune from anger."[23]

Lucretius goes further than his master and tries to do away with the myths altogether, hoping thus to free peo-ple from the "unfounded fear of the gods."[24] "There is no wretched Tantalus," he proclaims, "as the myth relates. . . . There is no Tityos lying in Hell forever probed by birds of prey. . . . But Tityos is here in our midst—that poor devil prostrated by love, torn indeed by birds of prey, devoured by gnawing jealousy or rent by the fangs of some other passion. Sisyphus too [is not a divine figure but] is alive for all to see, bent on winning the insignia of office. . . . As for Cerberus and the Furies and the pitchy darkness and jaws of Hell belching abominable fumes, these are not and cannot be anywhere at all. . . ."[25] There is no Prometheus anymore. For the "agent by which fire was first brought down to earth and made available to mortal man was lightning."[26]

Thus, he first treats the mythological figures as though his readers believed them to be real objects located in some place (which it is surely impossible to imagine Aeschylus believing). Then he psychologizes them—the myths are merely figurative expressions of subjective processes within each person. He was arguing here what every intelligent man knows—that the myth does indeed have one pole in the subjective dynamics of the individual's experience. But this is only a half-truth. It omits all the vast implications of the myth as man's way of trying to make sense of, and come to terms with, the troublesome fact that he *does* live in a finite universe in which the phenomenon of Sisyphus is objectively present for the normal as well as the morbidly anxious man. It is not merely that every workman toils over and over again at the same job ("and his fate is no less absurd than Sisyphus'," as Camus points out). It is that we are all engaged in eternal going and returning, laboring and resting and laboring again, growing and disintegrating and growing again. The myth of Sisyphus is present in my very heartbeat, in every change in my metabolism. The recognition of the myth as our fate is the beginning of finding meaning in an otherwise meaningless fatalism.[27]

But in his passion to explain away the myths, Lucretius himself is forced to fall into new myth-making. Ironic as this is, it is the fate of all those who engage in "mythoclasm," to borrow Jerome Bruner's phrase; they find themselves, in secret ways, constructing new myths again.[28] Time and again, Lucretius proclaims that if the reader can let himself be convinced of the natural "causes" in life, he will be relieved of his anxiety. And

if one cannot find adequate causes, it is better to assign
fictitious causes! For we cannot relinquish the belief that
"Whatever the senses may perceive at any time is all alike
true."[29] And when perceptions seem deceiving, "it is better, in default of reason, to assign fictitious causes . . .
than to let things clearly apprehended slip from our
grasp. This is to attack belief at its very roots—to tear
up the entire foundation on which the maintenance of
life is built."[30]

. This is the myth of the technological man. It is a set of
assumptions postulating that the human being is governed by what he can rationally understand, that his emotions will follow this understanding, and that his anxiety
and dread will thus be cured. It is a myth with which
we are exceedingly familiar in our day.

Since a myth must always have its aesthetic "form,"
we may think of Lucretius' whole poem as the embodiment of this myth. Lucretius himself is a Promethean figure in his brave defiance of what he felt to be superstition, ignorance, and the religions which play upon fears
and anxiety. The fact that his own myth has inner contradictions and that the very existence of his myth
disproves his thesis, namely, that it is possible to construct
a "myth of life without myths," make him particularly
important for our inquiry.

He is dedicated to the denial of the daimonic and the
irrational. It is ironic, indeed, that his own death is said
to have come from his participating in a magic act: "the
traditional story (immortalized by Tennyson) is that he
died by his own hand after being driven mad by a love
philtre."[31] Whether this is a factual truth or a legend, it
amounts to the same thing—an interpretation by history
of the death which "round[ed] out his life" by the most
irrational and daimonic symbol of all, a love philtre.

Lucretius' endeavor is brave indeed, and on the wings
of his superb poetic art, it seems to move nobly down
the royal road to enlightenment. But when we examine
it more closely, we find the road runs into an abyss, a
sudden void. That is the simple fact of death. Time and
again, Lucretius brings up death in his poem, and he
tries to explain to his readers that if they will accept his
proof that there is no hell in the hereafter and no demons
to burn them or in other ways give them eternal punish-

ment, they will not need to be afraid of death. But these "explanations" of the supposed causes of people's anxiety do not do justice even to Lucretius himself. For he is continually concerned with death because of his own deep human feelings and his own active sympathy for human kind, including himself.

It turns out that this conflict about death, which will not let him go, is like that of most men, not at all a question of locations of a future hell, but has its source in human love and loneliness and grief. The very last pages of his poem are unforgettably vivid pictures of a plague in Athens to which Lucretius returns and show death as close and horrifying as it ever was at the beginning of his poem,

> Lonely funerals were raced without a mourner to the grave. . . . One especially distressing symptom was this: as soon as a man saw himself enmeshed in the malady, he lost heart and lay in despair as though under sentence of death. In expectation of death, he gave up the ghost there and then. . . . The whole nation was beside itself with terror. Each in turn, when he suffered bereavement, put away his own dead as circumstance permitted. . . . Men would fling their own kinsfolk amid violent outcry on the pyres built for others and set torches to them. Often they shed much blood in these disputes rather than abandon their dead.'[32]

These very last lines of the poem—this picture of human beings in the violence of their grief, preferring to "shed [their own] blood . . . rather than abandon their dead," trying vainly to hang on to their loved ones—are the most powerful symbol that man's life transcends all the natural explanations. It is a vivid proof that the meaning of life is in the human emotions of pity, loneliness, and love. We end the poem with the conviction that this is the real evil, horror, and inevitable source of anxiety, which neither Lucretius nor anyone else can deny or negate or mitigate.

But it is a tribute of Lucretius' courage and honesty that he never flinches from the problem of death even though he cannot solve it. According to rational "rules," the end of the poem is exactly the wrong place to put such a description—one should conclude affirmatively! We see that Lucretius is governed not simply by "brain," but by profound human sensibilities; in the end, his poetry triumphs over his dogma. It is the beauty of his art that enables him not to "solve" or evade death, but to face it up to the last minute. The anxiety of death—prototypically the basic souce of all anxiety—still remains. All his life, Lucretius had his own share, and perhaps more than his share, of dreads and anxiety—a fact undoubtedly connected with the sensitivity and grace that made him such a superb poet.

But we cannot stop here. There is a sense in which Lucretius did transcend the problem of death. He transcended it by including in the picture *both love and death*, by reconciling the irreconcilables, uniting the antinomies, as we observe Aeschylus so nobly doing in his *Oresteia*. Lucretius does this by virtue of a new mythos[33] which emerges with particular clarity in the last pages of his poem.

It is not the dogma of his naturalistic explanations, to which we referred earlier, and what he consciously *intended* to get across. My psychoanalytic experience has made me dubious as to whether rational explanations ever quiet anxiety anyway; something else happens, namely, the explanation becomes the vehicle for a more profound mythos that does grasp people on levels deeper than rationality. The explanation, for example, becomes part of the mythos that I, the one doing the explaining, care for you, that you and I can trust and communicate with each other. This implication may be, as it surely is in psychoanalysis, a good deal more important than whether my "explanation" or interpretation is, in itself, entirely accurate or "brilliant" or whatever. I often notice, when I give an interpretation to a patient in a psychoanalytic session, that what impresses him most at the moment is not the theoretical truth or falsehood of what I say, but the fact that my saying it shows my belief that he can change and that his behavior has meaning. These are aspects of a positive myth. The deeper myth in such explanations may be that we can trust the meaning of our interpersonal universe, and that human consciousness can, in principle, be in touch with that meaning.

After reading Lucretius, we arise from our chairs better able to face death and to love. We finish the poem with the conviction that, despite death, there is meaning and nobility in the fact that we can admit together that we are not reconciled to the severing of our love. For our human love is even more precious when seen in the light of those Athenians clinging to the bodies of their loved ones. Together in the poem we affirm our love for each other and our mutual stand against death. The poem has not solved the problem of death at all, but we find ourselves better able to encounter it and less lonely because we encounter it together.

This is an illustration of how the myth carries *intentionality*. The myth is the language by which intentionality is made communicable. The reader will recall our original definition of intentionality; the structure by which experience becomes meaningful. What happens at the end of Lucretius' poem is that we are aware of a meaningful structure in the relationships of our lives to each other and to the universe in which death is an objective fact. We see here an illustration of how *intentionality* is to be clearly distinguished from conscious *intention*, which in Lucretius' case, was to get across certain explanations, many of which turn out to be false and most of which turn out to be irrelevant. But in his total dedication to his task, a deeper dimension, of which he himself is by no means wholly aware, comes into the picture, more important than what he learned from his master Epicurus, more important than his well-thought-out philosophy, even more important than his voluntary intentions. This lies not in what he says, but in the poem in which, as a totality, a gifted man, feeling, intuiting, loving, and willing, as well as thinking and writing, encounters the whole vast range of human experience.

This is the mythos of care. It is a statement which says that whatever happens in the external world, human love and grief, pity and compassion are what matter. These emotions transcend even death.

CARE IN OUR DAY

"In love every man starts from the beginning," wrote Søren Kierkegaard. This beginning is the relationship between people which we term care. Though it goes beyond feeling, it begins there. It is a feeling denoting a relationship of concern, when the other's existence matters to you; a relationship of dedication, taking the ultimate form of being willing to get delight in or, in ultimate terms, to suffer for, the other.

The new basis for care is shown by the interest of psychologists and philosophers in emphasizing *feeling* as the basis of human existence. We now need to establish feeling as a legitimate aspect of our way of relating to reality. When William James says, "Feeling is everything," he means not that there is nothing *more* than feeling, but that everything starts there. Feeling commits one, ties one to the object, and ensures action. But in the decades after James made this "existentialist" statement, feeling became demoted and was disparaged as merely subjective. Reason or, more accurately, technical reason was the guide to the way issues were to be settled. We said "I feel" as a synonym for "I vaguely believe" when we didn't *know*—little realizing that we cannot *know* except as we *feel*.

The development of psychoanalysis has led to a resurgence of the primacy of feeling. And in academic psychology, a number of papers have come out lately which show the drift of psychologists and philosophers toward a new appreciation of feeling. Hadley Cantril's paper, *"Sentio, ergo sum,"* is one, and Sylvan Tomkins' *"Homo patens"* is another. Susan Langer entitles her new book, *Mind, An Essay on Feeling.* And Alfred North Whitehead, Miss Langer's teacher, in pointing out that Descartes was wrong in his principle, *"Cogito, ergo sum,"* goes on:

> It is never bare thought or bare existence that we are aware of. I find myself rather as essentially a unity of emotions, of enjoyment, of hopes, of fears, of regrets, valuations of alternatives, decisions—all of these are my subjective reactions to my environ-

ment as I am active in my nature. My unity which is Descartes' "I am" is my process of shaping this welter of material into a consistent *pattern of feelings.*[34]

I have said that the romantic and ethical basis for love is not available to us any longer. We must seek to start from the beginning, psychologically speaking, with feelings.

To show how simply and directly feeling—care pointing toward love—comes into the therapeutic interivew, I offer the following excerpt from a psychoanalytic hour. This happens to be Preston, about whom I reported in detail in a previous chapter.

PRESTON. I'm a Judas. To my parents, to my sister. To art—I use it just for my own uses . . . I feel bad, discouraged . . . I am sick with lovelessness.

THERAPIST. [*I encouraged him to relax and let his associations come.*]

PRESTON. I'm not real. An impostor. A not me. Literally. I can't believe in myself . . . [*Silence*] . . . I'm stuck . . . Stuck in outside life, stuck with Beverly, stuck like Jiggs, immobilized. Beverly and I had great sex two weeks ago. But suppose she's pregnant—I'm stuck hunting for a new apartment . . . [*Silence*] . . . I shouldn't be talking, this is no good.

THERAPIST. Stick with the being stuck—at least that's real.

PRESTON. [*He agreed. Silence for several minutes. Then he turned around slightly and looked at me from the couch.*] I feel concerned about you. This must be hard, not to know what to do, whether to say something or not. It would be hard for Freud himself.

THERAPIST. [*What impressed me was the tone of voice, very different from his usual jaunty, triumphant sound. After a minute.*] Did I hear a new tone in what you said—a feeling of real sympathy for me rather than triumph?

PRESTON. Yes, it was sympathy. Just you were here with me. Both of us stuck . . . This feels different from the earlier hours.

THERAPIST. This is almost the first time I experienced a genuine human feeling from you . . . In *Waiting for*

Godot [*which he had mentioned earlier*] they feel
something for each other.
PRESTON. Yes, it's very important that they wait together.

This upsurgence of a genuine human feeling of sympathy, simple as it may be, is a critical point in psychotherapy. To appreciate what a step this is, we can see it
against the background of modern drama. Drama gropes
for this fundamental state of feeling. Our situation is that
in our heyday of rationalistic and technicalistic episodes,
we have lost sight of and concern for the human being;
and we must now humbly go back to the simple fact of
care. The critical issue presented by contemporary drama, for example, is the breakdown of communication.
This is the theme of our most serious plays, such as those
by O'Neill, Beckett, Ionesco, and Pinter. The mask is
fully removed and we see apparent emptiness, as in
O'Neill's *The Iceman Cometh.* The nobility of man which
is necessary for tragedy or for any genuine humanism is
felt on the stage as the fact that greatness has fled from
man—which means that it is there as a vacuum; *it is
present as a lack.* This is the paradoxical state of the
meaning of meaninglessness. The apparent vacuum, emptiness, and apathy are the tragic facts.

In *Waiting for Godot,* it is of the essence that Godot
does not come. We wait forever and the problem remains, Was there a tree there yesterday? Will there be
one there tomorrow? Beckett—not to mention the other
dramatists and visual artists—shocks us into the awareness of our human significance, forcing us to look more
deeply into our condition as men. We find ourselves caring despite the apparent meaningless of the situation.
Godot does not come, but in the waiting there is care
and hope. It matters that we wait and that we, like the
characters in the drama, wait in human relationship—we
share with each other the ragged coat, the shoes, the
piece of turnip. Waiting is caring, and caring is hoping.

This is a paradoxical situation which is lucidly grasped
by T. S. Eliot:

I said to my soul, be still, and wait without hope
For hope would be hope for the wrong thing; wait
    without love

For love would be love for the wrong thing; there is
   yet faith
But the faith and the love and the hope are all in the
   waiting,
Wait without thought, for you are not ready for thought:
So the darkness shall be light, and the stillness the
   dancing.[35]

Many of the contemporary dramas, to be sure, are
negations, and some of them tread perilously close to the
edge of nihilism. But it is the nihilism which shocks us
into confronting the void. And for the one who has ears
to hear, there speaks out of this void (the term now refers to a transcendent quality) a deeper and more immediate apprehension of being. It is the mythos of care—
and, I often believe, this mythos alone—which enables
us to stand against the cynicism and apathy which are
the psychological illnesses of our day.

This points toward a new morality not of appearance
and forms, but of authenticity in relationship. That the
vague outlines of such a morality are already upon us is
shown in that segment of the younger generation which
carries this problem as a genuine concern. These people
are not interested in money and success; these things are
now "immoral." They seek an honesty, openness, a gen-
uineness of personal relationship; they are out to find a
genuine feeling, a touch, a look in the eyes, a sharing of
fantasy. The criterion becomes the *intrinsic meaning* and
is to be judged by one's authenticity, doing one's own
thing, and giving in the sense of making one's self available for the other. No wonder there is a suspicion of
words in our day; for these states are determinable only
by immediate feelings.

The error in this new morality is the lack of content
for these values. The content *seems* present; but it turns
out to be based to some extent on whim and temporary
emotion. Where is the permanence? Where is the de-
pendability and lastingness? To these questions we now
turn.

THIRTEEN

COMMUNION OF CONSCIOUSNESS

Let them render grace for grace,
Let love be their common will.
                    —ATHENA, SUMMING UP THE DUTY OF
                    THE ATHENIANS, in the *Oresteia* of
                    Aeschylus.

When we look for answers to the questions we have been
discussing, we find, curiously enough, that every answer
seems to somehow impoverish the problem. Every answer sells us short; it does not do justice to the depth of
the question but transforms it from a dynamic human
concern into a simplistic, lifeless, inert line of words.
Hence, Denis de Rougement says, at the end of his *Love
in the Western World,* that there "probably aren't any answers."

The only way of resolving—in contrast to solving—the
questions is to transform them by means of deeper and
wider dimensions of consciousness. The problems must be
embraced in their full meaning, the antinomies resolved
even with their contradictions. They must be built upon;
and out of this will arise a new level of consciousness.
This is as close as we shall ever get to a resolution; and
it is all we need to get. In psychotherapy, for example,
we do not seek answers as such, or cut-and-dry solutions
to the question—which would leave the patient worse off
than he originally was in his struggling. But we seek to
help him take in, encompass, embrace, and integrate the
problem. With insight, Carl Jung once remarked that the
serious problems of life are never solved, and if it seems
that they have been solved, something important has been
lost.

This is the "message" of all three of the central emphases in this book: eros, the daimonic, and intentionality. As the function of eros, both within us and in the universe itself, is to draw us toward the ideal forms, it elicits in us the capacity to reach out, to let ourselves be grasped, to preform and mold the future. It is the self-conscious capacity to be responsive to what *might* be. The daimonic, that shadowy side which, in modern society, inhabits the underground realms as well as the transcendent realms of eros, demands integration from us on the personal dimension of consciousness. Intentionality is an imaginative attention which underlies our intentions and informs our actions. It is the capacity to participate in knowing or performing the art proleptically—that is, trying it on for size, performing it in imagination. Each of these emphases points toward a deeper dimension in human beings. Each requires a participation from us, an openness, a capacity to give of ourselves and receive into ourselves. And each is an inseparable part of the basis of love and will.

The new age which knocks upon the door is as yet unknown, seen only through beclouded windows. We get only hints of the new continent into which we are galloping: foolhardy are those who attempt to blueprint it, silly those who attempt to forecast it, and absurd those who irresponsibly try to toss it off by saying that the "new man will like his new world just as we like ours." There is plenty of evidence that many people do not like ours and that riots and violence and wars are necessary to force those in power to change it. But whatever the new world will be, we do not choose to back into it. Our human responsibility is to find a plane of consciousness which will be adequate to it and will fill the vast impersonal emptiness of our technology with human meaning.

The urgent need for this consciousness is seen by sensitive persons in all fields and is especially made real by the new consciousness in race relations, where we live if we transcend racial differences and die if we do not. I quote James Baldwin: "If we—and now I mean the relatively conscious whites and the relatively conscious blacks, *who must, like lovers insist on, or create, the consciousness of the others*—do not falter in our duty now, we may be able, handful that we are, to end the racial nightmare, and achieve our country, and change the history of the world. If we do not now dare everything, the fulfillment of that prophecy, re-created from the Bible in song by a slave, is upon us: 'God gave Noah the rainbow sign. No more water, the fire next time.' "[1]

Love and will are both forms of communion of consciousness. Both are also *affects*—ways of *affecting* others and our world. This play on words is not accidental: for affect, meaning affection or emotion, is the same word as that for *affecting* change. An affect or affection is also the way of making, doing, forming something. Both love and will are ways of creating consciousness in others. To be sure, each may be abused: love may be used as a way of clinging, and will as a way of manipulating others in order to enforce a compliance. Possibly always some traces of clinging love and manipulating will crop up in the behavior of all of us. But the abuse of an affect should not be the basis for its definition. The lack of both love and will ends up in separation, putting a distance between us and the other person; and in the long run, this leads to apathy.

LOVE AS PERSONAL

In the embracing and transformation of the antinomies of love and will, we have discovered that sexual love moves through *drive* to *need* to *desire*. Freud began with sex conceived as a drive, a push from the past, a stored-up set of energies. This concept came largely from the fact that his patients were victims of Victorian repression. But we now know that sexual love can evolve from drive, through primary need, to desire. As a *drive,* sexuality is essentially biological, has the character of force, and is physiologically insistent. *Need* is a less imperative form of drive. So long as a need is repressed, it tends to become a drive. We shall lump the two together here, as *need,* contrasting them both with *desire*.

The need is physiological in origin, but becomes imperious because of the constant stimulation of sexuality all about us. In contrast, the desire is psychological, and arises from human (in a total organismic sense) rather than physiological experience. The first is an economy of scarcity; the second is an economy of abundance. The need pushes us from the rear—we try to get back to something, to protect something, and we are then *driven* by this need. The desire, on the other hand, pulls us ahead to new possibilities. The need is negative, the desire positive. To be sure, if sexual love, or specifically sex, is unrelieved when the person is in a constant state of stimulation over a period of time, it reverts to its earlier status as a compelling need and may then become a drive.

We find, from sources where we would least expect, impressive evidence that even on infrahuman levels, sex is not the primary need we have thought it to be. In Harry Harlow's extensive work with rhesus monkeys, it becomes clear that the monkeys' need for contact, touch, and relationship takes precedence over the "drive" toward sex. The same is true of Masserman's experiments with monkeys, where sex turns out not to be the primary, all-encompassing drive. To be sure, sex *is* a primary need for the race, and its biological survival depends on sex. But as our world becomes less and less bound by the exigencies of that kind of biological survival—indeed *overpopulation* is our threat—and more and more open to the development of human values and choices, we find that this emphasis is not constructive, and that the individual does not depend upon sexuality as a primary need.

Now it is in the shift from drive to desire that we see *human* evolution. We find love as personal. If love were merely a *need*, it would not become personal, and will would not be involved: choices and other aspects of self-conscious freedom would not enter the picture. One would just fulfill the needs. But when sexual love becomes *desire*, will is involved; one chooses the woman, is aware of the act of love, and how it gets its fulfillment is a matter of increasing importance. Love and will are united as a task and an achievement. For human beings, the more powerful need is not for sex per se but for relationship, intimacy, acceptance, and affirmation.

This is where the fact that there are men and women—the polarity of loving—becomes ontologically necessary. The increased personal experience goes along with the increased consciousness; and consciousness is a polarity, an either/or, a saying "yes" to this and "no" to that. This is why, in an earlier chapter, we referred to the negative-positive polarity held in the theories of both Whitehead and Tillich. The paradox of love is that it is the highest degree of awareness of the self as a person and the highest degree of absorption in the other. Pierre Teilhard de Chardin asks, in *The Phenomenon of Man*, "At what moment do lovers come into the most complete possession of *themselves*, if not when they are *lost* in each other?"[2]

The polarity which is shown ontologically in the processes of nature is also shown in the human being. Day fades into night and out of darkness day is born again; yin and yang are inseparable and always present in oscillation; my breath expires and I then inspire again. The systole and diastole of my heartbeat echo this polarity in the universe; it is not mere poetry to say that the beat of the universe, which constitutes its life, is reflected in the beating of the human heart. The continuous rhythm of each moment of existence in the natural universe is reflected in the pulsating blood stream of each human being.

The fact that love is personal is shown in the love act itself. Man is the only creature who makes love *face to face*, who copulates *looking* at his partner. Yes, we can turn our heads or assume other positions for variety's sake, but these are variations on a theme—the theme of making love vis-à-vis each other. This opens the whole front of the person—the breasts, the chest, the stomach, all the parts which are most tender and most vulnerable —to the kindness or the cruelty of the partner. The man can thus see in the eyes of the woman the nuances of delight or awe, the tremulousness or the angst; it is the posture of the ultimate baring of one's self.

This marks the emergence of man as a psychological creature: it is the shift from animal to man. Even monkeys mount from the rear. The consequences of this change are great indeed. It not only stamps the love act as irrevocably *personal*, with all the implications of that fact, one of which being that the lovers can speak if they wish. Another consequence is the accentuation of the experience of intimacy in giving the side of the person closest to "ourselves" in the sexual experience. The two chords of love-making—one's experience of himself and his experience of the partner—are temporarily merged here. We feel our delight and passion and we look into the eyes of the partner also reading there the meaning of the act—and I cannot distinguish between her passion and mine. But the looking is fraught with intensity; it brings a heightened consciousness of relationship. We experience what we are doing—which may be play, or exploitation, or sharing of sensuality, or fucking, or lovemaking, or any form thereof. But at least the norm given by this position is personal. We have to block something off, exert some effort, to make it *not* personal. This is ontology in the psychological area: the capacity for self-relationship constitutes the genus *Homo sapiens*.

The banal word "relating" is lifted to an ontological level in this act which is anything but banal, in which male and female re-enact their counterpart of the age-old cosmic process, each time virginally and with surprise as though it were the first time. When Pythagoras talks of the music of the stars, he refers to a music which has as its obligato the basic act of sexual love.

One result of this personal aspect of sexual love is the variety it gives us. Consider, as an analogy, Mozart's music. In some portions of his music Mozart is engaged in elegant play. In other portions his music comes to us as pure sensuous pleasure, giving us a sheer delight. But in other portions, like the death music at the end of *Don Giovanni* or in his quintets, Mozart is profoundly shaking: we are gripped by fate and the daimonic as the inescapable tragedy rises before us. If Mozart had only the first element, play, he would sooner or later be banal and boring. If he presented only pure sensuality, he would become cloying; or if only the fire and death music, his creations would be too heavy. He is great because he writes on all three dimensions; and he must be listened to on all these levels at once.

Sexual love similarly can not only be play, but probably an element of sheer play should be regularly present. By this token, casual relationships in sex may have their gratification or meaning in the sharing of pleasure and tenderness. But if one's whole pattern and attitude toward sex is only casual, then sooner or later the playing itself becomes boring. The same is true of sensuality, obviously an element in any gratifying sexual love: if it has to carry the whole weight of the relationship, it becomes cloying. If sex is only sensuality, you sooner or later turn against sex itself. The element of the daimonic and tragic gives the depth and the memorable quality to love, as it does to Mozart's music.

Let us summarize how the love act contributes to the deepening of consciousness. First, there is the tenderness which comes out of an awareness of the other's needs and desires and the nuances of his feelings. The experience of tenderness emerges from the fact that the two persons, longing, as all individuals do, to overcome the separateness and isolation to which we are all heir because we are individuals, can participate in a relationship that, for the moment, is not of two isolated selves but a union. In this love act, the lover often cannot tell whether a particular sensation of delight is felt by him or his loved one—and it doesn't make any difference. A sharing takes place which is a new *Gestalt,* a new field of magnetic force, a new being.

The second aspect of the deepened consciousness comes from the affirmation of the self in the love act. Despite the fact that many people in our culture use sex to get a short-circuited, ersatz identity, the love act can and ought to provide a sound and meaningful avenue to the sense of personal identity. We normally emerge from love-making with renewed vigor, a vitality which comes not from triumph or proof of one's strength but from the expansion of awareness. Probably in love-making there is always some element of sadness—to continue an analogy suggested in an earlier chapter—as there is in practically all music no matter how joyful (precisely because it does not last; one hears it at that moment or it is lost forever). This sadness comes from the reminder that we have not succeeded absolutely in losing our separateness; and the infantile hope that we can recover the womb never becomes a reality. Even our increased self-awareness can also be a poignant reminder that none of us ever overcomes his loneliness completely. But by the replenished sense of our own personal significance in the love act itself, we can accept these limitations laid upon us by our human finiteness.

This leads immediately to the third aspect, the enrichment and fulfillment—so far as this is possible—of personality. Beginning with the expansion of awareness of our own selves and our feelings, this consists of experiencing our capacity to give pleasure to the other person, and thereby achieving an expansion of meaning in the relationship. We are carried beyond what we were at any given moment; I become literally more than I was. The most powerful symbol imaginable for this is *procreation* —the fact that a new being may be conceived and born. By new being I mean not simply a literal "birth," but the birth of some new aspect of one's self. Whether literal or partially metaphorical, the fact remains that the love act is distinguished by being procreative; and whether casual and ephemeral or faithful and lasting, this is the basic symbol of love's creativity.

A fourth aspect of new consciousness lies in the curious phenomenon that being able to give to the other person in love-making is essential to one's own full pleasure in the act. This sounds like a banal moralism in our age of mechanization of sex and emphasis on "release of tension" in sexual objects. But it is not sentimentality; it is rather a point which anyone can confirm in his own experience in the love act—that to give is essential to one's own pleasure. Many patients in psychotherapy find themselves discovering, generally with some surprise, that something is missing if they cannot "do something for," give something to, the partner—the normal expression of which is the giving in the act of intercourse itself. Just as giving is essential to one's own full pleasure, the ability to receive is necessary in the love relationship also. If you cannot receive, your giving will be a domination of the partner. Conversely, if you cannot give, your receiving will leave you empty. The paradox is demonstrably true that the person who can only receive becomes empty, for he is unable actively to appropriate and make his own what he receives. We speak, thus, not of receiving as a passive phenomenon, but of *active receiving:* one knows he is receiving, feels it, absorbs it into his own experience whether he verbally acknowledges it or not, and is grateful for it.

A corollary of this is the strange phenomenon in psychotherapy that when the patient feels some emotion—eroticism, anger, alienation, or hostility—the therapist normally finds himself feeling that same emotion. This inheres in the fact that when a relationship is genuine, they empathetically share a common field of emotion. This leads to the fact that, in everyday life, we normally tend to fall in love with those who love us. The meaning of "wooing" and "winning" a person is to be found here. The great "pull" to love someone comes precisely from his or her loving you. Passion arouses an answering passion.

Now I am aware of all the objections which will immediately be raised to this statement. One is that people are often repulsed by someone's loving them. Another is that my statement does not take into account all the added things one is motivated to *do* for the beloved and that it places too great an emphasis on passivity. The first objection, I answer, is the reverse proof of my point: we inhabit a *Gestalt* with the one who loves us, and to protect ourselves against his emotion, possibly with good reason, we react with revulsion. The second objection is merely a footnote to what I am already saying—that if someone loves us, he *will* do the many things necessary to show us that this is so; the actions are not the cause, however, but part of the total field. And the third objection will be made only by people who still separate passive and active and who have not accepted our understood active receiving. As we all know, the love experience is filled with pitfalls and disappointments and traumatic events for most of us. But all the pitfalls in the world do not gainsay the point that the given affect going out to the other does incite a response, positive or negative, in him. To quote Baldwin again, we are "like lovers [who] insist on, or create, the consciousness of the others." Hence, *making* love (with the verb being neither a manipulative nor accidental one) is the most powerful incentive for an answering emotion.

There is, finally, the form of consciousness which occurs ideally at the moment of climax in sexual intercourse. This is the point when the lovers are carried by-yond their personal isolation, and when a shift in consciousness occurs which they experience as uniting them with nature itself. There is an accelerating experience of touch, contact, union to the point where, for a moment, the awareness of separateness is lost, blotted out in a cosmic feeling of oneness with nature. In Hemingway's novel, *For Whom the Bell Tolls,* the older woman, Pilar, waits for the hero and the girl he loves when they have gone ahead into the mountain to make love; and when they return, she asks, "Did the earth shake?" This seems to be a normal part of the momentary loss of awareness of the self and the surging up of a sudden consciousness that includes the earth as well. I do not wish my account to sound too "ideal," for I think it is a quality, however subtle, in all love-making except the most depersonalized sort. Nor do I wish it to sound simply "mystic," for despite limitations in our awareness, I think it is an inseparable part of actual experience in the love act.

CREATING OF CONSCIOUSNESS

Love pushes us toward this new dimension of consciousness because it is based on the original "we" experience. Contrary to the usual assumption, we all begin life not as individuals, but as "we"; we are created by the union of male and female, literally of one flesh, produced by the semen of the father fertilizing the egg of the mother. Individuality emerges *within* this original "we," and by virtue of this "we." True, no one of us would actualize himself at all if he did not, sooner or later, become an individual, did not assert his own identity against his mother and father. Individual consciousness is essential for that. Though we do not begin as lonely selves, it is necessary—as we have lost the first freedom, the Garden of Eden at our mother's breast—that we be able to affirm our individuality as the Garden crumbles and the beginning of a man emerges. As the "we" is original *organically,* the "I" is original in human *consciousness.* This individual is a man because he can accept the crumbling of the first freedom, painful as it is, can affirm it, and can begin his pilgrimage toward full consciousness. The original "we" is always a backdrop against which we conduct the pilgrimage. As W. H. Auden puts it:

> Whatever view we hold, it must be shown
> Why every lover has a wish to make
> Some other kind of otherness his own:
> Perhaps, in fact, we never are alone.[3]

We have said that sex is saved from self-destruction by eros, and that this is the normal condition. But eros cannot live without philia, brotherly love and friendship. The tension of continuous attraction and continuous passion would be unbearable if it lasted forever. Philia is the relaxation in the presence of the beloved which accepts the other's being as being; it is simply liking to be with the other, liking to rest with the other, liking the rhythm of the walk, the voice, the whole being of the other. This gives a width to eros; it gives it time to grow; time to sink its roots down deeper. Philia does not require that we do anything for the beloved except accept him, be with him, and enjoy him. It is friendship in the simplest, most direct terms. This is why Paul Tillich makes so much of acceptance, and the ability—curious loss for modern man that this will sound strange—to *accept acceptance.*[4] We are the independent men who, often taking our powers too seriously, continuously act and react, unaware that much of value in life comes only if we don't press, comes in quietly when it is not pushed or required, comes not from a drive from behind or an attraction from in front, but emerges silently from simply being together. This is what Matthew Arnold refers to in his lines,

> Only—but this is rare—
> When a belovéd hand is laid in ours,
> When, jaded with the rush and glare
> Of the interminable hours,
> Our eyes can in another's eyes read clear,
> When our world-deafened ear
> Is by the tones of a loved voice caressed—
> A bolt is shot back somewhere in our breast,
> And a lost pulse of feeling stirs again;
> The eye sinks inward, and the heart lies plain,

And what we mean, we say, and what we would, we know. A man becomes aware of his life's flow.[5]

Hence Harry Stack Sullivan emphasized the "chum" period in human development. This period includes the several years, from about eight to twelve, before the heterosexual functioning of the boy or girl begins to mature. It is the time of genuine liking of the same sex, the time when boys walk to school with arms around each other's shoulders and when girls are inseparable. It is the beginning of the capacity to care for someone else as much as for yourself. If this "chum" experience is missing, holds Sullivan, the person cannot love heterosexually afterwards. Furthermore, Sullivan believed that the child cannot love anyone *before* the "chum" period, and held that if one forces it, one can get him to *act* as though he loves someone, but it will be a pretense. Whether or not one accepts these beliefs in their extreme form, the import is still clear.

An added confirmation of the importance of philia is also given in the experiments of Harry Harlow with rhesus monkeys.[6] Harlow's monkeys, who were not permitted to make friends in their childhood, who never learned to play with siblings or "friends" in all sorts of free and nonsexual ways, were those who later could not adequately function sexually. The period of play with peers is, in other words, an essential prerequisite to the learning of adequate sexual attraction and response to the opposite sex later. In his article, Harlow says, "We believe that the role of affection in the socialization of primates can only be understood by conceiving love as a number of love or affectional systems and not as a single emotion."

In our hurried day, philia is honored as a kind of vestige of bygone periods when people had time for friendship. We find ourselves so rushed, going from work to meetings to a late dinner to bed and up again the next morning, that the contribution of philia to our lives is lost. Or we get it mistakenly connected with homosexuality; American men are especially afraid of male friendship lest it have in it some trace of the homosexual. But, at least, we must recall that the importance of philia is very great in helping us to find ourselves in the chum period and begin the developing of identity.

Philia, in turn, needs agapé. We have defined agapé as esteem for the other, the concern for the other's welfare beyond any gain that one can get out of it; disinterested love, typically, the love of God for man. Charity, as the word is translated in the New Testament, is a poor translation, but it does contain within it the element of selfless giving. It is an analogy—though not an identity—with the biological aspect of nature which makes the mother cat defend to her death her kittens, and the human being love his own baby with a built-in mechanism without regard for what that baby can do for him.

Agapé always carries with it the risk of playing god. But this is a risk that we need to take and can take. We are aware that no human being's motivations are purely disinterested, that everyone's motivations are, at best, a blending of these different kinds of love. Just as I would not like someone to "love" me purely ethereally, without regard for my body and without any awareness of whether I am male or female. I also don't want to be loved *only* for my body. A child senses the lie when he is told that adults do something "only for your good," and everyone dislikes being told he is loved only "spiritually."

Each kind of love, however, presupposes care, for it asserts that something does matter. In normal human relations, each kind of love has an element of the other three, no matter how obscured it may be.

LOVE, WILL, AND THE FORMS OF SOCIETY

Love and will take place within the forms of the society. These forms are the myths and symbols viable at that period. The forms are the channels through which the vitality of the society flows. Creativity is the result of a struggle between vitality and form. As anyone who has tried to write a sonnet or scan poetry is aware, the forms ideally do not take away from the creativity but may add to it. And the present revolt against forms only proves the point in reverse: in our transitional age, we are hunting, exploring, reaching about, struggling to assert whatever we can find in the experiment for some new forms. In a homely illustration, Duke Ellington recounts that when he writes music, he must keep in mind that his trumpeter cannot hit the very high notes securely, whereas the trombonist is very good at them; and writing under these impediments, he remarks, "It's good to have limits." Not only with libido and eros, but other forms of love as well: full satisfaction means the death of the human being; love runs itself out with the death of the lovers. It is the nature of creativity to need form for its creative power; the impediment thus has a positive function.

These forms of the society are molded and presented first of all by the artists. It is the artists who teach us to see, who break the ground in the enlargement of our consciousness; they point the way toward the new dimensions of experience which we have, in any given period, been missing. This is why looking at a work of art gives us a sudden experience of self-recognition. Giotto, precursor to that remarkable birth of awareness known as the Renaissance, saw nature in a new perspective and for the first time painted rocks and trees in three-dimensional space. This space had been there all the time but was not seen because of medieval man's preoccupation with his vertical relationship to eternity reflected in the two-dimensional mosaics. Giotto enlarged human consciousness because his perspective required an individual man standing at a certain point to see this perspective. The individual was now important; eternity was no longer the criterion, but the individual's own experience and his own capacity to look. The art of Giotto was a prediction of the Renaissance individualism which was to flower a hundred years later.

The new view of space pictured by Giotto was basic for the new geographical explorations of oceans and continents by Magellan and Columbus, which changed man's relation to his world, and for the explorations in astronomy by Galileo and Copernicus, which changed man's relation to the heavens. These new discoveries in space resulted in a radical upheaval of man's image of himself. Ours is not the first age to be confronted with loneliness arising from man's discovery of new dimensions of external space and similarly requiring new extensions of his own mind. The psychological upheaval and spiritual loneliness in this period was expressed by the poet John Donne,

> And freely men confesse that this world's spent,
> When in the Planets, and the Firmament
> They seeke so many new; . . .
> 'Tis all in pieces, all cohaerence gone;
> All just supply, and all Relation:
> Prince, Subject, Father, Sonne, are things forgot,
> For every man alone thinkes he hath got
> To be a Phoenix. . . .[7]

The loneliness was also expressed in the philosopher Leibnitz's doctrine of isolated monads with no doors or windows by which one could communicate with the other. And by the scientist Pascal:

> On beholding the blindness and misery of man, on seeing all the universe dumb, and man without light, left to himself, as it were astray in this corner of the universe, knowing not who has set him here, what he is here for, or will become of him when he dies, incapable of all knowledge, I begin to be afraid, as a man who has been carried while asleep to a fearful desert island, and who will awake not knowing where he is and without any means of quitting the island.[8]

But just as these men were able to find the new planes of consciousness which did, to some extent, fill the new reservoirs of space, so in our day a similar shift is necessary.

Cézanne, at the beginning of our century, saw and painted space in a new way, not in perspective now but as a spontaneous totality, an immediate apprehension of form in space. He painted the *being* of space rather than its *measurements*. As we look at the rocks and trees and mountains on his canvases, we do not find ourselves thinking, "This mountain is behind this tree," but we are grasped by an immediate whole which is mythic in that it encompasses near and far, past and present, conscious and unconscious in one immediate totality of our relationship to the world. Indeed, I was recently intrigued to notice, when looking at one of Cézanne's oils in London, *Le Lac d'Annecy* (which I had never seen before), that he actually paints brushstrokes of the mountains *over* the tree, in complete contradiction to the literal fact that the mountain, as he looked at it, was twenty miles away. In Cézanne, the forms are not before us as compartmentalized items to be added up, but as a presence that grips us. The same is true in Cézanne's portraits—the subject is presented to us not as a face with a forehead and two ears and a nose, but as a presence. The eloquence of this presence beggars our naïve slavery to literalism, and reveals to us *more* truth about the human being than does realism. The significant point is that it *requires our participation in the picture itself if the painting is to speak to us.*

In Cézanne, we see this new world of spaces and stones and trees and faces. He tells us the *old* world of mechanics is gone and we must see and live in the *new* world of spaces. This is evident even with his seemingly banal apples and peaches on a table. But it is particularly clear and eloquent in his paintings of trees. In my college days, I used to walk to classes across the campus of my college under tall elms, whose size and strength I admired. Nowadays, I walk to my office under elm trees on Riverside Drive. Between these two, I saw and learned to love Cézanne's paintings of elms in their architectural grandeur, and what I now each morning see —or rather experience—is altogether different from the college campus. Now the trees are part of a musical movement of forms which has nothing to do with literal measurements of trees. The triangular white forms of the sky are as important as the tree limbs which give them their form; the sheer power hanging in the air has nothing to do with the size of the trees but consists of the lines the branches block in on the gray-blue of the Hudson River.

The new world which Cézanne reveals is characterized by a transcendence of cause and effect. There is no linear relationship in the sense of "A" produces "B" produces "C"; all aspects of the forms are born in our vision simultaneously—or not at all. This demonstrates the new form which will takes in our day. The painting is mythic, not literalistic or realistic: all categories of time, past, present, and future, conscious and unconscious, are included. And most important of all, I cannot even *see* the painting if I stand totally outside it; it communicates only if I *participate* in it. I cannot see Cézanne by observing his rocks as an accurate rendering of rocks, but only by looking at the rocks as patterns of forms which speak to me through my own body and my feelings and my perceptions of my world. This is the world that I must empathize with. I must give myself to it in a universe of basic forms in which my own life is grounded. This is the challenge to my consciousness which these paintings give.

But how do I know I will find myself again if I let myself go into the orbit of Cézanne's new forms and spaces? This question explains much of the rabid, irrational, and violent opposition many people feel toward modern art; it *does* destroy their old world, and must, therefore, be hated. They can never see the world in the old way again, never experience life in the old way; once the old consciousness is shattered, there is no chance of building it up again. Though Cézanne, bourgeois that he was, seems to present strong, solid forms on which life could look secure, we should not be lulled into failing to realize that in his paintings a radically different language obtains. It was a degree of consciousness which drove Van Gogh into psychosis a few years previously and with which Nietzsche struggled at great cost.

Cézanne's works are the opposite of the "divide-and-conquer" fragmentation which has characterized modern man's relation to nature since Bacon and has led us to the brink of catastrophe. There is in Cézanne a statement that we can, and must, *will* and *love* the world as an immediate, spontaneous totality. In Cézanne and his fellow artists, there is a new language of myth and symbol which will be more adequate to love and will in the new conditions we must confront.

It is the passion of the artist, of whatever type or craft, to communicate what he experiences as the subconscious and unconscious significance of his relation to his world. "Communicate" is related to "commune," and, in turn, both are avenues to the experience of communion and community with our fellowmen.

We love and will the world as an immediate, spontaneous totality. We *will* the world, create it by our decision, our fiat, our choice; and we *love* it, give it affect, energy, power to love and change us as we mold and change it. This is what it means to be fully related to one's world. I do not imply that the world does not exist *before* we love or will it; one can answer that question only on the basis of his assumptions, and, being a midwesterner with inbred realism, I would assume that it does exist. But it has no reality, no relation to me, as I have no effect upon it; I move as in a dream, vaguely and without viable contact. One can choose to shut it out—as New Yorkers do when riding the subway—or one can choose to see it, create it. In this sense, we give to Cézanne's art or the Cathedral at Chartres the power to move us.

What does this mean concerning our personal lives, to which, at last, we now return? The microcosm of our consciousness is where the macrocosm of the universe is *known*. It is the fearful joy, the blessing, and the curse of man that he can be conscious of himself and his world. For consciousness surprises the meaning in our otherwise absurd acts. Eros, infusing the whole, beckons us with its power with the promise that it may become our power. And the daimonic—that often nettlelike voice which is at the same time our creative power—leads us into life if we do not kill these daimonic experiences but accept them with a sense of the preciousness of what we are and what life is. Intentionality, itself consisting of the deepened awareness of one's self, is our means of putting the meaning surprised by consciousness into action.

We stand on the peak of the consciousness of previous ages, and their wisdom is available to us. History—that selective treasure house of the past which each age bequeaths to those that follow—has formed us in the present so that we may embrace the future. What does it matter if our insights, the new forms which play around the fringes of our minds, always lead us into virginal land where, like it or not, we stand on strange and bewildering ground? The only way out is ahead, and our choice is whether we shall cringe from it or affirm it.

For in every act of love and will—and in the long run they are both present in each genuine act—we mold ourselves and our world simultaneously. This is what it means to embrace the future.

NOTES

CHAPTER ONE. Introduction: Our Schizoid World

[1] Carl Oglesby, in *A Prophetic Minority*, by Jack Newfield (New York, New American Library, 1966), p. 19.

[2] Leslie Farber, *The Ways of the Will* (New York, Basic Books, 1965), p. 48.

[3] Anthony Storr, *Human Aggression* (New York, Atheneum, 1968), p. 85.

[4] *Ibid.*

[5] *Ibid.*, p. 88.

[6] Personal communication.

[7] Kenneth Keniston observes a parallel point, namely that the problems of our day bear down most heavily not upon the stupid and the bland, but upon the intelligent. "The sense of being inescapably locked in a psycho-social vise is often most paralyzing to precisely those men and women who have the greatest understanding of the complexity of their society, and who therefore might be best able to plan intelligently for its future." *The Uncommitted: Alienated Youth in American Society* (New York, Harcourt, Brace & World, 1960).

[8] Sir Herbert Read, *Icon and Idea: The Function of Art in the Development of Human Consciousness* (Cambridge, Mass., Harvard University Press, 1955).

[9] Maurice Merleau-Ponty, *Sense and Non-Sense* (Evanston, Ill., Northwestern University Press, 1964), p. 21.

[10] *Ibid.*

[11] Aeschylus, *Agamemnon,* from *The Complete Greek Tragedies,* eds. David Grene and Richmond Lattimore (Chicago, University of Chicago Press, 1953), p. 71.

[12] *Ibid.*, p. 70.

[13] The fact that pornography and other aspects of sexuality were also present in the Victorian period, as shown by Steven Marcus in *The Other Victorians* (New York, Basic Books, 1964), does not invalidate my thesis. In such a compartmentalized society there would always be repression which would come out in the underground in proportion to the blocking off of vital drives.

¹⁴ Published as *The Meaning of Anxiety* (New York, Ronald Press, 1950).

¹⁵ See May, *The Meaning of Anxiety,* pp. 6–7.

¹⁶ The drama that most clearly heralded the demise of the Horatio Alger values of work and success by which most of us had gotten our sense of individual identity and significance was *Death of a Salesman,* published by Arthur Miller in 1949. Willy Loman's basic trouble was, in Miller's words, that "he never knew who he was."

¹⁷ J. H. van den Berg, "The Changing Nature of Man," intro. to *A Historical Psychology* (New York, W. W. Norton & Co., 1961).

¹⁸ See David Shapiro, *Neurotic Styles* (New York, Basic Books, 1965), p. 23.

¹⁹ P. H. Johnson, *On Iniquity: Reflections Arising out of the Moors Murder Trial* (New York, Scribners).

²⁰ Rollo May, *Man's Search for Himself* (New York, W. W. Norton & Co., 1953), p. 14. The problem which seemed to me to be emerging in a new and unique form I first called the patients' "emptiness," not an entirely well-chosen phrase. I meant by it a state closely allied to apathy.

²¹ *Ibid.,* p. 24.

²² *Ibid.*

²³ *Ibid.,* pp. 24–25.

²⁴ *Ibid.,* p. 25.

²⁵ *The New York Times,* March 27, 1964.

²⁶ *Ibid.,* April 16, 1964.

²⁷ *Ibid.,* May 6, 1964.

²⁸ Keniston, in *The Uncommitted,* speaking of this anomie, writes: "Our age inspires scant enthusiasm. In the industrial West, and increasingly now in the uncommitted nations, ardor is lacking; instead men talk of their growing distance from each other, from their social order, from their work and play, and from the values and heroes which in a perhaps romanticized past seem to have given order, meaning, and coherence to their lives."

²⁹ James H. Billington, "The Humanistic Heartbeat Has Failed," *Life Magazine,* p. 32.

³⁰ *Ibid.*

³¹ *Ibid.*

³² "Public apathy," says Dr. Karl Menninger, "is itself a manifestation of aggression." Karl Menninger at a conference of the Medical Correctional Association on violence, covered by *The New York Times,* April 12, 1964.

³³ The vast need of our society for touch and the revolt against its prohibition are shown in the growth of all the forms of touch therapy, from Esalen on down to the group therapy in

the next room. These rightly reflect the need, but they are in error in their anti-intellectual bias and in the grandiose aims which they assert for what is essentially a corrective measure. They are also in error in their failure to see that this is an aspect of the whole society which must be changed, and changed on a deeper level involving the whole man.

34 Harry Stack Sullivan, *The Psychiatric Interview* (New York, W. W. Norton & Co., 1954), p. 184.

35 Bruno Bettelheim, *The Informed Heart* (Glencoe, Ill., The Free Press, 1960), pp. 20–21.

36 Arthur J. Brodbeck, "Placing Aesthetic Developments in Social Context: A Program of Value Analysis," *Journal of Social Issues,* January, 1964, p. 17.

CHAPTER TWO. Paradoxes of Sex and Love

1 William James, *Principles of Psychology* (New York, Dover Publications, 1950; originally published by Henry Holt, 1890), II, p. 439.

2 *Atlas,* November, 1965, p. 302. Reprinted from *The Times Literary Supplement,* London.

3 *Ibid.*

4 Howard Taubman, "Is Sex Kaput?," *The New York Times,* sect. 2, January 17, 1965.

5 Leon Edel, "Sex and the Novel," *The New York Times,* sect. 7, pt. I, November 1, 1964.

6 *Ibid.*

7 See Taubman.

8 John L. Schimel, "Ideology and Sexual Practices," *Sexual Behavior and the Law,* ed. Ralph Slovenko (Springfield, Ill., Charles C. Thomas, 1965), pp. 195, 197.

9 Sometimes a woman patient will report to me in the course of describing how a man tried to seduce her, that he cites as part of his seduction line how efficient a lover he is, and he promises to perform the act eminently satisfactorily for her. (Imagine Mozart's Don Giovanni offering such an argument!) In fairness to elemental human nature, I must add that as far as I can remember, the women reported that this "advance billing" did not add to the seducers' chances of success.

10 That the actual Puritans in the sixteenth and seventeenth centuries were a different breed from those who represented the deteriorated forms in our century can be seen in a number of sources. Roland H. Bainton in the chapter "Puritanism and the Modern Period," of his book *What Christianity Says About Sex, Love and Marriage* (New York, Reflection Books, Association Press, 1957), writes "The Puritan ideal for the relations of man and wife was summed up in the words, 'a tender respectiveness.'" He quotes Thomas Hooker: "The man whose

heart is endeared to the woman he loves, he dreams of her in the night, hath her in his eye and apprehension when he awakes, museth on her as he sits at table, walks with her when he travels and parlies with her in each place he comes." Ronald Mushat Frye, in a thoughtful paper, "The Teachings of Classical Puritanism on Conjugal Love," *Studies from the Renaissance,* II (1955), submits conclusive evidence that classical Puritanism inculcated a view of sexual life in marriage as the "Crown of all our bliss," "Founded in Reason, Loyal, Just, and Pure" (p. 149). He believes that "the fact remains that the education of England in a more liberal view of married love in the sixteenth and early seventeenth centuries was in large part the work of that party within English Protestantism which is called Puritan" (p. 149). The Puritans were against lust and acting on physical attraction outside of marriage, but they as strongly believed in the sexual side of marriage and believed it the duty of all people to keep this alive all their lives. It was a later confusion which associated them with the asceticism of continence in marriage. Frye states, "In the course of a wide reading of Puritan and other Protestant writers in the sixteenth and early seventeenth centuries, I have found nothing but opposition to this type of ascetic 'perfection' " (p. 152).

One has only to look carefully at the New England churches built by the Puritans and in the Puritan heritage to see the great refinement and dignity of form which surely implies a passionate attitude toward life. They had the dignity of controlled passion, which may have made possible an actual living with passion in contrast to our present pattern of expressing and dispersing all passion. The deterioration of Puritanism into our modern secular attitudes was caused by the confluence of three trends: industrialism, Victorian emotional compartmentalization, and the secularization of all religious attitudes. The first introduced the specific mechanical model; the second introduced the emotional dishonesty which Freud analyzed so well; and the third took away the depth-dimensions of religion and made the concerns how one "behaved" in such matters as smoking, drinking, and sex in the superficial forms which we are attacking above. (For a view of the delightful love letters between husband and wife in this period, see the two-volume biography of John Adams by Page Smith. See also the writings on the Puritans by Perry Miller.)

[11] This formulation was originally suggested to me by Dr. Ludwig Lefebre.

[12] *Atlas,* November, 1965, p. 302.

[13] Philip Rieff, *Freud: The Mind of the Moralist* (New York, Viking Press, 1959), quoted in James A. Knight's "Calvinism

and Psychoanalysis: A Comparative Study," *Pastoral Psychology*, December, 1963, p. 10.

[14] Knight, p. 11.

[15] Cf. Marcus, *The Other Victorians*, pp. 146–147. Freud's letter goes on: "Our whole conduct of life presupposes that we are protected from the direst poverty and that the possibility exists of being able to free ourselves increasingly from social ills. The poor people, the masses, could not survive without their thick skins and their easy-going ways. Why should they scorn the pleasures of the moment when no other awaits them? The poor are too helpless, too exposed, to behave like us. When I see the people indulging themselves, disregarding all sense of moderation, I invariably think that this is their compensation for being a helpless target for all the taxes, epidemics, sickness, and evils of social institutions."

[16] Paul Tillich, in a speech, "Psychoanalysis and Existentialism," given at the Conference of the American Association of Existential Psychology and Psychiatry, February, 1962.

[17] Schimel, p. 198.

[18] Leopold Caligor and Rollo May, in *Dreams and Symbols* (New York, Basic Books, 1968), p. 108n, similarly maintain that today's patients, as a whole, seem to be preoccupied with the head and genitals in their dreams and leave out the heart.

[19] *Playboy*, April, 1957.

[20] These articles by notable people can be biased, as was Timothy Leary's famous interview which *Playboy* used broadly in its advertising, holding that LSD makes possible a "hundred orgasms" for the woman, and that "an LSD session that doesn't involve an ultimate merger isn't really complete." Actually, LSD seemingly temporarily "turns off" the sexual functions. This interview inspired a rejoinder from a writer who is an authority on both LSD and sex, Dr. R. E. L. Masters, who wrote, "Such claims about LSD effects are not only false, they are dangerous. . . . That occasional rare cases might support some of his claims, I don't doubt; but he suggests that he is describing the rule, not the exception, and that is altogether false" (mimeographed letter privately circulated).

[21] "*Playboy's* Doctrine of the Male," in *Christianity and Crisis*, XXI/6, April 17, 1961, unpaged.

[22] Discussion in symposium on sex, Michigan State University, February, 1969.

[23] *Ibid.*

[24] Gerald Sykes, *The Cool Millennium* (New York, 1967).

[25] A survey of students on three college campuses in the New York/New Jersey area conducted by Dr. Sylvia Hertz, chairman of the Essex County Council on Drug Addiction,

reported in *The New York Times* on November 26, 1967, that "The use of drugs has become so prominent, that it has relegated sex to second place."

As sex began to lose its power as the arena of proving one's individuality by rebellion and merged with the use of drugs as the new frontier, both then became related to the preoccupation with acts of violence. Efforts crop up anachronistically here and there to use sex as the vehicle for revolt against society. When I was speaking at a college in California, my student chauffeur to the campus told me that there was a society at the college dedicated, as its name indicates, to "Sex Unlimited." I remarked that I hadn't noticed anybody in California trying to limit sex, so what did this society do? He answered that the previous week, the total membership (which turned out to be six or seven students) got undressed at noon and, naked, jumped into the goldfish pool in the center of the campus. The city police then came and hiked them off to jail. My response was that if one wanted to get arrested, that was a good way to do it, but I couldn't see that the experience had a thing in the world to do with sex.

[26] Marshall McLuhan and George G. Leonard, "The Future of Sex," *Look Magazine*, July 25, 1967, p. 58. The article makes a significant point with respect to the polls about sex: "When survey-takers 'prove' that there is no sexual revolution among our young people by showing that the frequency of sexual intercourse has not greatly increased, they are missing the point completely. Indeed, the frequency of intercourse may decrease in the future *because of* a real revolution in attitudes toward, feelings about and uses of sex, especially concerning the roles of the male and female" (p. 57).

[27] Not being an anthropologist, I conferred with Ashley Montague on this point. The judgment was expressed orally to me.

[28] McLuhan and Leonard, p. 58. The words are italicized by McLuhan and Leonard.

[29] Eleanor Garth, "The A-Sexual Society," *Center Diary*, published by the Center for the Study of Democratic Institutions, 15, November–December, 1966, p. 43.

[30] *Ibid.*

[31] *Ibid.*

CHAPTER THREE. Eros in Conflict with Sex

[1] U. S. Department of Health Statistics *Medical World News*, March, 1967, pp. 64–68. These reports also inform us that venereal disease is also increasing 4 per cent a year among adolescents. This increase may have different causes from those for illegitimate pregnancy, but it bears out my general thesis.

The second statistic—that this is an increase from one in fifteen of ten years ago—is from a report of the Teamsters Joint Council 16, covered in *The New York Times*, July 1, 1968.

² Kenneth Clark, *Dark Ghetto: A Study in the Effect of Powerlessness* (New York, Harper and Row, 1965). This excerpt is from sections of the book quoted in *Psychology Today*, I/5, September, 1967, p. 38.

³ The same is true among the Indians of South America, where the symbol of being able to father babies is so important that it defeats all the efforts of enlightened nurses and doctors to spread birth control. The woman will readily confess that she *wants* not to have any more babies, but the "husband"—generally of the common-law variety—feels it a mark. against his *machismos* if he cannot father a baby a year, and so leaves her in favor of others if he cannot prove his potency with her.

⁴ T. S. Eliot, "The Hollow Men," *Collected Poems* (New York, Harcourt, Brace & Company, 1934), p. 101.

⁵ The gripping thing about the movie *La Dolce Vita* was not its sex, but that while everyone was feeling sexy and emoting all over, no one could *hear* any other person. From the first scene when the noise of the helicopter blots out the shouting of the men to the women, to the last scene in which the hero strains to hear the girl across the stream but cannot because of the noise of the ocean waves, no one hears another. Just at the moment in the castle when the man and the woman are at the point of declaring authentic love for each other in a communication by echoes, she cannot hear his voice from the other room and immediately drugs herself by promiscuous sexual titillation with a chance passerby. The dehumanizing thing is the so-called emotion without any relatedness; and sex is the most ready drug to hide one's terror at this dehumanization.

⁶ Joseph Campbell, *Occidental Mythology*, vol. III from *The Masks of God* (New York, Viking Press, 1964), p. 235.

⁷ *Webster's Collegiate Dictionary,* 3rd ed. (Springfield, Mass., G. & C. Merriam Company).

⁸ *Webster's Third New International Dictionary* (Springfield, Mass., G. & C. Merriam Company, 1961).

⁹ To the argument that Plato was actually speaking of pederasty, the love of men for boys, and that the Greeks valued homosexuality more than heterosexuality, I reply that eros has the same characteristics regardless of the form the love about which you are speaking. I do not believe that this is any disparagement of Plato's insights into love. Furthermore, "There is evidence that Socrates did not practice pederasty," writes Professor Morgan, and "no convincing evidence that Plato did either. The issue seems to me to interest only scholars of Athenian cultural history. Plato's philosophical interpretation of love

stands wholly outside the problem of homosexuality and heterosexuality. . . . Were Plato living today, his language would
presumably reflect our differing social customs, but would not
require any fundamental revision on this account. . . . In
either cultural environment, the man who is consumed with
merely carnal hungers and gratified in merely carnal manners
is properly and identically condemned as bestial, foolish, childish, and infrahuman; Plato's presentation of love can stand as
strong today as it ever stood." Douglas N. Morgan, *Love:
Plato, the Bible and Freud* (Englewood Cliffs, N.J., Prentice-
Hall, 1964), pp. 44–45.

[10] W. H. Auden, ed., *The Portable Greek Reader* (New York,
Viking Press, 1948), p. 487.

[11] *Ibid.*, p. 493.

[12] *Ibid.*, pp. 493–494.

[13] *Ibid.*, p. 495.

[14] This fits the binding function of eros; the origin of the
word religion *(re-ligio)* means binding together.

[15] Albert Camus, *The Myth of Sisyphus* (New York, Alfred
A. Knopf, 1955), p. 123.

[16] Surely Freud himself had no desire to render sex and love
banal. He would have been perplexed by how his emphasis on
the sexual basis of life was pursued with a vengeance in our
society, indeed carried to its *reductio ad absurdum*. And he
would have been appalled by Kinsey and Masters, who define
sex in a way which omits exactly what Freud wished most to
preserve—the intentionality of sexual love and its wide significance in the psychological constellation of human experience.
No matter how much Freud talked in such physicalistic phrases
as the "filling and emptying of seminal vesicles," there was
always in his views of sex a sense of the *mysterium tremendum,*
a sense of Schopenhauer's proclamation, "the sexual passion is
the kernel of the will to live."

[17] Morgan, p. 136.

[18] *Ibid.*, p. 139.

[19] Sigmund Freud, "On the Universal Tendency to Debase-
ment in the Sphere of Love" (1912), *Standard Edition* of *The
Complete Psychological Works of Sigmund Freud,* trans. and
ed. James Strachey (London, Hogarth Press, 1961), XI, pp.
187–188.

[20] Sigmund Freud, *Beyond the Pleasure Principle* (1920),
Standard Edition (London, Hogarth Press, 1955), XVIII, p. 7.

[21] *Ibid.*, p. 35. Freud himself italicized these sentences.

[22] *Ibid.*, p. 38.

[23] It is not within our purpose here to discuss the merits of
this theory of the death instinct, which has been so fervently
attacked and rejected by Freudians as well as by Horney and

others of the cultural school. I can only repeat what I have said elsewhere, that though the theory may not make sense biologically or with the literal definition of "instinct," it makes very important sense as a myth expressing the tragic nature of human life. Here, Freud's voice is in the great tradition of Ecclesiastes, Nietzsche, Schopenhauer, and all those thinkers through the ages who were motivated by their profound respect for the inexorable character of *Ananke,* or Necessity, in nature.

[24] Morgan, p. 144.

[25] Sigmund Freud, *The Ego and the Id* (1923), *Standard Edition* (London, Hogarth Press, 1961), XIX, p. 47. (New York, W. W. Norton & Co., Norton Library, 1962, p. 37)

[26] *Ibid.,* p. 46. (Norton Library, p. 36)

[27] *Ibid.,* p. 47. (Norton Library, p. 37) (It is here, incidentally, that Freud refers to the fact that the drone bee and the praying mantis die after copulation, and uses this as an illustration of death after satisfaction.)

[28] Such as Ernest Jones, *The Life and Work of Sigmund Freud* (New York, Basic Books, 1957), III, p. 276: "The aim was to establish a relationship between Fechner's principle of stability, which Freud had identified with his Nirvana principle and ultimately with the death instinct, and the second law of thermodynamics. This sinister law, the bogey of all optimists, can strictly speaking be expressed only in mathematical language, such as a quantity of heat divided by a temperature; the law of entropy states that *in a self-contained system* this number increases with time. This is true, however, only of a hypothetical closed system such as is never met with in nature, least of all in living beings where, as the eminent physicist Schrödinger has insisted, by taking in energy from without they actually acquire a negative entropy."

[29] Morgan, p. 173.

[30] *Ibid.*

[31] *Ibid.,* p. 165.

[32] *Ibid.*

[33] *Ibid.,* p. 164.

[34] *Ibid.,* p. 165.

[35] *Ibid.*

[36] Professor Morgan, p. 174, expresses astonishment that Freud, knowing the classics as he did, could have made such an extraordinary error. One can only remark the obvious: that so great are the pressures in any society to see reality through the eyeglasses of our own predelictions, that we tend to reinterpret the past in terms of our biases, which, in Freud's nineteenth-century culture, was Helmoltz's physics. "In his *Three Essays on Sexuality,* Freud commits still another remarkable error, betraying an almost uncanny misconception of Athenian love:

'The most striking distinction between the erotic life of antiquity and our own no doubt lies in the fact that the ancients laid stress on the instinct itself whereas we emphasize its object. The ancients glorified the instinct and were prepared on its account to honour even an inferior object; while we despise the instinctual activity in itself, and find excuses for it only in the merits of the object.' [*Standard Edition*, VII, p. 149, n. 1.] If by 'ancients' we are to read Plato, it is difficult to discredit Freud with so extraordinary a misreading. For Plato, the dynamism of love derives all its value from its ultimate object; 'inferior objects' were honored not because of love, but rather because they revealed in a limited manner the ultimately and properly beloved object. And Freud appears here to be as mistaken about psychoanalysis as he is about Plato!"

³⁷ Abraham Maslow has made this point well in his various writings.

³⁸ Paul Tillich, *Love, Power and Justice* (New York, Oxford University Press, 1954), p. 22.

³⁹ Helene A. Guerber, *Myths of Greece and Rome* (London, British Book Centre, 1907), p. 86.

⁴⁰ "Eros," *Encyclopaedia Britannica*, vol. VIII (1947), p. 695.

⁴¹ Rollo May, in a review of Vance Packard's *The Sexual Wilderness: The Contemporary Upheaval in Male-Female Relationships* (New York, David McKay Company, 1968), appearing in *The New York Times Book Review*, October 13, 1968: "Packard here cites J. D. Unwin's massive, if almost forgotten, 'Sex and Culture' (1934), a study of 80 uncivilized societies and also a number of historically advanced cultures. Unwin sought to correlate various societies' sexual permissiveness with their energy for civilized advancement. He concluded that the 'amount of cultural ascent of the primitive societies closely paralleled the amount of limitation they placed upon the nonmarital sexual opportunity.' Virtually all the civilized societies Unwin examined—the Babylonians, Athenians, Romans, Anglo-Saxons, and English—began their historical careers in a 'state of absolute monogamy.' The one exception was the Moors, where a specific religious sanction supported polygamy. 'Any human society,' Unwin writes, 'is free to choose either to display great energy or to enjoy sexual freedom; the evidence is that it cannot do both for more than one generation.' Packard points out that this is supported in different ways by other historians and anthropologists, such as Carl C. Zimmerman, Arnold J. Toynbee, Charles Winick and Pitirim A. Sorokin."

⁴² From Denis de Rougement's *The Myths of Love* (New

York, Pantheon Books, 1963), quoted in *Atlas,* November, 1965, p. 306.

CHAPTER FOUR. Love and Death

1 Campbell, III, p. 67.

2 Hesiod, *Theogony,* lines 120–122, trans. Richmond Lattimore (Ann Arbor, University of Michigan Press, 1961), quoted by Joseph Campbell, III, p. 234.

3 *Ibid.*

4 Love's effect can parallel that of the drug LSD. Both break down the walls of the customary world and crumble our defenses, leaving us naked and vulnerable. In LSD, the experience may be one of awe and discovery, or it can be one of paranoia and disintegration with no delight at all. That parallel, too, holds in love. Jealousy, envy, suspicion, rage, and even hatred can be more powerful when love is present. Many couples stay together ostensibly motivated more by hatred than by love. As in Edward Albee's *Who's Afraid of Virginia Woolf?,* it is sometimes very hard to tell whether hatred masks love or the reverse.

5 Sigmund Freud, "The Two Classes of Instincts," in *The Ego and the Id.* (Hogarth, p. 47, Norton Library, p. 37)

6 Campbell, III, p. 235. Also see treatment of Tristan and Iseult in Denis de Rougement, *Love in the Western World,* trans. Montgomery Belgion (New York, Pantheon Books, 1956).

7 *Ibid.*

8 Cf. Robert Lifton, "On Death and Death Symbolism," *Psychiatry,* published by The William Allison White Foundation, Washington, D. C., 27, 1964, pp. 191–210. Also Geoffrey Gorer, "The Pornography of Death," in *The Berkley Book of Modern Writings,* eds. W. Phillips and P. Rauh, 3rd ed. (New York, Berkley Publishing Corp., 1956), pp. 56–62.

9 Erich Fromm's later writings are clear examples of this avoidance of the reality of death. "Grief is sin," he writes, giving the psychological rationale for the repression of death. He goes on to urge that man keep himself from even thinking about death. I do not see how such an evasion can escape being destructive to the personality. Cf. *The Heart of Man* (New York, Harper & Row, 1964).

10 For a satire of this, see Aldous Huxley, *After Many a Summer Dies the Swan.*

11 The tendency to repress death also has its history. After the loss of belief in immortality in the eighteenth and nineteenth centuries, we repressed death by our belief in progress; if we could conquer nature, conquer diseases, why should not

progress be extrapolated to also include, some day far off in the glowing future, our conquering death?

12 Tillich, p. 23.

13 See Freud, *Beyond the Pleasure Principle,* p. 58.

14 I am aware that some women will protest at Buytendijk's data. True, the cultural parallels should be taken as *illustrations,* not as firmly culturally-conditioned ways of behaving. But it would be an error to reject the differences in the sexes, as some members of the women's liberation movement do, simply because the particular forms of behavior are culturally-conditioned.

15 Frobenius in *Der Kopf als Schicksal* (Munich, 1924), quoted by Jung-Kerenyi, *Introduction to a Science of Mythology.*

16 Seymour L. Halleck, "The Roots of Student Despair," *THINK,* published by IBM, XXXIII/2, March–April, 1967, p. 22.

CHAPTER FIVE. Love and the Daimonic

1 This word can be spelled "demonic" (the popularized form), or "daemonic" (the medieval form often now used by the poets —Yeats, for example), or "daimonic" (the derivitive from the ancient Greek word "diamon"). Since this last is the origin of the concept, and since the term is unambiguous in its including the positive as well as the negative, the divine as well as the diabolical, I use the Greek term.

2 Plato, *The Apologia,* from *The Works of Plato,* ed. Irwin Edman, trans. Jowett (New York, Tudor Publishing Co., 1928), pp. 74, 82–83.

3 William Butler Yeats, *Mythologies* (New York, Macmillan Co., 1959), p. 332.

4 Johann Wolfgang van Goethe, *Autobiography: Poetry and Truth from My Own Life,* trans. R. O. Moon (Washington, D. C., Public Affairs Press, 1949), pp. 683–684.

5 *Webster's Collegiate Dictionary.*

6 E. R. Dodds, *The Greeks and the Irrational* (Berkeley, University of California Press, 1968), p. 120.

7 Henry Murray, "The Personality and Career of Satan," *The Journal of Social Issues,* XVIII/4, p. 51.

8 Henrik Ibsen. *Peer Gynt,* trans. Michael Meyer (New York, Doubleday Anchor, 1963), p. xxviii.

9 William Butler Yeats, *Selected Poems,* ed. M. L. Rosenthal (New York, Macmillan Co., 1962), p. xx.

10 Yeats, *Mythologies,* p. 332.

11 Storr, p. 1.

12 From the Presentation at the Annual Convention of the

American Psychiatric Association, 1967, Atlantic City, partially published in *The American Journal of Psychiatry,* 124/9, March, 1968, pp. 58–64. Dr. Prince, we should add for those of us who tend to take the usual pejorative view of primitive therapy and ceremonies, had a high regard for the skill of the native mental healers. When a native could not be helped by the psychiatric facilities of the hospital, Dr. Prince would send him to a native healer in whom he had confidence. These healers seemed to have quite a good idea of the different types of ailments we call schizophrenia, and had some idea of which types they could cure and which not. I believe we should not judge this kind of therapy by comparing it to our contemporary techniques, or see it simply as "primitive" healing in the derogatory sense, but as an expression of archetypal ways of dealing with human problems which were, to some extent, adequate for their tribal situation as our methods are relatively adequate for us. This so-called earlier form can cast significant light on our contemporary problems.

¹³ I am indebted through here to Dr. Wolfgang Zucker for ideas in his unpublished paper, "The Demonic from Aeschylus to Tillich," *Theology Today,* XXV/1, April, 1969.

¹⁴ ηθος αγθρωπω σαιμων, Dodds, p. 182. This phrase is often mistranslated "Man's character is his fate." Dodds translates "daimon" here as "destiny." While these give different aspects of the daimonic, it is well to keep in mind that the Greek term is σαιμων.

¹⁵ Aeschylus, *The Eumenides,* trans. John Stuart Blackie (London, Everyman's Library, 1906), p. 163.

¹⁶ Dodds, p. 183. "On that issue [the springs of human conduct] the first generation of Sophists, in particular Protagoras, seem to have held a view whose optimism is pathetic in retrospect, but historically intelligible. 'Virtue or Efficiency *(arête)* could be taught': by criticizing his traditions, by modernising the *Nomos* which his ancestors had created and eliminated from it the last vestiges of 'barbarian silliness', man could acquire a new Art of Living, and human life could be raised to new levels hitherto undreamed of. Such a hope is understandable in men who had witnessed the swift growth of material prosperity after the Persian Wars, and the unexampled flowering of the spirit that accompanied it, culminating in the unique achievements of Periclean Athens. For that generation, the Golden Age was no lost paradise of the dim past, as Hesiod had believed; for them it lay not behind but ahead, and not so very far ahead either. In a civilised community, declared Protagoras robustly, the very worst citizen was already a better man than the supposedly noble savage. Better, in fact,

fifty years of Europe than a cycle of Cathay. But history has, alas, a short way with optimists. Had Tennyson experienced the latest fifty years of Europe he might, I fancy, have reconsidered his preference; and Protagoras before he died had ample ground for revising his. Faith in the inevitability of progress had an even shorter run in Athens than in England."

[17] Herbert Spiegelberg, ed., *The Socratic Enigma* (Indianapolis, Bobbs-Merrill Co., 1964), p. 127.

[18] *Ibid.*, pp. 127–128.

[19] *New English Dictionary*, ed. James A. H. Murray (Oxford, 1897).

[20] Zucker.

[21] *Ibid.*

[22] Goethe, p. 682.

[23] This translation is by Wolfgang Zucker. The parallel passage in Goethe's *Autobiography*, cited above, is on pp. 683–684.

[24] Sigmund Freud, "Analysis of a Case of Hysteria," *Collected Papers* (New York, Basic Books, 1959), III, pp. 131–132.

[25] Morgan, p, 158. Let those psychologists and social scientists who, several decades ago, used to side-step these hard sayings of Freud by means of the easy shibboleth of his "pessimism" now recall what has happened since he argued this tragic state of life: Hitler and Dachau, the atom bomb and Hiroshima, and now the spectacle of the most powerful nation in the world mired in destruction in Vietnam with no possible constructive solution.

Freud gives a concrete illustration of the daimonic in the sense of partial aspects of the personality taking power over the whole, with disintegrating effects upon the total self: "It is in sadism, where the death instinct twists the erotic aim in its own sense and yet at the same time fully satisfies the erotic urge, that we succeed in obtaining the clearest insight into its nature and its relation to Eros. But even where it emerges without any sexual purpose, in the blindest fury of destructiveness, we cannot fail to recognize that the satisfaction of the instinct is accompanied by an extraordinary high degree of narcissistic enjoyment, owing to its presenting the ego with a fulfillment of the latter's old wishes for omnipotence." *Civilization and Its Discontents* (1927–1931), *Standard Edition* (London, The Hogarth Press, 1961), XXI, p. 121. (New York, W. W. Norton & Co., Norton Library, 1962, p. 68)

[26] James, II, pp. 553–554.

[27] I say lungs because the anxiety in loneliness seems to affect the breathing apparatus, and the pain seems to be a sharp stab of constriction of the lungs rather than, as we say in grief

or sadness, a pain "in the heart." There is a greater basis for this usage than mere localization of felt pain, for anxiety in general has been connected with the narrow passage which the infant must go through in birth, and the difficulties in breathing that may be associated (whether "caused by" or not we don't need to go into for this purpose) with the confined channel, the "straightened gate." The French root for anxiety—*angoisse*—is connected literally with the meaning of going through a narrow channel, as is the English word "anguish" (L. *angustia*, narrowness, distress; Fr. *angoisse*, to press together). Cf. Rollo May, *The Meaning of Anxiety*.

²⁸ That we are afraid because we run, rather than that we run because we are afraid. James believed that the experiencing of an emotion was our awareness of the inner chemical and muscular changes in the body produced by our action, such as running away.

CHAPTER SIX. The Daimonic in Dialogue

¹ Spiegelberg, p. 236. Hegel sees the positive side of this also. The threat in a Socrates is not only the disaster; it is "the principle which includes both the disaster and the cure," Hegel adds.

² Socrates designated himself by the humble symbol "midwife," since his function was not to *tell* the people the ultimate truth but to draw out of them, by questions, their own inner truth. How much irony there is hiding behind the humility in Socrates nobody knows. In any case, he would have described the function of the psychotherapist in general as a midwife.

³ Prof. Paul Ricoeur, in a personal conversation with me.

⁴ Ex. 32:32; Ps. 69:28; Rev. 3:5.

⁵ John 8:32.

⁶ *Webster's Collegiate Dictionary*

⁷ James, I, p. 565. Italics James's.

⁸ I owe this observation to Thomas Laws of Columbia University.

⁹ *The Holy Bible*, rev. stand. ed. (New York, Thomas Nelson, 1952), Gen. 32:30, p. 34.

¹⁰ *The New York Times*, October 10, 1967, p. 42.

¹¹ When a prince is crowned king, or a pope is installed, he assumes a new being and is given a new name. When a woman gets married in our society, she takes on the name of her husband, symbolically reflecting her new being.

¹² Jan Frank, "Some Aspects of Lobotomy Under Analytic Scrutiny," *Psychiatry*, vol. 13, February, 1950.

¹³ Aeschylus, *The Eumenides*, in *The Complete Greek Tragedies*, p. 161.

[14] *Ibid.* p. 152.

CHAPTER SEVEN. The Will in Crisis

[1] Sigmund Freud, *General Introduction to Psychoanalysis,* trans. Joan Riviera (New York, Garden City Publishing Co., 1938), p. 95.

[2] Alan Wheelis, "Will and Psychoanalysis," *Journal of the American Psychoanalytic Association,* IV/2, April, 1956, p. 256. Wheelis' solution to the problem, in this article and in the last chapters of *The Quest for Identity* (New York, W. W. Norton & Co., 1958), falls short of the penetrating quality of his analysis.

[3] *Modern Man Is Obsolete* is also the title of a book by Norman Cousins, written directly after the explosion of the first atomic bomb.

[4] From the movie *Seven Days in May.*

[5] Prof. L. S. Feuer, "American Philosophy Is Dead," *The New York Times Magazine,* April 24, 1966.

[6] Friedrich Nietzsche, *The Gay Science.* See Walter Kaufmann, *Nietzsche: Philosopher, Psychologist, Antichrist* (Princeton, N. J., Princeton University Press, 1950), p. 75.

[7] Sylvano Arieti, "Volition and Value: A Study Based on Catatonic Schizophrenia," delivered at the mid-winter meeting of the Academy of Psychoanalysis, December, 1960, and published in *Comprehensive Psychiatry,* II/2, April, 1961, p. 77.

[8] *Ibid.,* p. 78.

[9] *Ibid.,* p. 79.

[10] *Ibid.,* p. 80.

[11] *Ibid.,* p. 81.

[12] See Wheelis. See also Bruno Bettelheim, *The Informed Heart.*

[13] Cf. speeches of Jules Masserman and Judson Marmor at the American Psychiatric Convention, May, 1966, and the American Academy of Psychoanalysis, May, 1966.

[14] It is significant, and only fitting, that the issue of power was recently brought into psychology by a Negro psychologist who speaks out of the conflicts of race relations. Here it cannot be avoided. See Clark, *Dark Ghetto.*

[15] Robert Knight, "Determinism, Freedom, and Psychotherapy," *Psychiatry,* 1946/9, pp. 251–262.

[16] Freud, *The Ego and the Id* (Hogarth; n. p. 50, Norton Library, n. p. 40).

[17] Wheelis, p. 287.

[18] Vera M. Gatch and Maurice Temerlin, "The Belief in Psychic Determinism and the Behavior of the Psychotherapist," *Review of Existential Psychology and Psychiatry,* pp. 16–34.

[19] See Knight.

[20] Hudson Hoagland, "Science and the New Humanism," *Science,* 143, 1964, p. 114.

CHAPTER EIGHT. Wish and Will

[1] William James states in his chapter on will in *Principles of Psychology,* that the problem of free will is insoluble on the psychological level. It is a metaphysical question; and if the psychologist takes a stand on the free-will—determinism issue as such, he should know that he is speaking metaphysics and take the appropriate safeguards.

[2] Wheelis, p. 289.

[3] Ernest Schachtel informs me that baby seagulls will give the feeding response upon seeing a yellow mark, painted on wood or in other form, similar to the mother seagull's mark on her throat.

[4] From an unpublished paper by William F. Lynch, given orally at a conference on will and responsibility in New York, 1964.

[5] From the discussion and criticism of *The Waste Land,* by Wright Thomas and Stuart Brown, *Reading Poems: An Introduction to a Critical Study* (New York, Oxford University Press, 1941), p. 716.

[6] *Ibid.*

[7] William Lynch, in a speech at the Annual Convention of the American Association of Existential Psychology and Psychiatry, 1964. This reminds me of Spinoza's teaching, that we should "hold in the forefront of our minds the virtue we wish to acquire," so that we may then see how it is applied to each situation which arises, and the virtue will then gradually become imprinted on us. How literally that advice can or should be followed I do not know: but the import we want to underline of both Spinoza and Father Lynch above is the transitive, active aspects of consciousness.

[8] *Ibid.*

[9] *Ibid.*

[10] Leslie Farber, from a paper given at a conference on will and responsibility in New York, 1964. Later printed in *The Ways of the Will: Essays Toward a Psychology and Psychopathology of Will* (New York, Basic Books, 1966), pp. 1–25.

[11] E. R. Hilgard, "The Unfinished Work of William James," paper presented at the American Psychological Association Annual Convention, Washington, D. C., September, 1967. (To be published.)

[12] In *Principles of Psychology,* James's masterpiece, published in 1890, ten years before Freud published his *Interpretation of Dreams.*

[13] James believed that the pleasure-pain system of motivation

—i.e., we will certain things because they give us pleasure and decide against other things because they give us pain—has two grave flaws. One is that, though pleasure and pain are motivations on the superficial level, they are only two among many different motives. Second, on the more basic level, pleasure and pain are accompaniments rather than causes: I act to achieve some self-fulfillment, and if my action contributes to this, it brings me pleasure. As James says, I do not keep writing because I get pleasure out of it, but I find myself writing and filled with mental excitement and I continue this project or task for its own reasons; though I may, indeed, get pleasure of several different sorts out of the fact that I have continued.

14 James, II, p. 546.

15 *Ibid.*, p. 321.

16 *Ibid.*, p. 322.

17 *Ibid.*, p. 524. Italics mine.

CHAPTER NINE. Intentionality

1 This was read and translated for me from a German dictionary of philosophy by Paul Tillich.

2 See n. 1 above.

3 Here, the word "con-form" is exceedingly interesting, meaning to "form with."

4 As quoted by Arthur Koestler, *The Act of Creation* (New York, Macmillan Co., 1964), p. 251.

5 As quoted by Quentin Lauer, *The Triumph of Subjectivity* (New York, Fordham University Press, 1958), p. 29.

6 *Webster's Collegiate Dictionary.*

7 *Ibid.*

8 Quoted by Prof. Paul Ricoeur in a seminar.

9 Personal communication.

10 Speech at the Annual Convention of the New York Psychological Association, February, 1953.

11 See Prof. Robert Rosenthal's many papers on experimental bias, Harvard Social Relations Department.

12 Quoted by Paul Ricoeur in personal communication.

13 Eugene Genlin, "Therapeutic Procedures in Dealing with Schizophrenics," Ch. 16 in *The Therapeutic Relationship with Schizophrenics,* by Rogers, Genlin, and Kiesler (Madison, Wis., University of Wisconsin Press, 1967).

14 From Sonnet 27. Italics mine.

15 The studies and seminars of Paul Ricoeur, Professor of Philosophy at the Sorbonne, are an exceedingly important contemporary contribution to the understanding of will. Some of Ricoeur's thinking will be available in English with the publication of his Terry Lectures at Yale. I am grateful for a num-

ber of ideas from Prof. Ricoeur in seminars and personal discussion.

16 This fits Dr. Robert Lifton's concept that psychic illness is due to an "impaired sense of symbolic immortality." Also, Dr. Eugene Minkowski has constructed a theory of depression as the distortion of the future time dimension, not as the *result* of the depression, but as the cause. (See Chapter 4 in *Existence: A New Dimension of Psychiatry and Psychology*, eds. Rollo May, Ernest Angel, and Henri Ellenberger, New York, Basic Books, 1958.) Our being concerned with the patient's hopes, as one side of his wants, is one sound and constructive aspect of psychotherapy. These hopes and wants may of course be romantic, unreal or may be filled with dog-in-the-manger resentfulness; but this is all the more reason for bringing them into the open. Or his condition may approach a genuine, sheer lack of hope, in which case he is apt to show pronounced symptoms of apathy. In any case, his intentionality, with respect to his future, will largely condition what he remembers of, and how he deals with, his past, as I have indicated in Chapter 4 of *Existence*, mentioned above.

17 May *(The Meaning of Anxiety).*

18 Paul Tillich, *The Courage to Be* (New Haven, Yale University Press, 1952), pp. 81–82.

19 *Ibid.*, p. 83.

CHAPTER TEN. Intentionality in Therapy

1 This is taken from a tape recording of the session.

2 Ernest Keen, formerly my graduate assistant in my course at Harvard during the summer of 1964, now professor at Bucknell. To be published.

3 Dr. Robert Knight is in error when he cites the determinism of Spinoza as a determinism which destroys human freedom. This is a misunderstanding that identifies all determinism with scientific, cause-and-effect processes. These can, indeed, be inimical to human freedom if they are made, unjustifiably, into ultimate principles. But as Spinoza's determinism is a deepening of human experience, an added dignity if you will, it makes freedom dearly bought but all the more real for that. "Necessity," for Spinoza, is the fact of living and dying, not the necessity of a technical process such as Dr. Knight proposes.

4 James, II pp. 578–579.

CHAPTER ELEVEN. The Relation of Love and Will

1 David Riesman, Reuel Denney, and Nathan Glazer, *The Lonely Crowd* (New Haven, Yale University Press, 1950).

2 I am aware that I describe this type mythically, and that

there are many exceptions—like William James and his parents —to this rule. Making all allowances for the fate of each of us to hate the age just before ours, I believe that my point is still generally sound.

³ This is why if there is psychological malignancy on the part of the mother at this time—serious depression or some other upset—the consequences can be paranoid tendencies or some other serious disorder for the infant.

⁴ Anaximander wrote in one fragment: "Every individual does penance for [his] separation from the boundless."

CHAPTER TWELVE. The Meaning of Care

¹ Kant, states that " 'only a rational being has the power to act in accordance with his idea of laws—that is, in accordance with principles—and only so has he a will.' He [Heidegger] immediately adds that, 'since reason is required in order to deduce actions from laws, the will is nothing but practical reason.' Yet his use of the word 'power' indicates that will is also understood as energy." John Macquarrie, "Will and Existence," *The Concept of Willing,* ed. James N. Lapsley (New York, Abingdon Press, 1967), p. 76.

² Martin Heidegger, *Being and Time,* trans. John Macquarrie and Edward Robinson (New York, Harper & Row, 1962), p. 370.

³ Macquarrie, p. 78.

⁴ Heidegger, p. 227.

⁵ Macquarrie, p. 82.

⁶ Heidegger, p. 319.

⁷ *Ibid.,* p. 242.

⁸ Macquarrie, p. 82.

⁹ Ronald Latham's introduction to Lucretius, *The Nature of the Universe* (London, Penguin Books, 1951), p. 7.

¹⁰ Some of the writers we shall be referring to lived a century or two later—Plutarch, second century, A.D.; Epictetus, a Greek living in Rome in the second century A.D.; Lucretius, first century B.C. But these men were writing to the best of their knowledge about the earlier period—Lucretius explicating Epicurus of the third century B.C., and Epictetus interpreting Zeno's Stoicism. We are dependent, at least for quoted references, on the literature which survived and was handed down. Dodds and other scholars believe that these men do faithfully represent the mood and tone of their sources in the Hellenistic period.

¹¹ Epictetus, in *The Stoic and Epicurean Philosophers,* ed. Whitney J. Oates (New York, Random House, 1940), p. 306.

¹² Lucretius, p. 208.

13 C. G. Jung, *Memories, Dreams, Reflections,* ed. Aniela Jaffé (New York, Vintage Books, 1965), pp. 212, 334. The point is not the anxiety about satellites and space ships and trips to the moon in themselves, but what they symbolically represent in the change of our relationship to heavenly bodies. The same kind of anxiety came out at the transitional point between the Middle Ages and modern times, when new interpretations of heavenly space were made. The citizen of Copernicus' or Galileo's time experienced no less warmth and light from the sun and the earth was no less earthy after the new theory was proved that the earth goes round the sun. But there was a profound impact on man's image of himself, his relation to his church, and other cultural forms through which he had made sense out of his life. I agree with Lewis Mumford when he writes, in reviewing Jung's autobiography, that Jung "made perhaps a more realistic appraisal of these unidentified objects (flying saucers) than those who had expected them to contain visitors from another planet." Mumford goes on: Jung "saw them as unconscious projections of modern man's need for the intervention of higher powers in a world menaced by its own scientific-mechanical ingenuities—typical hallucinations of an age that could conceive of Heaven only in the forces that threatened it." Lewis Mumford, *The New Yorker,* May 23, 1964.

14 Lucretius, p. 217.

15 Italics mine.

16 Dodds, p. 240.

17 Lucretius, p. 218.

18 Dodds, p. 248.

19 Lucretius, p. 61.

20 *Ibid.,* p. 128.

21 *Ibid.,* p. 128.

22 *Ibid.,* p. 98.

23 *Ibid.,* p. 79.

24 *Ibid.,* p. 126.

25 *Ibid.,* pp. 126–127.

26 *Ibid.,* p. 204.

27 It is especially difficult for us, as modern men, to come to terms with the myth of Sisyphus because of our strong faith in the myth of perpetual progress. We have rejected the myth of God's providence only to come up in its place with the myth of progress—"every day in every way we become better and better."

28 The term "mythoclasm" is used by Jerome Bruner, "Myth and Identity," *The Making of Myth* (New York, Putnam, 1962), and is referred to in Chapter V of this book. I find

mythoclasm to be a very interesting word. I think that what happens is that the person turns against the failing myths, as against a parent, with the violence and sense of hurt of one betrayed. The myths *ought* to have stood me in good stead and they have let me down! This expresses itself in a defiant iconoclasm (e.g., "God is dead") and in a turning of one's energy toward the destruction of the very myths on which one longed to depend. This, in turn, goes with the defiant vow, "I'll live without myths!" This process in itself is a most vivid and meaningful, if self-defeating, form of mythologizing. We also see this mythoclasm in those psychoanalysts who have turned against their old faith.

[29] The absurdity to which Lucretius' passionate faith in the therapeutic effects of naturalistic explanations leads him is shown in the following: *"The Nile,* for instance, unlike any other river on earth, rises on the threshold of summer and floods the fields of Egypt. The reason why it normally irrigates Egypt at the height of the heat may be because in summer there are north winds blowing against its mouths—the winds that are said to be Etesian or 'seasonal' at that time. These winds, blowing against the stream, arrest its flow. By piling up the water they raise its level and hold up its advance. There is no doubt that these breezes do run counter to the river. They blow from the cold stars of the Pole." Lucretius, p. 239.

[30] Lucretius, p. 146. This assignment of fictitious causes reminds us of the argument of some analysts which maintains that the patient should be helped to believe in the "illusion of freedom" in order to get the necessary commitment to change. (This is discussed in Chapter VII.) Also, we are reminded of the contention of a number of psychotherapists that whether or not an interpretation that is given to the patient is true is not relevant to its curative value. The effect depends upon the patient's faith, hope, and other things rather than its accuracy. This is a partial truth which needs to be placed in a larger context, namely, that of the "intentionality" present in the therapeutic relationship at the moment as determinative of the curative value of the interpretation.

[31] Latham, p. 9.

[32] Lucretius, pp. 254, 256.

[33] I use the term *mythos* to distinguish the myth which still has viability, is partly unconscious, and is now in a process of being formed. *Mythopeic* is the name of this process of forming myths.

[34] Alfred North Whitehead, in *Alfred North Whitehead: His Reflections on Man and Nature,* ed. Ruth Narda Anshen, (New York, Harper & Row, 1961), p. 28.

[35] T. S. Eliot, "East Coker," *Four Quartets* (New York, Harcourt, Brace, 1943), p. 15.

CHAPTER THIRTEEN. Communion of Consciousness *

[1] James Baldwin, *The Fire Next Time.*

[2] Quoted by Dan Sullivan in "Sex and the Person," *Commonweal*, 22, July, 1966, p. 461.

[3] W. H. Auden, *Collected Shorter Poems* (New York, Random House, 1967).

[4] Tillich, *The Courage to Be,* Chapt. 6.

[5] *The Buried Life,* lines 77–89.

[6] Harry Harlow, "Affection in Primates," *Discovery,* London, January, 1966, unpaged.

[7] John Donne, "The First Anniversary: An Anatomy of the World," *The Complete Poetry of John Donne,* ed. John T. Shawcross (New York, Doubleday & Co., Anchor Books, 1967), p. 278, lines 209–217.

[8] Blaise Pascal, *Pensées,* ed. and trans. G. B. Rawlings, (Mount Vernon, N.Y., The Peter Pauper Press, 1946), p. 7.

* I owe the title of this chapter to Mr. John Bleibtreu.

Index

From the publisher who brought you
the 6 million copy bestseller
The Doctor's
Quick Weight Loss Diet

THE TRUTH ABOUT WEIGHT-CONTROL

by NEIL SOLOMON, M.D.

In this informative guide, a Johns Hopkins-trained specialist who has spent ten years treating the problems of obesity in more than 1000 patients tells how to lose excess pounds—and how to keep them off. Dr. Solomon covers such topics as fad diets, the health hazards of obesity, the reasons one overeats, and the dangers of diet clubs and diet pills. This is the first weight-control book to pass the rigorous standards of the Book-of-the-Month Club.

A DELL BOOK $1.50

If you cannot obtain copies of this title from your local bookseller, just send the price (plus 25c per copy for handling and postage) to Dell Books, Post Office Box 1000, Pinebrook, N. J. 07058.

BURNT OFFERINGS

A novel by
ROBERT MARASCO

WHEN MARIAN ROLFE FOUND THE LISTING IN
THE WANT ADS, IT SEEMED ALMOST TOO GOOD TO
BE TRUE:

> *Unique summer home. Restful, secluded.
> Perfect for large family. Pool, private
> beach, dock. Long season. Very reason-
> able for the right people.*

AND THE ROLFES WERE THE RIGHT PEOPLE.
MARIAN KNEW IT THE SECOND SHE FELT HERSELF
SURROUNDED BY THE AUBUSSONS AND CRYSTAL.
AS FOR BEN, HIS DOUBTS ABOUT SOME "CATCH"
SEEMED SILLY. UNTIL, STEP BY STEP, THE HOUSE
AND GROUNDS BEGAN TO EXERT THEIR POWER AND
PLUNGE THE ROLFES INTO A NIGHTMARE OF
EXQUISITELY MOUNTING HORROR.

*"BURNT OFFERINGS terrifies. Even by day-
light it makes your flesh crawl."*

—*New York Times*

A DELL BOOK $1.50

THE TAKING OF PELHAM ONE TWO THREE

a novel by
John Godey

HOW MANY OF THESE DELL BESTSELLERS HAVE YOU READ?

1. **THE TAKING OF PELHAM ONE TWO THREE**
   by John Godey $1.75

2. **A DAY NO PIGS WOULD DIE**
   by Robert Newton Peck $1.25

3. **QUEEN VICTORIA** by Cecil Woodham-Smith $1.75

4. **ELEPHANTS CAN REMEMBER**
   by Agatha Christie $1.25

5. **TREVAYNE** by Jonathan Ryder $1.50

6. **RAMBLING ROSE** by Calder Willingham $1.50

7. **THE MAN WHO LOVED CAT DANCING**
   by Marilyn Durham $1.75

8. **MEAT ON THE HOOF** by Gary Shaw $1.50

9. **SOLDIER** by Anthony B. Herbert $1.75

10. **11 HARROWHOUSE** by Gerald A. Browne $1.50

11. **THE CAR THIEF** by Theodore Weesner $1.50

12. **THE GREAT EXECUTIVE DREAM**
    by Robert Heller $1.75

13. **TARGET BLUE** by Robert Daley $1.75

14. **THE GLOW OF MORNING**
    by Irving A. Greenfield $1.50

If you cannot obtain copies of these titles from your local bookseller, just send the price (plus 25c per copy for handling and postage) to Dell Books, Post Office Box 1000, Pinebrook, N. J. 07058.